SEECO'S STORY

My Father's Heroic Journey through
Bulgaria, Israel, and America.

Jonathan Varsano

Seeco's Story: My Father's Heroic Journey through Bulgaria, Israel, and America

By Jonathan Varsano

Crespi Street House
c/o Jonathan Varsano
10736 Jefferson Boulevard #250
Culver City, CA 90230

ISBN: 978-0-578-03198-9

Printed and bound in the United States of America

Credits

Editor: Eric Wasserman
Proofreaders: Mark Sundahl, Alan Rosenblatt, Merle M. Singer

Acknowledgements

This book is dedicated to the memory of my dad, Mordecai Varsano. I hope that my family and future generations read this book to learn about my father's historic life.

I would like to thank my mom, Elaine for providing me with a lot of unknown information about my father and for her love and support during through the writing process.

My aunt in Israel, Sarah Gerecht, provided me with most of the material for the Bulgarian and early Israeli portions of the book. Thanks to her for putting up with my constant questions about difficult times in the past.

Thank you to my editor, Eric Wasserman, who patiently guided me through the writing process and learned more about my family than he ever thought he would.

Thank you to Mickey Wolf who provided me insight into my father's personal life during his later years. Leonard Chesler, David Zollman, Bob Sirkin, and Harvey Levine were other friends that provided anecdotes.

Shalom Eitan, whom I never met in person, was kind enough to provide me with email correspondence regarding my father's service in the Israeli Army. Marcel and Lina Braha were Israeli friends that provided valuable content. Marc Varsano, who is of Greek heritage and makes great chocolate, provided me with genealogical information regarding the Varsanos of Spain.

Thank you to my friends that read early drafts and offered me sound advice: Mark Sundahl, Alan Rosenblatt, and Merle M. Singer.

Authors Frederick B. Chary, Stephane Groueff, Guy H. Haskell, Marshall Lee Miller, A.J. Barker, Howard M. Sachar, and Idith Zertal provided additional research information.

CONTENTS

PROLOGUE

Ship of Opportunity

In the fall of 1964, a curious young lady named Elaine Schneider from suburban Los Angeles boarded an airplane for the first time in her life. Her destination was New York City. She had not been to New York, or anywhere in the Eastern United States, since she was only five years old. On the flight out, she was extremely nervous, so she read the best-selling book titled "Sex and the Single Girl" by Helen Gurly Brown—the eventual editor of Cosmopolitan Magazine. The book gave advice to young single women about their career, fashion, entertainment, love, and sex emphasizing the positive benefits of unmarried life. With new ideas about becoming a liberated woman freshly planted in her head, she approached her journey with an optimistic, if not aggressive attitude.

When she arrived in the overwhelming metropolis of New York City, she had the comforting shelter of staying overnight at her grandmother's home in Brooklyn. She hadn't seen her grandmother in years, but all she could think about was the great adventure that would start tomorrow morning. Her itinerary consisted of a voyage across the Atlantic Ocean to France by ship followed by a flight to Israel where she would live on a Kibbutz, which was a communal farm.

She decided to take a ship rather than fly because her friend told her that you will meet lots of single men on a long voyage by boat.

5

Reservations for the expedition were made well in advance, but she had no way of knowing that the ship was chartered by Hadassah, a group consisting of primarily older women. The large pool of eligible young bachelors never panned out with this group of travelers. The vast majority of the passengers were old ladies with blue hair and gaudy jeweled sweaters that play lots of mahjong. In fact, there were not too much passengers on the ship at all. It was a luxury liner stocked with more than an ample amount of staff members that seemed to out number the passengers.

The ship was named the Shalom (a Hebrew word meaning hello, good-bye, and peace) and it was built to the exacting standards of an American or European first class vessel but was made in Israel. It possessed all the amenities of a cruise ship, but technically it was a trans-Atlantic sailing vessel because it didn't stop at any ports of call. Her cabin was smartly decorated with turquoise, crimson, lime, and golden colored modern style furniture, as well as a color television set which was considered a feature of extreme comfort. In the 1960s, traveling by ship was considered very glamorous. There were only a few cruise lines and low budget excursions did not exist. Traveling in style on the high seas was considered sophisticated, as well as costly. Initially, the young single lady was frustrated about spending her hard earned money and making reservations months in advance to be stuck on a long trip with people her grandmother's age.

Trying to disregard the septuagenarian vacationers and the throngs of deck hands, she just needed to find one available young man. The massive ship proudly blew its booming horn, as it slowly ambled out of the chilly waters of the New York harbor. It was a crisp autumn morning and the wind was blowing stiffly on the main deck. A young man dressed in a dapper brown wool suit with a thin black tie and a pressed white shirt leaned against the railing staring pensively into the distance. Across the deck, Elaine who was wearing a colorful mod style dress noticed the handsome man and she looked for a chance to approach the apparently eligible bachelor. While nervous tension started to brew within the shy young lady's mind, the Shalom calmly cut through the thick Atlantic Ocean as it crept by the quintessential symbol of freedom, the Statue of Liberty.

The famous structure standing on a small island in the water gave the young lady the opportunity that she was seeking. She coyly approached the serious looking man and naively inquires, "I didn't know the Statue of Liberty was green." The black haired and olive skinned gentleman warmly responded with a logical yet flirtatious explanation. As the conversation progressed, it was obvious that there was a strong physical attraction and they became irreversibly enamored with each other. It was a classic case of love at first sight, and it was how my parents first met.

It almost seemed scripted. Meeting the love of your life on a ship in front of the Statue of Liberty, it was both cliché and romantic with a dash of patriotism added for good measure. Real life doesn't usually resemble a movie, but in the case of my parents, it actually did. When my parents first told me this story, it was hard to imagine my parents as young adults that were full of hopes and dreams, craving adventure and willing to take chances. I only knew them as the overprotective parents that had their safe daily routine. Even in my earliest memories of them, they seemed middle aged. My mother, most certainly, never flirted with anyone, so the image of her picking up my father, was almost unimaginable. I also had trouble conjuring up an image of my father as a bachelor trolling around the deck of a ship in search of single women. I suppose it was a glimpse of my parents before parenthood, an incarnation that no child ever really experiences. They were just two cool cats that dug each other on a groovy boat in the 1960s.

After the ice was broken, my mother began to inquire about the origin of my father's accent. He explained that he was currently living in Israel, but grew up in Bulgaria, and was also fluent in several other languages. My mother was utterly intrigued by this globetrotting cosmopolitan man. How did this complex man wind up in New York on this fateful autumn day?

PART I
Bulgaria

CHAPTER 1

The Great Depression and a Rich Jewish Life

My father, Mordecai Varsano, was born into a world of economic upheaval and political uncertainty on December 2, 1932 in Sofia, Bulgaria. The world was suffering through the midst of the Great Depression and Bulgarians fared no better than the rest of the struggling European countries. Mordecai, the son of Isaac and Rachel Varsano, was a Jew in a largely Eastern Orthodox Christian country which meant that he would never be fully integrating into the majority.

The Jewish community in Bulgaria was a tight knit group that merely represented less than one percent of the total population. The Jews of Bulgaria were a united and organized community that had adapted the millet system from the previous Ottoman rule where the Jews were governed by wealthy families and other designated notables such as rabbis. Changes in modern Judaism, such as the Reform movement, that occurred throughout the 19th and early 20th Century had little effect on the unique brand of Jewish culture in Bulgaria. Most Jewish families in Bulgaria, including the Varsanos, emigrated from Spain in the 15th Century and were known as Sephardic Jews. The Sephardim were a small percentage of the total amount of Jews in the world, most of whom were Ashkenazim that originally lived in Germany, Russia, and neighboring areas.

My family retained the traditionally Sephardic way of life in many ways, still speaking Ladino which was Medieval Spanish combined with Hebrew and other regional dialects. Ladino for Sephardim was similar to Yiddish for Ashkenazim which combined German with Hebrew and other languages. As a small minority in Bulgaria, the Jewish families helped each other both financially and spiritually which helped soften the blow of the tough economic conditions. Fortunately for my father, he had little recollection of the really hard times because he was merely a baby during the depths of the worldwide financial crisis. His earliest memories were of the mid to late 1930s living in the relatively booming city of Sofia with all the comforts of modern life. Bulgaria was on the road to economic recovery and the Varsano family was living a rich Jewish life.

Just a few years earlier, the Great Depression was the first hurdle for my newlywed grandparents to overcome. Things would certainly get worse before they got better for the young couple. Even during the most difficult of times, my grandfather provided an above average life for his family. He owned a hardware store in central Sofia and my grandmother was a traditional homemaker. They named their first born child, Mordecai, after his paternal grandfather who was supposedly Bavarian. It was a grandiose name for a little baby, so his parent's nicknamed him Morris. Morris was also a rather mature name, so it was adapted to Moriseeco. Finally, for the sake of simplicity his name was shortened to Seeco, which stuck with him the rest of his life. When my father was a young boy, he remembered living in a proud country on the rebound from economic devastation. By the second half of the decade, Bulgarian industry was growing faster than the European average.

The Varsano family - considered upper middle class during that era - lived in a luxury apartment in the capital city of Bulgaria where Jews were almost ten percent of the population. Their home in Sofia was located on Dragoman Boulevard in the center of town, not far from my grandfather's hardware store. The relatively affluent family hired non-Jewish, usually ethnic Turks, as domestic help that lived in the servant's quarters of the apartment and acted as Nannies, cleaning ladies, and kitchen helpers. My father never said too much about the luxury of having servants, it was just accepted lifestyle of anyone of moderate means. It was also showed that my family was able to maintain their affluence, even in the midst of the Great Depression.

In any society, there always seems to be an underclass that does the menial jobs. No matter the overall level of wealth, there was always a relative association with job duties. Jews were a minority but generally more affluent than other minority group such as Gypsies, Turks, or Armenians. In modern day Israel, my cousins have hired a Nanny from Moldova that is impoverished, not well educated, and doesn't speak Hebrew well. I grew up with a part time cleaning lady, but had many friends that had live-in maids, most of whom were Latino, impoverished, not well educated, and didn't speak English well. I would guess that my family's servants in Bulgaria bared a resemblance to the Latinos in America and the former Soviet immigrants in Israel in that they were hard working and became essential components to the family but were generally poor and not formally educated.

Both Seeco and his younger sister Sarah, nicknamed Seli, attended the American College in Sofia which also taught grade school. They began learning to speak English at early age and were quite advanced in the other subjects compared to their counterparts in the traditional Bulgarian schools. Both my father and his sister dressed for school in typical outfits of the times. He would often wear a brown woolen button suit jacket with a white shirt buttoned stiffly to the top. Brown wool shorts matched the jacket and his exposed skinny pale legs. Wrinkled socks and brown short leather boots finished the daily attire. My aunt would wear a navy blue short wool jacket over a little white dress with a blue scarf tied around her neck, complimented by white school girl shoes and a white bow.

On Sundays and after school, Seeco would often accompany his father to work and to run errands around the urban center of Sofia. Isaac's hardware store, Magazine Stomano, was a bustling center for local builders and merchants.   Located on 31 Grobarska Ulitza, it served both Jews and non-Jewish Bulgarians alike. Passing by the Magazine Stomano was like a glimpse at the comparative prosperity of the Jews of Sofia during uncertain economic times. The store front was overflowing with goods of all types. From the street approaching customers would see buckets stacked in rows, shovel heads arranged on the wall like game trophies, spooled wire for all needs, a mini lumber yard of poles and wood, chains of various length and thickness, and an assortment of specially priced items for sale.   The signs on front windows boasted of the state-of-the-art tools and specialty items that would be found inside the shop.

Customers to the hardware depot would be greeted by the well-groomed owner, who always sported a fashionable hat and a heavy coat for the chilly Bulgarian climate. He worked in a rugged industry and was quite handy, but had a style that was both sensible and elegant. He might wear work boots and a leather petticoat, but underneath would be a white shirt and tie. For he was the boss, so he felt he must present an image of authority while having the practicality of getting dirty and doing what must be done. My father would later dress in the same adaptable manner during his stint as a small business owner. He instilled the same common sense values in his only son, who at a very early age learned valuable lessons from his astute father that would last a lifetime. He helped his extended family and his community through his store. His brother Shlomo and others were periodically employed at Magazine Stomano, which helped several families within the Jewish community of Sofia.

Business connections through Jewish and non-Jewish colleagues would play a critical role as a great crisis developed throughout Europe in the coming years. There were always discriminatory laws against minority groups in Bulgaria in one form or another. As the burgeoning Fascist State grew, the discrimination became more severe and the penalties grew harsher. To overcome restrictions against Jews pertaining to property rights, my grandfather would commonly use bribery as a standard practice of business. He also would pay Bulgarian Christians to act as a front for him, in order to bypass the limits on Jewish rights. In a jurisdiction where corruption

14

and discrimination rule, bribery and deceit were weapons of the common businessman. My grandfather was not crooked or immoral, he just engaged in the generally accepted business practices of the time and place.

Several times every year, my grandfather would take a break from working at the hardware store and bring his family on a domestic vacation. Sometimes it was a short trip in his 1930 Fiat 514 convertible "horseless carriage" to the frozen heights of Mount Vitosha just outside Sofia and other times it was a cross-country excursion to the Black Sea. The coastal town of Varna was a popular resort destination of the day. Before turning in for the night, Isaac and little Seeco would take advantage of the plentiful natural resources of Bulgaria by stringing a fishing line with several hooks and bait across a river. The line would be left over night and in the morning it would usually be filled with dangling fish. Rachel and Seli would make a wonderful meal with the local vegetables and the fresh catch while the whole family enjoyed the simple pleasures of the countryside.

During other non-working hours, the two Varsano men would often drive around town in my grandfather's convertible car. Other times, they would take my grandfather's motorcycle with an attached sidecar that my father would ride in while wearing his little leather helmet and goggles. They would dress with a different sense of fashion while on these excursions than everyday attire. Isaac would wear a black wool fedora hat with a thick black wool four button overcoat covering a formal grey wool suit with tie and black leather dress shoes. He would dress his son in a black "paperboy" wool cap that matched his suit, a black wool coat covering a turtleneck sweater and wool

15

knickers with black leather dress shoes completed with a curious glare of a small child in the big city.

They would usually go to the traditional male domains of the day such as coffee shops and barbershops. About once a month, my grandfather Isaac would bring his into the heart of the city for a haircut. Every time he went into the "guy's only" hangout, he would get the same urban cut for boys, shortly cropped around the ears with the bangs slightly longer. A dominating featuring of downtown Sofia that my father distinctly remembered was the large and imposing lion statutes that stood guard in front of the government buildings. That entire area of the city was paved with yellow cobblestones which symbolized that it was a special area for all Bulgarians. Many of the side streets had a variety of street vendors pushing carts about and carnival-like performers in search of tips. Tame bears roamed the streets with their trainers and organ grinding monkeys entertained children of all backgrounds. There were even photo booths so Seeco could take home a little souvenir. In the days before amusement parks, going to downtown Sofia with his dad was almost like a trip to the circus. On Friday afternoons, Isaac would always pick up something special for Shabbat.

Bulgaria was known for their yogurt and their produce. Yogurt was not packaged in small plastic containers like it is today, though. The pride of Bulgarian food was sold in bulk and the vendor would slice off a piece with a taut wire in the same manner that clay was cut. My grandmother would usually do most of the shopping because she was the doing the vast majority of the cooking. Everyday was a farmers market in Bulgaria and there was always a plentiful supply of

16

fresh vegetables because it was still a largely agricultural society. Peppers, eggplants, quinces, apricots, peaches, tomatoes, cucumbers, onions piled into round baskets were staples of the Bulgarian diet. All meat products, lamb being the most prevalent, were purchased at the kosher butcher in Jewish quarter.

In preparation for Shabbat, my grandmother Rachel, nicknamed Shella, would usually complete about three meals by Friday afternoon, so the food may be eaten and not worked on from Friday night until Saturday evening, which was the official period of observance. The home also needed to be cleaned in preparation for the holy resting day which was done mostly by the servants. Again, the servants were an essential part of the family, but did not take part in the rituals because they weren't Jewish and were only hired help. Even though the servants were constantly around the home, there was an understood disconnection when it came to including them in family events.

At nightfall on Friday, the Shamash, who was warden of the synagogue, would shout "Shabbat, Shabbat!" from the grand synagogue in central Sofia which was situated only a few blocks from the main square. It was designed in the Byzantine-Oriental style of the great Sephardic synagogue in Cordoba, Spain. Its exterior had a square shaped beige base surrounded by iron gates topped with a round dome engraved with a large Star of David. The sanctuary was breathtaking with its painted wooden arches and cornices. A massive ornate chandelier dominated the center of men's seating area while a canopied balcony for the women overlooked the ark where the Torahs were kept. After the Shamash made his announcement, he proceeded to march down the tree lined cobblestone streets beating in time with a silver headed mace. This was the signal that all work must stop and women were to kindle the Shabbat candles.

My grandmother and her daughter would light the two ceremonial candles while their flowing brown hair glistened in the natural light and the day of rest officially began. The evening of Shabbat was traditionally celebrated with family and guests of honor. The predominate dish served during a Sephardic Shabbat celebration was huevos haminados, which are hard boiled or oven eggs cooked with the outer skins of onions, olive oil, and tea or coffee grounds which added a brown color.

On Saturday, the morning would begin with a table laden with bread, olives, cheese, haminados, cucumbers, and sliced tomatoes. The next meal of Shabbat was usually some combination of beef, lamb, beans, vegetable pies, and sweets such as nut and raisin cake as well as sutlach which was a succulent form of rice pudding. Meals were usually preceded by a copious amount of appetizers such as fried eggplant and burekas which were filo dough pastries usually stuffed with potato, cheese, or spinach. Following the first course of appetizers, the main meal would be brought out consisting of a smorgasbord of traditional dishes. Ouzo and Rake were the spirits from the Balkan region that were drunk to wash down the feast. No one in my family consumed much alcohol, so the toasting beverage of choice was usually just a little sip of ceremonial wine. The dishes were normally put out on the table and everyone helped themselves which allowed the women to socialize rather than serve. Sephardic families, in general, felt that sitting at the table and sharing the meal experience with family and guests were the most important part of the dining experience.

Following the third meal, the men would say prayers in synagogue while the women waited at home. When three stars could be seen in the night sky, the Havadallah ceremony would commence. The ceremony involved a cup of wine, a special braided candle, and an aromatic spice box, which signified the conclusion of the week's Shabbat observance.

Saturday nights were traditionally a time for celebration with friends and neighbors. Turkish coffee served with dulces; special ones prepared for late arrivers symbolized a new week of sweetness. After sufficiently filling their bellies, my grandfather would start to sing a traditional Ladino song while Seeco would play accompaniment on the accordion. Then others would start to sing along and the rest of the party would gleefully dance for the rest of the evening.

The year round observance of ancient traditions served as the framework for vibrant Jewish life which bonded the community together. Once a year in the fall, the High Holy Days arrived, which were a solemn time of religious observance for all the Jews of Bulgaria. The high holy days of Rosh Hashanah and Yom Kippur were the most significant on the Jewish calendar and followed a particular custom according to ancient laws. The commercial district of Sofia would be shut down on the high holy days because of the shear amount of observant Jewish merchants.

Rosh (meaning head in Hebrew) Hashanah was the self reflective observance of the New Year of the Hebrew calendar. It was customary to serve the head of the household, who was Isaac, a head of a fish as a symbolic ritual. Intensive prayers would follow and the hope for a new spiritually beginning.

During Yom Kippur, the Day of Atonement, a twenty-four hour fast was started with a large ceremonial meal and completed by a another special meal. During the painful hours of not eating, there were many hours of prayer and self examination before God. The fast was often broken with a cool drink of Ayran a mixture of yogurt, ice water, salt, and mint. The fast was one of the few observances of strict Judaism that my father kept throughout his entire life. I started to fast at the age of twelve to continue the tradition that was past down from my father's roots in Bulgaria.

Sukkoth was the autumn harvest festival that invoked prayers for winter rains. The harvest and seasonal availability determined what foods were eaten but it usually consisted of sweets made with apples, quinces, and grapes, cakes filled with cinnamon and pumpkin, and also baklava. Many families temporarily constructed a Sukkah which was an outdoor spiritual hut that had representations of nuts, pomegranates, citron, and palm branches. Since my family lived in an apartment in the middle of a bustling city, erecting a Sukkah was not practical but the holiday was still observed to the best of their abilities. Possibly because of this lack of a Sukkah, the central component to the holiday, my father never really celebrated this holiday later in life. The only Sukkah I ever saw was on the lawn of the synagogue grounds, not in our backyard like many other American Jewish families.

Hanukkah was considered a minor holiday on the Jewish calendar, and did not become the "Jewish Christmas" until the latter half of the twentieth century. A simple lighting of the eight candled menorah and a few special dishes were the extent of the festival of lights. Traditionally, fried foods were served on Hanukkah to symbolize the miracle of the oil in the lamps of the ancient Israelites lasting eight nights when it was only suppose to last one. Hanukkah specialties included loukoumades (fried donut holes) and halva (sesame seed sweets). Potato pancakes, which are common for Hanukah in America, were not served by Sephardic families because it was Askanazi fare. My mother, who was Askanazi preferred potato pancakes over the Sephardic dishes for Hanukah, so my father allowed this "foreign cuisine" in our house. Thankfully, my father reluctantly gave me costly presents on Hanukah despite his childhood memories of a gift-free holiday.

Purim, celebrated in the beginning of spring, was a favorite holiday of children like Seeco and Seli, because they were encouraged to dress up in costumes. Masquerade parties would reenact the ancient story of the saving of the Jews of Persia from the wicked Haman. Cookies in various shapes were served to symbolize the defeat of Haman. Paflas, or small tin coins, were made in the synagogue and sold to members of the congregation. The children's objective was to try to collect as many paflas from the adults as they could. At the end of the day, the children would sell back the paflas for tasty treats and toys to complete the ritual. Purim was similar to Halloween because children were allowed to dress up but like all other Jewish holidays it also told an important historical lesson. Purim set Jewish kids apart from the rest of the Bulgarian children in a most visual way because they were all donning costumes. Even though most families knew who was a Jew and who wasn't, this children's oriented holiday made it abundantly clear to my father that he was a minority in his homeland.

Later in the springtime, the harvest festival of Shavuot and the great meal of the Pesach Seder were celebrated throughout the heavily agrarian region of the Balkans. Pesach, or Passover, was the biggest feast of all the holidays where my grandmother would literally spend days preparing elaborate homemade Sephardic rice dishes, various lamb kabobs and pies, haminados, date and raisin haroset, spinach pastries, and walnut cake. Matzah was prepared from scratch in large communal ovens in the Jewish quarter of Sofia. The entire city could smell the fumes of the baked unleavened bread. To recall the suffering of the Israelites, the family would eat only unleavened products for eight days which resulted in many interesting culinary adaptations such as the fried matzah pancakes known as boumwelos.

My father would prepare boumwelos with a chocolate chateau sauce for me during the eight days of Passover in America. One of the few traditions that my father did keep from his childhood in Bulgaria was the Passover Seder, although the American celebration was quite different from the Bulgarian one. Besides the boumwelos, everything served was American or Askanazi dishes such as gefilte fish from a jar with horseradish, potato kugel, beef brisket, sweet Manischewitz Grape wine, canned coconut macaroons, and Jello. During the American Seder, the prayers and stories were mostly told in English with a little Hebrew, and lasted less than an hour before the meal started. In Bulgaria, the prayers and stories portion of the Seder lasted several hours and was conducted almost exclusively in Hebrew. The meal was followed by singing which was a tradition my father tried to carry on in America, but none of the Ashkenazi half of my family knew the words or was enthusiastic about learning them. He would start singing "Quienso Penso ..." which was the beginning of a song that was reminiscent of *The Twelve Days of Christmas.* He would get the part of the song of "Dos Moshe y Aron ..." which only represented the second of many verses before the rest of the Ashkenazi family would start to roll there eyes.

Shavuot was the springtime holiday where houses and synagogues were decorated with flowers. During this time of year, sheep and goats in rural Bulgaria were feeding their young so there was a prevalence of milk products like yogurt and cheese in the cities. The special bread known as Los Siete Cielos, or seven heavens, was prepared with heavy symbolism to the themes of biblical stories. The process of helping her mom to cook for the holidays would teach my aunt the meaning of the Jewish tradition. My father did more eating than cooking, but the ceremonial way food was consumed with prayers, storytelling, and song, taught him a more about the history of his people than reading a textbook ever could. Shavuot was never celebrated in my family in America, and I didn't even know the holiday existed until learning about it in Hebrew School. It seemed sad to me that all these traditions that lasted for centuries could just disappear in one generation.

The Bulgarian word for self knowing, Samopoznanie, helped describe the Jewish community in Bulgaria. The age old traditions gave them identity and a focus that allowed them to prosper within a system in which they were a minority. They would always be considered Jews of Bulgaria rather than Bulgarian Jews because

Judaism came first and the Bulgarians would not fully integrate them into leadership of the nation. Although the Varsano family was not considered more devout than the average Jewish family in Bulgaria, the following of rituals and the basic understanding of the biblical teachings formed a moral order to their daily lives. A Jewish sense of spirituality was simply an inherited way of life for my father. There were no Orthodox, Conservative, or Reform congregations in Bulgaria like there was in America. The Bulgarian form of Judaism fell somewhere in between Orthodox and Conservative, but every family chose how observant they would be. The men of my family had a long history of being merchants and business people, so becoming a Rabbi or Cantor was never even considered by my father.

A little bit of faith coupled with a keen sense of values helped the Varsanos integrate with the multi-ethnic Bulgarian society for business purposes while being a proud member of an insulated Jewish social community. The family hired mostly Turkish assistants for domestic duties while my grandfather had customers and business associates that were Bulgarian Christians. As a young boy, my father knew very little about the evil and prejudice that existed in the past and which would soon ostracize his people from their previously accepting neighbors. For a brief time in his young life, he believed he lived in a fair world where a good moral foundation and hard work would bring you happiness and prosperity. Although he followed the traditional customs, he did not fully realize the symbolism within those rituals because the suffering of his people seemed like ancient history. In the next few years, he would learn first hand that the discrimination and persecution of the Jewish people was a perpetual problem.

CHAPTER 2

A Fifteen Hundred Year Voyage through Europe

My family, like most Jewish families, was forced to migrate to various countries around the world, mainly due to religious persecution. My father, as well as his hereditary ancestors, sought a land where they could freely practice their Judaism and enjoy the utmost economic opportunity. He was well aware of the injustices suffered by his Sephardic predecessors over their uneasy history, but never imagined that he would be persecuted in a similar fashion as the dark cloud of Fascism rose over his sunny Bulgarian childhood. The parallels between the anti-Semitics of the middle ages and the mid twentieth century were horrifically similar.

Following their exile from the land of Israel, most Jews—including my ancestors—relocated within the parameters of the Roman Empire. The empire extended to a region known as Gaul, the area of modern day France. Most of the Jews, including the Varsanos, relocated to communities along the Mediterranean. Varsano literally translated from medieval Spanish was "one who is from Vars." Vars County was in the Dauphine Province, the region of Province Cote d'Azur; it was bordered by Nice from the East and Marseille to the West. Historical records indicate that the cities of Draguignan and Toulon within Vars County had Jewish populations from as early as the 4th Century of the Common Era up to the 14th Century.

The Gaul's considered the Jews as Romans and thus they enjoyed the freedom of worship, the right to serve in the military, and the right to hold public office. Jews were integrated into the greater society in both language and appearance. My father spoke French even though he never lived anywhere near France because French was considered a sophisticated language that sounded classy compared with the Slavic tongue of Bulgarian. Even those that weren't fluent in French would learn a few words just to add a slight touch of perceived erudition to their lifestyle. The overall influence of French culture on my family was slight compared with the culture of Spain which would be their next destination.

As the reach of Christianity and the Crusades expanded, the rulers of France began to impose stricter anti-Jewish laws because all non-believers of Christ needed to be converted or banished. First, they were subjected to onerous taxation which denied them the prosperity that they once enjoyed. The policy of economic deprivation was followed by an absolute order of exile for all Jewish residents. The strategy of progressively denying rights and imposing escalating punishments was a mirror of official anti-Semitic laws that swept across Europe during my father's childhood.

Ultimately, my family was forced to move elsewhere in order to live freely as Jews. My ancestors from Vars County most likely started immigrating from France to Spain after the onslaught of the Crusades, but no later than the expulsion order of 1394. When they arrived in Spain, they were absorbed into a pre-existing and flourishing Jewish community. Since Vars county was in the south of France on the Mediterranean Sea, my family made a relatively short journey around the Gulf of Lions to Northeast Spain. Hundreds of years later, my father would also sail the seas of uncertainty in search of a better life. The Varsanos settled in a city with a sizable Jewish population that had a similar climate of warm mild weather and feel to Toulon or Marseilles along the Mediterranean. My family found safe harbor in Barcelona and Gerona in the region of Catalonia. Interestingly, my father also lived in Tel Aviv, Israel, and Los Angeles, California, both of which have similar climates to Barcelona and Marseilles. The pleasant weather was definitely a factor in his eventual move to Southern California. Perhaps his Sephardic blood was predisposed to enjoying a Mediterranean climate.

Jewish communities experienced a "Golden Age of Sephardim" during the Moorish, or Moslem, rule of Spain. Jews were tax officials, doctors, merchants, and craftsmen. Most of the Jews of Spain lived in the so called royal cities of Cordova, Granada, and Toledo. However, Barcelona and other urban concentrations had significant scientific, artistic, and intellectual circles of Jews. In Cordova, the capital of Moslem Spain, the main mosque stood adjacent to the Juderia, or Jewish quarter, which was symbolic of the peaceful coexistence of the two faiths.

While the Jewish people lived in Spain, they spoke Ladino which was essentially Medieval Castilian Spanish with some influences of Portuguese, Catalan, and Aragonese. As the Sephardim migrated to other countries, words from the languages of those countries were incorporated into the ever evolving Ladino dialect. Ladino, until recent years, was written in Hebrew rather than Roman characters which made it difficult for non-Jews to read. However, folk

27

songs and prayers were chanted in Ladino which most Spaniards could understand. The Ladino language and traditions were passed down for hundreds of years in my family. My father was fluent in Ladino and well versed in the ancient songs and customs. "Boca dulce abre puertos de hierro," or "Kind Words open iron gates," was a popular saying through the years and was a philosophy that helped the Sephardim live harmoniously with their Christian and Moslem neighbors.

The rich culture and adaptive nature of the Sephardim allowed them to prosper in Medieval Spain. A unique Sephardic Cuisine was developed starting around the 12th Century which incorporated Arabic influences of Moslem Spain into the Kosher Laws of Judaism. Sephardic food utilized the grains, nuts, seeds, vegetables, fruits, and meats of the Mediterranean region. In the Sephardic culture, rituals and traditions were often stronger than the religious beliefs. A different menu to correspond to each holiday was often more meaningful than the religious teachings of the holiday itself. The dishes were named according to biblical stories that integrated the eating experience with Jewish study to create a "Holy Cuisine." Food became both ceremonial and celebratory. Following the traditional prayers, the Varsano family dinners in Medieval Spain would burst out into Ladino folk songs and dances in a similar manner to the festive meals of the 20th Century Bulgaria.

From cuisine to theology, from painting to poetry, from politics to business; Judaism in Spain blossomed. My ancestors wished for "anyos muchos y buenos" meaning good years and many more in Ladino, but unfortunately many struggles were ahead. During the

Reconquista which was a series of campaigns by Christian states from the north to recapture territory from Moslem ruled areas of the Iberian Peninsula, the Jews of Moorish Spain scattered throughout Moslem and Christian regions, and slowly regained some of their previous stature but longed for the golden days of Cordova rule.

To the Christian Church, Jews were to be kept separate and urged to convert. My father would experience the same form of religious pressure and forced separation during the grim days of WWII. Jews were never allowed to be at the top levels of government. Following the Christian conquering of Moslem regions in the mid 13th Century, the Jewish learning centers of Granada and Cordova were destroyed, but a rich cultural life for a large number of Jews, including the Varsanos, persisted in Barcelona and Toledo. Synagogues were still full, the observance of Shabbat persisted, art and literature continued to develop, and many Jews even acted as culturally bridges between the Christian and Moslems, but the tolerance of a Jewish existence under Christian rule was merely a temporary strategy.

In 1263, at the Cathedral of Barcelona there was a debate between Judaism and Christianity which was halted after four days with the Jews being charged with blasphemy for not accepting Christ as their Lord and Savior. As a result, Jewish books were subsequently censored and other restrictions were imposed. Conditions for Jews would continually deteriorate over the next few years just as they would during the Holocaust in twentieth century Europe. To make matters worse, the Bubonic Plague, or Black Death, would take the lives of droves of people throughout Europe during the following decades. The combination of ignorance, fear, and hate caused many people to blame the Jews for the disease epidemic. Out of revenge, many innocent families were slaughtered simply because they were Jews just like in the extermination camps of the Holocaust during my father's childhood.

In addition to the Jews suffering the consequences of being the plague scapegoat, the Catholic Church was stepping up its efforts to convert Jews to Christianity. The 700,000 Jews that lived in Spain were sliced into thirds. One third were killed or exiled. One third converted to Christianity and one third survived as Jews. Jews in Barcelona, such as Victoria Lopez Varsano (or Barsano, a common mispronunciation of our family name), were burned at the stake for observing the Shabbat and her sister was put in "perpetual prison." Also, the old Spanish records reveal that Rogelio Varsano was punished for prayer in "Jude mode." My family was punished for numerous "religious crimes" over the centuries. Hundreds of years later, my father was persecuted for not wearing the proper Jewish identification.

In 1412, the preacher monk named Vincent Ferry strongly urged Jewish conversion. Reformatory laws were imposed that stated Jews and Christians must live separately. Jews were required to wear a badge, an oppressive practice that would be repeated during my father's childhood in the mid 20th Century. Christians could not be treated by Jewish doctors. Jews could not do business with Christians. The Jews' communal autonomy was taken away. Many Jews felt that they had no choice but to convert. Because of many logistical problems some of the laws were eventually revoked or softened and a smaller Jewish population persisted, the Varsanos were among them.

The anti-Jewish laws were difficult to enforce over such a large area and it caused major disruption to the greater society. Jewish merchants were essential to the distribution of products and services for the greater economy. Again, it was strikingly similar to Bulgaria during WWII when some of the political leaders sought to eliminate the Jews from their society, but the common man saw them as fellow countryman and useful components of the national order. Eliminating them would make life more difficult for everyone. Achieving a "pure" nation was not worth the sacrifice of eradicating the benefits of the Jewish contribution to society.

Unfortunately, widespread democracy did not exist yet, and the unelected leadership would ultimately decide the fate of the Jews despite the will of the people or the best interests of the nation. In 1412, Haranimo de Santa Fe, a former Jew, issued a memorandum on the Jewish "problem." A few months later, Pope John XXIII ordered Jewish representatives of Aragon to the Papal Court to answer the questions of Haranimo's Memorandum. The blatantly biased proceedings were conducted by Haranimo himself in "debate" sessions where he tried to convince the Jews that Jesus was the messiah and upon conclusion of his preaching declared a victory for the church which was politically damaging to the legitimacy of Judaism. The church seemed poised to finally solve the Jewish problem, but the Pope was forced to abdicate for unrelated reasons and the Jews received a temporary reprieve due to the internal crisis within the Papacy. When my father was only eleven years old, the Nazis seemed poised to "solve the Jewish problem" within Europe, but the Jews of Bulgaria were granted a delay in being transported to the

31

extermination camps because of a technicality in the wording of a law. Whether it was simple luck or divine intervention, there has always been one small break, a tiny miracle perhaps, which has saved my family from perishing.

Jewish communities were at the mercy of the ruling Catholic monarchs. Ambitious Jews in cities chose to convert because they had no power or real opportunity otherwise. In the countryside, there was a stronger Jewish tradition and Conversos practiced "secret" Judaism. Conversos were accepted by Jews. Men were circumcised and many received a Jewish burial.

To the Christians, the Conversos were considered Christians. Many achieved high levels of power. During my father's early teenage years, about ten percent of the Jews of Bulgaria became communists or married non-Jews following WWII. Rather than taking a risk for their beliefs like my family did, they opted for the path of least resistance and remained in their familiar surroundings. However, the Conversos of Spain as well as the intermarried of Bulgaria were resented by many because it was believed that on the outside they were Christians but on the inside they were Jewish.

In 1469, Princess Isabella I of Castille wed Ferdinand V of Aragon in her hometown of Segovia. Both Jews and Christians were welcome at the national wedding and celebration. A decade later, Ferdinand ascended to the throne of Aragon and the two major kingdoms of Spain united. The main goals of the new rulers were to conquer Granada, the last stronghold of Moslem Spain, and to start an inquisition to solve the Jewish problem, thus fully integrating all Conversos.

32

The most forceful step towards complete societal integration and homogenization was the inquisition. The Spanish Inquisition was an ecclesiastical tribunal established by the Pope at the request of the Catholic Kings to combat former Jews, Muslims, and Illuminists, as well as those accused of witchcraft or sorcery. The Spanish Inquisition officially began in 1484 in the city of Toledo. However, forced conversions and unfounded killing of Jews began centuries earlier. The inquisition was merely a horrific escalation of these injustices. My father would experience a similar intensification of discrimination and religious persecution in Europe during the 1940s. Beginning with the rise of the Nazi party and the violent rampage of Kristallnacht, there was a steady organized progression to a final solution complete with a network of concentration camps that eventually extended to the Fascist country of Bulgaria.

Just like in Nazi Germany, the Spanish persecution of the Jews was officially sanctioned and well organized. The authorization to name inquisitors was given and the Grand Inquisitor of Domican Tomas de Torquemada was named. The inquisition sought to exile Jewish heretics and save the souls of lapsed Conversos by burning their bodies at the stake. Information and testimony were obtained by the use of torture and confiscation. Several thousand innocent people were burned at the stake through elaborate ceremonies during the public sentencing in the town center. The atrocities of the Holocaust were mostly done out of the public eye, but most people knew that the Jews were being murdered.

In 1491, the Moslems at Granada surrendered to the Christians and a Royal Procession through the streets of Granada followed to commemorate the uniting of Castille and Aragon. With the Moslems defeated, a united Catholic Spain sought to vanquish any trace of Judaism from its country. On March 31, 1492, the edict of expulsion for the Jews of the Spanish Kingdom was signed by Ferdinand and Isabella. Although not imposed during modern times, the Spanish edict of expulsion remained officially in force until 1968 when it was rescinded by the Spanish government. Spain never regained a sizable Jewish population again, and my family never really considered returning to their former home to live. My father did visit the country once later in life, but did not feel much of an historical attachment or an urge to spend more time there.

On May 1, all the Jews of Spain were given three months to leave every region within the Catholic Kingdom. They were not allowed to take gold, money, livestock, guns, or anything of tangible value. The only items they were allowed to keep were the essentials of food and clothes which were similar terms to the forced relocations during WWII that my family would fall victim to. King Ferdinand and Queen Isabella managed to expel the entire Jewish population within four months of their edict. The Jews that were expelled represented about ten percent of the total Spanish population. During that period, the vast majority of Western Europe was closed to Jews with few exceptions. With exile to a strange land imminent, thousands of Spanish Jews converted to Christianity at the eleventh hour to avoid facing the unknown. The Port of Cadiz on the southern coast of the province of Andulsia was the main departure point of exiles who could arrange travel by boat. Contracts with Basque, Portuguese, and Genoese ship owners were made to sail Jews to Italy and North Africa.

The Port of Palos was the departure point for the ships carrying thousands of exiled Jews as well as the Nina, the Pinta, and the Santa Maria of Christopher Columbus' famous voyage. Columbus' voyage was supposedly partly financed by confiscated property of Jewish exiles. In fact, Columbus' historic journey was delayed several days because of the mass exodus of the Jews. On October 11, the last Jews left Spain, followed by Columbus one day later.

Most Jews, however, were not fortunate enough to leave by ship and simply walked away from the country that had been their home for hundreds of years. 120,000 Jews went on foot to neighboring Portugal, which would exile them again only a few years later. My family remembered the temporary sanctuary of the Jews in Portugal when they were considering whether to immigrate to a new Jewish state in the land of Palestine or hope for fair treatment somewhere else. Rather than depending on the whims of a non-Jewish government, they would take a chance on securing a long term Jewish homeland.

Establishing a Jewish state was not feasible for the Jews of Spain and Portugal. My father's family ceased the opportunity that his ancestors never had. The Jewish castaways of Isabella and Ferdinand merely wanted to drift to a land where they were somewhat welcome. 50,000 exiles crossed the straits of North Africa into the Moslem regions of the unfamiliar continent. The Varsano family was among the 30,000 destined for the friendly Mediterranean regions. The Sultan Beyazit II extended the invitation of expelled Jews from Spain to Ottoman territories. The area consisting of modern day Turkey, Greece, Bulgaria, Bosnia, Serbia, Albania, parts of Romania, Egypt, Lebanon, Syria, and Jerusalem were the new Ottoman homes for much of

Spanish Jewry. Most exiles were welcomed into pre-existing Jewish communities within the empire. The Turkish leadership of the empire had high esteem for the Jewish people. In fact, over the course of recent history Israel has enjoyed better relations with Turkey than just about any other Moslem nation. My parents traveled to Turkey during the 1990s and felt comfortable despite being Jews in a land where the star and the crescent reigned. The Ottoman Muslims regarded the Jews as "people of the book," who were part of the monotheistic tradition which eventually led to Islam. Moslems and Jews managed to live together in relative peace over the next 500 years.

The Jews were tolerated under the Moslem system while the Christians were discriminated against. The Jews were considered a stateless people with no military defense which garnered sympathy from the Ottomans. A similar rationale would help bring together world support for the creation of Israel following the helplessness that the Holocaust tragically exposed. My father would later become one the early members of an organized military defense for the sake of the Jewish people. After centuries of persecution, the Jews of my father's generation vowed "Never Again!" and established the defense forces to uphold that motto. As a consequence, the Moslem nations lost any hint of previously held sympathy towards the Jews once they were actually able to defend themselves and determine their own destiny.

As the defenseless Sephardim settled along the welcoming Mediterranean communities, the extended Varsano family settled in several Balkan countries. The Balkan region was a caldron of nationalities and the hub of the Ottoman Empire. Immigration records reveal citizens with the Varsano surname in Bulgaria and Greece. Our particular branch of the family migrated inland to the non-Mediterranean and unfamiliar region of Bulgaria. Since the Bulgaria nation did not exist during the Ottoman period, the Balkan Jews within the empire were considered one people. The immigrants to Bulgaria came in four separate waves via Salonika, Constantinople, Adrianople, and Ragura. The third wave of Sephardic immigrants, including my family, settled in Sofia some time after 1497.

The Sephardic culture of the Spanish Jews mixed with Romaniot—descendants of Jewish communities of the Byzantium and the Hellenistic world—and Ashkenazi culture of the native Jews in Bulgaria. Some of the native Bulgarian Jews had had been exiled from Provence, like my ancestors, but went directly to the Ottoman Empire instead of Spain. The rich tradition of the Spanish Jews quickly spread and Ladino became the predominant language of the Balkan Jews. The longevity of Ladino was evident during my father's lifetime because almost every Jew in Bulgaria regularly conversed in this adapted form of Spanish despite it being over four hundred years since his ancestors lived in Spain. The new Jewish community of the Ottoman Empire mostly lived in cities, working as merchants and artisans. They had little contact with the majority of the Bulgarian people who were illiterate peasants living in the countryside. The same basic conditions of Jews in the cities separate from most of the other Bulgarians persisted into my father's childhood.

The Jews of Bulgaria had almost no need to even speak the dying Bulgarian language. Trade was conducted in Turkish, Greek, or Ladino. Jewish religion and scholarly pursuits were taught in Hebrew. The Bulgarian cities during the middle ages were multi-ethnic but had a Turkish majority. The multi-ethnicity and the usage of several languages was also a part of my father's early life in Bulgaria. He could speak Bulgarian, Ladino, and Hebrew by the time he was a teenager and was lumped together by the government with other minority groups such as Turks and Armenians.

The great Sephardic culture had overcome adversity and thrived once again. The culinary tradition of the Spanish Jews now incorporated dishes from the heritage of Greek, Roman, Byzantine, Persian, Arab, and Ottoman culture. The rice based dishes that originated from Spain continued to be a staple of the cuisine for the Jews of the Ottoman Empire and many generations later during my father's lifetime. The flexible language of Ladino borrowed words from Greek, Turkish, French, Arabic and even some Bulgarian and Slavic additions.

There was a separate Jewish millet in the Ottoman system through which Jews enjoyed some measure of self-government. A few politically adept Jews even became influential advisors to the sultans. In the area of Northern Greece, the city of Solonika became an Ottoman Center for Jewish life and the Jewish residents briefly held a majority in the population which was a rarity for this sparse group of people. A portion of the Varsano family originating from Spain was among the sizable Jewish population in Greece until the early 20th Century.

Meanwhile, the Ashkenazi Jews in Western and Northern Europe were exposed to an entirely different civilization. On one hand, the Renaissance theoretically led to a more "enlightened" view of religions and the invention of the printing press made popular the studies of ancient texts such as Hebrew, Greek, and Roman. Unfortunately, the reality of the times was the constant struggle between the different sects of Christianity and Judaism.

The Roman Church wanted to stamp out all heresy and reform movements. In the Pope's eyes, the Jews appeared to be the allies of the Protestants. Starting in Italian cities, Jewish communities which were previously in a loosely demarked quarter and allowed to mingle with others for mostly business purpose were confined to ghettos, places of deprivation and isolation. The xenophobic practice of banishing Jews to clearly defined ghetto areas quickly spread throughout Italy, then throughout the rest of Christian Europe. The oppressive practice of forced isolation would be repeated in the same countries in Europe during WWII and eventually spread to my father's historically tolerant home in Bulgaria.

Militant Christian sects from the imperialist nations of the north attacked the Moslem nations of the Ottoman Empire, causing the displacement of many Jews. After years of Ottoman taxation and resentment from other nations, economic stagnation and external pressure forced the power of the empire into decline. European foes from the North repeatedly attacked regions of Bulgaria, hitting the port cities first. The Jewish residents, mostly merchants in these Danube River port towns, were subject to anti-Semitic persecution by their Northern European conquerors. Most of these Jews fled inland to the safety of cities like Sofia. My ancestors were exposed to the nearby persecution of Jews for the first time in centuries but they were confident that the open-minded city of Sofia would be a safe haven for them. In reality, my ancestors had few options since most Jews were being treated in a much worse manner in virtually all other places in Europe. By the end of the 16th Century, the Ottoman Empire was an economic disaster and over taxation only worsened the problem. Scapegoating became more common and religious tolerance dwindled. The Jewish community suffered with the rest of the empire and became disillusioned.

The Sephardim turned to blind faith and false hope. In 1665, Shabeti Savee, a Turkish Jew, proclaimed himself the messiah. Many Jews drew inspiration and hope from this apparent messiah. Unfortunately, he was charlatan. The Turks eventually arrested him and forced him to convert to Islam. The Jewish community became disillusioned and religious teaching lost credibility. The effects of the decline of religious orthodoxy in Bulgaria were felt during my father's lifetime because his country remained skeptical about religious zealotry. My father never spoke about the coming of the messiah or alluded to any other theological prophesies. The earthly moral teachings and the daily rituals were always more important to my family than finding the answers to existential questions or the promise of a blissful afterlife.

Since Bulgaria was not a central part of the Ottoman Empire, the Jews in Bulgaria received a diluted form of the spiritual movements within the empire. The changes brought about by the Reformation, Renaissance, and Enlightenment to the Christian community were barely felt in Bulgaria. The Bulgarians were always individualistic and lacked an enthusiasm for the trends of the rest of the empire. Therefore, the Jews of Bulgaria—including my ancestors—did not have faith in the apparent messiah like the rest of the Balkan Jews. My father had a common sense view of religion and only believed what he could actually verify. He would rather rely on his family and own personal diligence than the uncertain proclamations of a rabbi.

By the 18th Century, the Christian nations of Europe were growing stronger, while the Ottoman Empire was crumbling. In Western Europe, many Jews became integrated into the greater society by being involved in commerce and government. Generally, they were elegant, wealthy, and accepted. The Enlightenment purportedly eased social repression and religious intolerance, as well as enabled scientific breakthroughs. The American Declaration of Independence of 1776 and the French Revolution of 1789 allowed religious freedom to spread to a wider area of the globe, which provided even more opportunities for Jews seeking freedom.

In Russia, however, over half of the Jews enjoyed no freedom and languished under medieval customs and institutions. The Pale of Settlement was established which was an area the Jews could not leave. Jewish commerce was suppressed and they were forced into a rural agricultural based existence. Jews and Christians occasionally mingled in business but were completely separate both politically and socially. My family kept the memory of the Pale in mind when Bulgaria became a Soviet Bloc nation following WWII. The Jews of the Pale, as well as the Jews of the Soviet Union were treated poorly by their Russian rulers. My family was not going to fall into the trap of trusting communist promises of equality because history taught them the truth about the Russians.

The industrial revolution of the late 19th Century saw artisans and farmers lose their careers to new technologies. Assembly line factories mass produced products that relied on a distribution network of merchants and the financing of banks. Some banks and industrial plant owners were high profile Jews who became tremendously wealthy in the new economy. However, the vast majority of Jewish businessmen were relatively low volume merchants who were only considered middle class. Although most Western European Jewish families were modest, they became a symbol of the new power and wealth to many people. Anti-Semites blamed the problems of the modern world and the causes of poverty on the Jews which resulted in hate crimes and a tremendous amount of discrimination. Similar to the Conversos of Spain, many prominent European Jews simply converted to Christianity so that they could be more accepted into the culture and avoid the wrath of the Jew haters.

In Russia, Tsar Alexander II allowed the Jews to leave the Pale and go to universities. He sought to modernize the nation as the farmers gravitated towards the cities. In 1881, Alexander was assassinated by anarchists and the Jews were blamed. A pogrom, or riot, against the Jews ensued. Many Jews left Russia—mostly for the US—and some to Palestine. Two million Jews, about one third of Eastern European Jews, went to the United States over the next forty years on steamboats across the Atlantic Ocean. My mother's family was among those Ashkenazi Jews that immigrated to America, while my father's family remained in the relevantly tolerant and prosperous city of Sofia.

An environment of uncertainty and impending war caused many Ottoman Jews to flee with their Russian neighbors to the Americas. The precariously unstable Ottoman Empire was not comforting to the content group of Jews in the region. However, Jews were not active among the growing number of Bulgarian nationalists due to their relatively favorable situation under Ottoman rule. There was a fear that their position would worsen in a state that was Bulgarian in ethnicity and Christian Orthodox in faith. It was ironic to think that my family liked the Moslems while they feared the Christians because the exact opposite was true during the second half of the twentieth century.

In 1878, the Bulgarians and Russians defeated the ruling Turks of the debilitated Ottoman Empire, and an independent Bulgarian State was declared. When Bulgaria gained autonomy, the vibrant Jewish community retained a special status with substantial self-administration under a chief rabbi which was somewhat reminiscent of the millet system under the Ottomans. Historically, Sofia was a city on a major trade route with Constantinople where there was a significant Jewish population. Following the demise of the Ottomans, the displaced Jewish merchants of the Danube River towns inundated the already sizable Jewish community of the capital city of Sofia. My family weathered the storm and stayed in Bulgaria for several more decades. Perhaps the Varsano family's historical ability to persevere through hardships and have confidence in the leadership of Bulgaria was the reason they stayed in the Balkan nation even as the fascism of the 1940s deprived them of the good life that they had enjoyed for centuries.

Every Jewish family has a nomadic story filled with oppression and triumph. The Varsano family finds its origins in France, Spain, Bulgaria, and Greece. Although generation after generation was subjected to the whims of history, my ancestors weave a unique quilt of experience over the years that explain who we are today. The traditions were a reflection of the past and an explanation of the present. Mordecai Varsano, a Sephardic Jew living in Bulgaria, was a man bred to deal with the adversity that he would face him as a child and young man.

CHAPTER 3

The Rise of the Fascist Pirates

After Bulgaria received its independence from the Ottoman Empire, it was forced to cope with the problems of modernizing an underdeveloped nation. The result was a nation with untested economic systems and precarious alliances. The ensuing fascist experiment would ultimately have a terrifying effect on my father's childhood.

Following the establishment of an independent Bulgaria, the West became leery of a unified pro-Russian Bulgaria and sought to divide the country into segments. Bulgaria proper was now a separate region from Eastern Rumelia, Thrace, and Macedonia. The Bulgarian authorities felt they had the historic rights to these lands but begrudgingly agreed to the new constrictive borders. The Bulgarian leadership continually thirsted for the concept of a "greater Bulgaria," which became a key factor in their alliances with Germany eventually resulting in the cooperation in the persecution of the Jewish population, including my family, in all Bulgarian held territories.

Compared to the rest of European Jewry, however, the Bulgarians were sheltered and backwards. The national language of Bulgarian and medieval language of Ladino were taught to children while very few Jews even bothered to learn Hebrew. Similar to the late 20th Century in United States, the late 19th Century in Bulgaria saw many synagogues empty except for weddings, births, funerals, and the High Holy Days. For my great grandparents, contributing to the new independent country of Bulgaria became a higher priority than going to synagogue on a daily basis.

In 1912, the Bulgarians would instigate the Balkan Wars in order to recapture the "disputed" lands. The First Balkan War involved the Balkan League of Bulgaria, Serbia, Greece, and Montenegro successfully dividing what remained of the Ottoman Empire. The Second Balkan War of 1913 resulted in Bulgaria being defeated by Serbia, Greece, and Romania primarily over the control of Macedonia and Thrace. Approximately 5,000 Jewish citizens of Bulgaria proudly served in the country's military for these wars and suffered many causalities. The Jews of Bulgaria were mostly patriotic and the Bulgarian government appreciated their contributions until fascism took hold.

The Bulgarian leader prior to WWI was Tsar Ferdinand Radoslavov who professed an official policy of "strict and loyal neutrality" in the burgeoning war, but economic dependence on foreign nations and internal political pressures forced them to take sides. In 1914, the Bulgaria government accepted a loan of 500 million gold lev from Germany, while rejecting a similar offer from France because the French wanted the Bulgarians to pledge their loyalty to the Western powers in exchange.

Germany fully expected Bulgaria to join their war coalition as compensation for the loan. German companies also began to receive railroad construction contracts and mining rights within Bulgaria which would later be worked on by Jewish slave labor, which included my grandfather during WWII.

46

The Central Powers of Germany, Austria-Hungary, and the Ottoman Empire wanted Bulgaria to join their coalition because Constantinople and the Straits could be controlled and Serbia could be attacked through Bulgaria. Bulgaria officially changed their ambiguous foreign policy to "armed neutrality" which was shortly followed by joining the Central Powers. By the fall of 1915, the Central Powers appeared poised for victory and the Germans offered Bulgaria the territorial gains of Macedonia and most of Thrace as a reward.

There were over 7,000 Jewish soldiers killed in action in WWI. My father's maternal grandfather, Samuel Leon, proudly served in the Bulgarian forces of WWI and managed to survive "the war to end all wars." Twenty-eight Jewish soldiers reached the distinction of being officers and three Jewish men even achieved the high rank of colonel. My great grandfather's valiant service in the Bulgarian military stood in stark contrast to his son's participation in WWII, a generation later. My grandfather, along with the rest of the Jews of Bulgaria, wasn't welcome in the armed services of their own homeland which illustrates the decline in social progress that would occur in Bulgaria following WWI.

As the devastation of war grew, the Bulgarian enthusiasm shifted to despair. The military began appropriating supplies from the civilian population to serve the troops. Inflation started to take its toll and a pre-existing black market exploded with ensuing corruption that lasted several generations. The financial reliance on the Central Powers tightened while public dissatisfaction and war causalities continued to rise. French and British troops led an invasion into war torn Bulgaria and by September of 1919, Bulgaria was forced to sign the Armistice of Salonika which gave back all of the "new territories." A few days later, Ferdinand resigned in disgrace and abdicated his throne to his young son, Boris III. Followed shortly by the signing of the Treaty of Neuilly between Bulgaria and the victorious Allied Powers in which Bulgaria was forced to cede land to Greece and Yugoslavia, thus depriving it of an outlet to the Aegean Sea.

Most of the treaties that ended WWI sought to punish rather than rebuild the defeated nations which resulted in more radical forms of government. The downtrodden states of the former Central Powers were fertile grounds for fascism to take root. The years immediately following the war in Bulgaria were marked by servicing war debt, uneasiness with their Balkan neighbors, slow economic growth, temporary political coalitions, and a rise of socialism. The disgruntled Bulgarian people replaced the existing government with a new ruling party whose main goal was to consolidate power in order to promote economic growth which followed the model of the Italian Fascists.

Thankfully for my great grand parents, the early form of a fascist government in Bulgaria was short-lived. While authoritarian governments and extreme anti-Semitism in the rest of Europe metastasized, the low profile Balkan nation of Bulgaria remained fairly insulated until WWII began. The Jews of Bulgaria were allowed the freedom to educate themselves as they saw fit and practice their religion without legal restrictions.

Most of the Bulgarian Jewish children of my great grandparent's generation were educated in part by a French school known as Alliance Israelite Universelle (AIU). Although it taught

48

Jewish studies, it was more of a secular education that spread the French culture. My great grandfather could fluently speak Bulgarian, French, and Ladino while many Jewish adults also spoke Greek and Turkish for business purposes. Although it had been centuries since anyone in the Varsano family lived in France, the French traditions had been reintroduced to us. Bits and pieces of the French culture and language were eventually passed down to my father's generation, but to a far lesser extent than the Sephardic culture of Spain.

The French cultural imperialism died out after several years and was replaced by Jewish Nationalism with an emphasis on learning Hebrew. In the early 20th Century, Zionist youth organizations captured the spirit and political diversity of the Jewish families of Bulgaria. In addition to educating the children, these groups were also a social outlet and a center of activity best illustrated by the sports oriented group Maccabi. The Maccabi club was modeled after the Yunak Bulgarian Athletic Youth group and the Sokol organizations of other Slavic countries. As a child, my grandfather wore the Maccabi uniform which was the colors of the Zionist flag splashed with Bulgarian pride; white shirt, blue pants, a Bulgarian flag ribbon, and finished off by a blue and white hat. An intermingling of loyalties was a common practice among the Jews of Bulgaria.

My grandparent's generation was loyal to their country, but wanted democratic change. They sought Jewish schools that were independent from the local synagogues. They strove for equal voting rights and representation regardless of position or wealth. They wanted to change their own Jewish community at home while seeking to establish a Zionist infrastructure with other Jews around the world.

49

The urge for a creating a better life was instilled in my father at a very early age. His parents taught him the importance of his heritage and the need to secure a homeland for the Jewish people.

The Bulgarian government before WWII was very tolerant of Zionist activity compared to other European nations. This phenomenon can be explained by the historical tolerance of the Bulgarian nation and the lack of political disturbances by Jews. Few Jews in Bulgaria were involved in national politics compared to other European nations. The main political cause of most Jews was Zionism, but they still remained loyal and patriotic citizens of Bulgaria. Eventually, assimilation and Zionism helped erode the traditional Sephardic culture and religious observances.

Jews experienced very little anti-Semitism in Bulgaria due to the multi-ethnic tradition of the country. The Turks and the Greeks were traditional enemies and a larger minority group than the Jews, so they received the brunt of Bulgarian xenophobia. Most Bulgarian politicians did not promote anti-Semitism and the average Bulgarian did not even come in contact with the mostly insulated Jewish community. Jews did not have high positions in the Bulgarian government and did not exercise significant economic influence over the country as their counterparts did in other Western European countries. Therefore, they did not experience economically based anti-Semitism like other Jews in Europe.

However, there were scattered anti-Semitic incidents within Bulgarian cities targeting Jewish populations mostly instigated by racist organizations from Vienna, St. Petersburg, and Berlin. The multiethnic Bulgarian populace was not a receptive audience to these

50

forces and the intelligentsia publicly celebrated their policies on Jews and their tolerance of other cultures. Despite the nation's resistance, the state sponsored anti-Semitism of foreign nations would continue to infiltrate and expand in Bulgaria throughout my father's childhood.

While systematic anti-Semitism wasn't prevalent, my father did experience isolated incidents of bigotry and discrimination. Christian boys would make derogatory comments about "Seeco the Jew," and he would respond by getting the kid in a headlock with his left arm then punching him in the face with his right fist. He once demonstrated that move to me when I was a child to show me how to defend myself against the bully's. He also said that throwing rocks was a good tactic against a larger opponent. Sometimes he unable to fight back against a more imposing force like when he was on the receiving end of some beatings from schoolmasters. Even though he attended secular schools, he was still a Jewish minority student in a predominately Christian school. While the teachers did not express overt anti-Semitism, some clearly had their prejudices. Corporal punishment was an accepted form of discipline and my father received spankings and was hit with a ruler for bad behavior. The more the teacher disliked Jews, the more severe the punishment was. However, corporal punishment wasn't only restricted to non-Jewish teachers; my grandfather also would strike his son as a form of discipline. Achieving results through the use of force helped to formulate my father's value system. Physical intimidation and negative reinforcement were the acceptable parenting tools to enforce respect for authority and punish insubordination.

Meanwhile on the national scale, the Bulgarian leaders were governing their people in a similar manner to parents disciplining their children: authoritatively. The experimental fascist regime was short lived and was eventually forced from power by military factions that took over the government and imposed dictatorial measures. They abolished all political parties and changed the representation of the Subranie (Bulgarian Parliament). Instead of political parties, Subranie members would represent classes of people such as peasants, workers, artisans, merchants, intelligentsia, bureaucrats, and professionals. Since my grandfather owned a hardware store, his family was designated a merchant class.

Meanwhile in nearby Germany, the popularity of the Nazi party spelled the end for millions of Jews on German lands, and would eventually directly affect the Jews of Bulgaria. In 1935, the Nuremberg Laws and the Law for the Protection of German Blood and Honor were instituted which denied German Jews rights of citizenship, as well as the right to marry German citizens. While Germany blamed it problems on minorities, Bulgaria tried to establish a system that would be fair to all of its citizens.

In the midst of my father's otherwise pleasant childhood, the economic crisis had led to an alliance between the workers and the peasants against bourgeois domination and fascism. The resented bourgeoisie consisted of former political party activists and leaders from the professions such as lawyers, financiers, industrialists, merchants and statesmen Even though some merchants were considered bourgeois, my grandfather was a Jew with no political ambitions and could not have been blamed by any reasonable person for the economic problems of the peasant and worker classes. The rise of communism and the strike movement helped to bring a demise to the government. The Bulgarian public was alarmed by the authoritarianism of the existing ruling party, so a coalition of various political factions effectively removed them from power. Consequently, a royal dictatorship headed by Tsar Boris III was declared—who would be the ruler had the power of life or death over my family.

The royal dictatorship was not an absolute monarchy, but a government of compromise. The three major political factions were the ruling party, the "legal" opposition of old bourgeoisie party men, and the illegal opposition consisting of Agrarians, Communists, and political exiles. The Fascists were a much smaller faction which did not attain the same level of popularity as they did in Germany and Italy.

Boris was relatively popular and created an economically stable country. He allowed an election in 1938, but the policy of no political parties was kept in place. The new government forced diversification which led to the dwindling of large state sponsored industries and started the growth of small private industries. Since my grandfather owned a modest hardware store, the current economic trend was favorable for his business.

However, by the late 1930s, times were not good for all Bulgarians. Bulgarian commerce was still largely state controlled and centralized in Sofia despite diversification efforts. The social and political gap between the peasants in the rural regions and the modern urbanites grew wider. Most Bulgarian Jews, as well as the Varsano family, enjoyed the fruits of modern Europe in the late 1930s because

53

they resided mostly in the prosperous cities and didn't share the discontentment with the rest of the country.

By 1938, a second set of Nuremberg Laws in Germany was set forth that further persecuted and humiliated the Jewish population. Jews were forced to wear a Star of David and to live in ghettos. They were not allowed to ride public transportation or possess an automobile. Less than a year later, the Third Reich's policies of rounding up Jews in an orderly manner began expanding to the new lands that they dominated and eventually to allied nations like Bulgaria.

Notwithstanding the royal monarchy, Bulgaria was collaborating with the other fascist regimes in Europe. Bulgaria had a social dependence on Italy because Boris was married to the daughter of King Victor Emanuel III of Italy. Bulgaria also had an economic and military reliance on Germany since WWI. Germany purchased two thirds of Bulgarian agricultural exports and provided Bulgaria with loans, industrial trade, and armaments. Many middle class Bulgarians were educated in Berlin, Munich, and Vienna. From the German strategic perspective, the Balkan nations were not an immediate military priority but economic domination was essential.

In early 1939 following Germany annexation of Czechoslovakia, Boris began to realize that an alliance with the Third Reich was the only way to avoid forced occupation even though he was more philosophically attuned to the Western powers. Tsar Boris and Adolph Hitler began to secretly negotiate the terms of their pact. Bulgaria wanted the land lost in the Treaty of Neuilly, including Dobrudja from Romania and Thrace from Greece. The Germans agreed to let the Bulgarians acquire these "new territories" in exchange for mining rights within rural Bulgaria and other forms of non-official cooperation.

Throughout the early years of the war, Bulgaria positioned itself with the anti-Western forces which also turned out to be extremely anti-Semitic forces as well. Following the formation of the Nazi-Soviet Alliance, the Bulgarian-Soviet Commercial Treaty was signed and the pro-Western Prime Minister, Georgi Kioseivanov, was deposed in favor of the pro-German Bogdan Filov.

Filov's regime was pro-German and Anti-Semitic from the outset which set the tone for Bulgaria's participation in WWII. Bulgaria had indeed emerged from the shadows of Turkish rule to become a more modern and more militant nation. After being soundly defeated in the Balkan Wars and WWI, the still recovering nation turned to a more brutal and long term form of fascism for what they believed would be an expedient ascension to world prominence. The Bulgaria people were desperate to recover from failed military campaigns and prosper economically by any means possible.

The Jews and other minority groups of Bulgaria would suffer greatly under Filov's government. The unfolding of events within Bulgaria following their independence in 1878 until WWII, points to clear alliances with the Germans and their susceptibility to a form of government that emphasized nationalism and authority centered around one leader known as fascism. However, Bulgaria's alliances of convenience contradicted the region's centuries-old policy of tolerance and would prove to be detrimental to the nation for many years to come.

During Filov's reign of terror, my father would have his dreams shattered and his innocence robbed. The Varsano family had been contently settled in Bulgaria for about 450 years. They were patriotic and law abiding citizens that directly contributed to the well being of the community by gainfully employing Jews and non Jews alike. No one in my family was ever a radical or revolutionary, and they even passively accepted their role as discriminated minority group as long as they could earn a living and keep their traditions. They weren't interesting in ruling Bulgaria and were satisfied being willing subjects in a multi-ethnic society. After so many years of good standing, the faltering of the political structure throughout Europe would turn my family and their Jewish neighbors into unwilling enemies of their own nations.

CHAPTER 4

The Sinking Vessel

In the latter half of the year 1939, my father turned seven years old and Adolph Hitler began his camcjmpaign of hate and subjugation across Europe. WWII would transform my father's life from that of a privileged son of an affluent Jewish family to an impoverished child, lucky to escape the war with his life. At the onset of fighting, Bulgaria was already controlled by the Fascist Party which made joining the Axis powers inevitable. The next four arduous years saw the Jewish citizens of Bulgaria used as bargaining chips with the Nazi regime, with an ultimate deal that was unpredictably better for the Jews of Bulgaria than majority of European Jewry.

The vast majority of the Jews of Bulgaria were not accustomed to severe anti-Semitism, so as the war began, they were not too concerned about religious persecution. My father was transformed from a naive boy to a child that was mature beyond his years and well aware of his enemies. He spent his precious formative years under a brutal regime that deprived him of an authentic childhood.

The fall of 1939 marked the beginning of official government sponsored anti-Semitic legislation. Starting in September, 4,000 Jews from Central Europe were temporarily in Bulgaria on route to Palestine. Instead of allowing them safe passage, they were deported to uncertain and problematic destinations. The next month, Aleksandur Belev, a pro-Nazi and rabid anti-Semite became head of the Bulgarian

Government's Agency regarding Jewish matters. Belev's appointment was a terrible blow to the Jewish citizens of Bulgaria, and his policies would certainly become more inhumane as the fascist machine became more powerful.

In July of 1940, Bulgaria adopted the "Law for the Defense of the Nation," or ZZN (Bulgarian acronym), which was a Slavic version of the Nuremberg Laws. Although there was some debate in the Subranie over whether anti-Mason and other anti-union type legislation should be included in the law, the sections regarding restrictions on Jews passed rather easily. Filov instituted a Nazi-type youth league that would fundamentally divide all of the children of Bulgaria into the majority Christians against the other minority groups. The honeymoon of my father's youth was over by his eighth birthday. It was clear that Tsar Boris and the Bulgarian government felt that the Jews were expendable and were prepared to use them as a negotiating tool for international diplomacy.

Financially, the Bulgarian people had no problem exploiting their Jewish neighbors. Confiscation of Jewish property under the ZZN was aggressively enforced. Special taxes were imposed on Jewish families and businesses. In spite of the government's new policies, my family was still able to live a decent lifestyle, but the constrictive net of anti-Semitic legislation was slowly closing in on them and depriving them of the amenities and achievements that my grandfather had worked so hard to achieve.

The ZZN was humiliating for Jews, but all parts of the law were not stringently enforced at first. Article 33 stated that Jews that served in the Bulgarian military or converted to Christianity enjoyed special privileges and were exempt from restrictions in some cases. This loophole helped many families, including the Varsanos. My father's maternal grandfather, Samuel Leon, was a WWI veteran which slightly helped the whole family in the early days of WWII.

The leaders of the well organized Jewish community in Bulgaria began making attempts to transfer their people to a safer country with the most logical destination for those seeking refuge: Palestine. However, British, Bulgarian, Arab, and German officials made mass emigration to the Holy Land nearly impossible. The entire Jewish community of Europe tried to get a limited number of children to the safety of Palestine, but with only scattered success. The SS Salvator from Bulgaria, overcrowded with desperate Jewish passengers, barely reached its destination of Haifa, Palestine. The British port authorities sent the unstable ship back to sea and she eventually sank in the Turkish straits, killing 280 passengers and dealing a devastating blow to the hopes of the Zionists. My family decided that they would ride out the war in Bulgaria and hope for the best.

Meanwhile, authorities within Bulgaria had made a deal that would essentially trade land for Nazi cooperation. Bulgaria would comply with Germany political plans, and in return Germany coerced Romania to cede Bulgaria the region of Dobrudja with its 5,000 Jewish residents.

The Reich forcefully encouraged its neighbors to fully embrace their Nazi ideologies. Boris gladly accepted the spoils of fascist conquests and became a good friend of the Germans. He began renaming the streets of Sofia to identify the country's new heroes.

Adolph Hitler, Benito Mussolini, and Victor Emanuel III all became new street names in my father's hometown. Practically overnight, the familiar avenues of his innocence vanished.

In October of 1940, Italy invaded Greece, but Bulgaria which was officially neutral declined any obvious involvement in the military action. The Bulgarians were still interested in re-acquiring Thrace and would be passive during the Italian operations. Greece would be a tragically brave example of a Balkan country that fought the tyrannical forces of fascism rather than embracing them.

Italy's attempt to conquer Greece failed. The battle of the two empires of antiquity ended in a Roman defeat, but the modern day Nazi storm troopers accomplished what the Italian legions could not. In order for the German invasion - known as Operation Marita - to be effective, the Axis troops would have to go through Bulgaria. Lured by the promise of territorial gain, Boris allowed the Germans safe passage and support on their way to fighting the Greeks. As a reward for their complicity, Bulgaria would receive the region of Thrace which had about 6,000 Jewish residents.

Bulgarian support of Operation Marita effectively ended their tenuous neutrality, and in March of 1941 Bulgaria entered the Three Power Pact Alliance with the Axis countries. A few weeks later, Yugoslavia signed the Three Power Pact for similar reasons as Bulgaria. However, shortly after the Yugoslavian decision, an internal coup instituted an anti-Nazi government in the capital city of Belgrade. Berlin responded by including Yugoslavia in their invasion and conquest plans of Operation Marita. The Yugoslavian coup furthered Bulgaria's alliance with Germany because of the prospect of even more territorial gains from their neighbor to the west. Bulgaria went a step further in December when it declared war on the United States and Great Britain, but stopped short of a war declaration on their Slavic brothers in the Soviet Union.

With the help of German advances in Yugoslavia, Bulgaria annexed Macedonia which it added to its war chest of "recently liberated territories." The Macedonian region, along with their 8,000 Jewish residents, would be governed by Bulgaria rather than locally controlled. The fate of the Jews in the new territories would help delay the persecution of my father in coming years. Every asset of a nation, including its people, became negotiating tools to be exploited for strategic importance. The location of Bulgaria was a major asset and its leaders intended to use their geopolitical position for the maximum amount of gain.

Before the German invasion of Russia began, both sides courted Bulgaria for their political support. The Soviets, led by Joseph Stalin, were pressuring the Bulgarians to sign a mutual defense pact. Boris, clinging to the unrealistic notion of neutrality, refused Stalin's request and thus angered many Bulgarian communists. Great Britain also wanted Bulgarian support in order to create a second front to the war in the Balkans for their strategic advantage. Germany, on the verge of committing tremendous resources to the Soviet offensive, did not want to exhaust troops and supplies to occupy the Balkan Peninsula. Germany needed to exert control of the Balkans while expending a minimal amount of capital and effort.

The German invasion of the Soviet Union had a severe impact on the Communist Party of Bulgaria (BKP). The party leaders, some of whom were Jewish, were rounded up and put into political concentration camps. In response, underground guerrilla militias consisting of an unusual coalition of communists, Greeks, Yugoslavians, and Jews began springing up throughout the country. Although there were only about 400 Jews in approximately 10,000 partisans, this represented twice their percentage of the total population. With the aid of the Western Allies and the USSR, the partisans became an overt nuisance and a significant internal political problem for the Bulgarian government.

By September of 1941, the government closed the American College in Sofia, which had been allowing more than the mandated five percent maximum enrollment for Jewish students. Consequently Seeco and Seli were forced to attend the remedial Bulgarian public schools. Previously, the ZZN required Jewish men of working age to serve in labor groups supervised by the Ministry of War, which was considered a somewhat patriotic duty because it contributed to the war effort. Under the new rules, Jewish men, including my grandfather, were put into forced labor crews under the Ministry of Public Works which was viewed as an obvious punishment that was not related to helping national aspirations. The slave laborers were also forced to shave their heads and many were treated in a degrading manner. On July 19, 1942 all Jewish men ages twenty to forty-five were to report for labor service on roads and railway beds in strategic parts of Bulgaria. My grandfather was sentenced to work in a remote section of railroad near the Bof station. My grandfather was relatively lucky because he was not physically abused; he just had to work long grueling days for no pay.

My father was traumatized by the breakup of his nuclear family by the government authorities whose anti-Semitic net continued to close in every Jew. Even though my grandfather was in a forced labor camp, he could still visit his family occasionally. His appearance shocked my father because his freshly shaven head gave him an unusually depersonalized look—similar to concentration camp victims. A few years later, the Israeli military would not require their soldiers to have short hair cuts because of the Holocaust imagery of the bald headed captive. While my grandfather spent hours of hard labor building railroads, my family heard rumors of other camps in Romania, Germany, and Poland where Jews were being exterminated. The labor camps in Bulgaria were viewed as a lesser evil, but there was a constant fear that they would be transformed into extermination camps.

In Germany, the brain trust of the Nazi Party reached a "Final Solution to the Jewish Problem." Justifying that it was not possible to deport all the Jews to Palestine, Adolph Hitler and Hermann Goering—a leader in the Nazi Party and prime architect of the Nazi police—officially gave orders to kill all the European Jews. The Fuehrer and Schutzstaffel (SS) Commander Heinrich Himmler also made the decision to kill all the Jews in Russia during their planned invasion. The genocide of the Jewish people would be carried out in an orderly German manner which was outlined at the Wannsee Conference in January of 1942. Jews from various European countries were to be identified, rounded up, and deported to extermination camps in Poland with the cooperation of Nazi and local officials.

By the spring of 1942, Jews of Bulgarian citizenship living within the Reich and its protectorate (a masked form of annexation) were deported to the exterminations camps in Poland. Tsar Boris was again sacrificing Jewish rights at the behest of Hitler and was held up to other European leaders as a model of cooperation. In a meager attempt to appeal to humanitarian concerns, Boris temporarily refused to give up the Jews of Bulgaria citizenship that were living in France, Yugoslavia, and other occupied territories. Later, the Bulgarian authorities acquiesced to the Nazi plans, and stated that all Jews of Bulgarian citizenship living in conquered foreign countries were subject to German law. My father began to get the sense that no one was safe. Any citizen of country associated with the Reich, especially Jews, was merely at the mercy of their government's whims and had little chance to voice opposition or exercise political rights. He heard that Jews across Europe were having their basic human rights unceremoniously stripped from them. Nothing was guaranteed because he had to rely on rumor and innuendo for news. The authoritarian regime controlled the media and truthful information was suppressed and manipulated for propaganda purposes. All that was certain was what was happening in your community that very instant. The future was fully dependent on how the battles in the war turned out and how the politician postured accordingly. He learned to trust only people close to him, namely Jews. He also learned to rely on himself at an early age because his father might be taken away or murdered at any time. The basic traits of self reliance and distrust of outsiders stayed with him for the rest of his life. As matters became worse, his distrust intensified into outright loathing.

The engulfing Bulgarian wave of Jewish maltreatment grew more powerful with the Decree of August 26, 1942. The decree strengthened the ZZN regulations and established a body within the Ministry of Internal Affairs called Komisarstvo za Evreiskite Vuprosi (KEV), or the Commissariat for Jewish Questions. The KEV would legally have the power to enact rules regarding Jews without the approval of the Subranie or the king. The familiar enemy of the Jews, Aleksandur Belev, would run the newly empowered government agency.

The KEV under Belev was a nightmare for the Jewish people, no matter how religious or politically active they were. A central point to the August 26 Decree was that a person's ancestry rather than their religion was the key factor in determining who was a Jew. Unlike the Spanish Inquisition, conversion to Christianity could not dispel the hatred of the fascists. Article 29 stipulated that any unemployed Jews of working age would be expelled from Sofia. Consequently, Magazine Stomano became the employer of several Varsano family members and friends. Seeco and Seli curiously peeked through the keyhole of their parent's room as they hid the French gold bullion coins in the hollowed out cores of the furniture from confiscation by the KEV treasury.

To combat this financial plundering, my grandfather covertly made arrangements to funnel his savings to Swiss Bank accounts. These accounts were considered safe because Switzerland was neutral and the accounts were secretly number. Unfortunately, the Varsano deposits into Swiss accounts were never recovered despite the efforts of the legal community from the 1940s through the 1990s.

The KEV actively pursued the seizure of all Jewish assets. Cash, marketable securities, precious metals and stones were placed in separate accounts for "safekeeping" under the control of the commission. The bookkeeping for seized assets was corrupt and sloppy with the rampant misappropriation of Jewish funds to conspiring banks. KEV lackeys were even legally allowed to live in Jewish apartments. Objects of attributed value such as musical instruments and rugs were registered and placed at the disposal of KEV officers. My father's accordion and other furnishings of the Varsano family apartment were never to be seen again. The frivolous sounds of the wheezing accordion keyboard were replaced by the melancholy prayers for freedom that so many Jewish generations lamented.

The net of authoritarian confiscation had scooped up the cherished possessions of the entire family. The progressively intensifying persecution of the Jews of the mid 20th Century mirrored the censuring, restrictions, inquisition, and exile that our ancestors in Spain experienced 450 years earlier. No one ever imagined that history would repeat itself in such modern and apparently civilized times. My family realized that man was capable of committing atrocities no matter what era it was.

The commission sought to restrict Jews from participating in the formerly integrated Bulgarian society. By the end of 1942, Belev ordered the confiscation of all Jewish owned automobiles, motorcycles, bicycles, radios, and home telephones. My grandfather's convertible Fiat automobile and motorcycle with side car which gave him a great sense of personal pride were unceremoniously repossessed from him. Like the pre-Civil Rights Movement discrimination against "colored people" in the United States, Jews in Bulgaria were also restricted from visiting certain hotels, parks, theaters, and other public places.

In order to further their plans, an essential step for the KEV was to determine the designation and location of all Jews within the country. The ultimate goal of this information gathering process was to arrange for deportation with the SS. Stars of David marked all Jewish homes, businesses, and people. When the rule requiring the wearing of yellow stars was first established, there was a shortage of government issued stars. Some Jews decided to make their own custom stars to wear, complete with a picture of the King and Queen of Bulgaria. Even though the stars were meant to alienate and ridicule the Jews, many of them still felt patriotic towards the country that treated them as enemies

In spite of the Germans aggressively pressing for deportations, the Bulgarian government was somewhat apprehensive to deport all the Jews for several reasons. Legally, the Subranie was concerned with the precedent of deporting law abiding citizens of their country. Economically, they claimed the Jews were needed for road building and railway beds. Socially, deportations might cause unrest and political upheaval among the civilian population.

In the winter of 1942 Walter Schellenberg, head of espionage services (RSHA) for the Third Reich sent Berlin a secret report regarding the treatment of the Jews. The very critical and demanding report stated that Bulgarians were disinterested in deporting and persecuting Jews. It also said that the King's royal court had Jewish connections that were reassuring their people that the worst was behind them. Although some of the report was accurate, much of it was hyperbole meant to incite anti-Semitic forces into action. Following the Schellenberg report, Theodor Dannecker was sent to Bulgaria by the foreign office and RSHA to accelerate the Final Solution in Bulgaria. Dannecker -- who was previously the problem solver in charge of Jewish affairs in Paris -- was an SS officer under the command of Nazi extermination expert Adolph Eichmann. In February of 1943, Belev and Dannecker sent a plan to Gabrovski, the Bulgarian Minister of Internal Affairs, outlining a nine month schedule of deportation for all the Jews of Bulgaria.

The Dannecker-Belev agreement would be carried out in two stages with a contingency plan for second stage. The first phase of the plan involved the Jews living in Bulgaria's new territories. The Jews of Thrace, Macedonia, and additional 6,000 "undesirable" Jews in Bulgaria proper would be transferred to deportation camps and lose their Bulgarian citizenship. Since the Jews in recently annexed Dobruja were considered ethnically Bulgarian, they were grouped with Bulgaria proper. The process was to begin in March and last approximately one month. The Jews were to be told they were being relocated within Bulgaria and not deported; a deceptive tactic similar to telling gas chamber victims they were going to the showers.

The second phase of the plan stated that all the Jews in Bulgaria proper, or "old Bulgaria," were to be deported in a similar manner. Armed with the whereabouts of every Jew in Bulgaria, the KEV grouped them into ghettos. However, Warrant Number 127 stated that German authorities had the right to deport 20,000 Jews "inhabiting the recently liberated territories," but made no mention of

Bulgaria proper. This qualified choice of words might have unknowingly saved my father's life.

My father and aunt were merely children that were probably oblivious to the technicalities of the laws. The adults in the family, however, were aware and actively lobbied the Jewish political and economic groups to pressure the authorities while trying to ride the fine line of not being a partisan. They were just a regular law abiding family that wanted to work hard and have a peaceful life, not political radicals or violent protestors. The extent of their political involvement was isolated to issues of self preservation and they had no designs on ascension to power.

The loophole in the law bought my family some precious time which allowed more debate about Bulgaria's policies on Jews. The totalitarian drive to legislate discrimination and genocide was a tricky legal maneuver, especially when years of human rights laws were already on the books. The rule of law still existed, corrupted as the system might have been.

More potential perils still lay ahead for my family, though. It's like a defendant getting acquitted because of a small point in the law rather than being found innocent by a jury of his peers. Lives might have been spared temporarily but they certainly did not return to their pre-war routine.

Many Jews tried to find loopholes in the legislation to save their own lives. Jews that married non-Jews were exempt from wearing stars and deportation. So a marriage of convenience became another tactic that could save a family's doom. Certain Jews living in Bulgaria were exempt from many of the discriminatory laws because

69

they held foreign citizenship. Many Sephardic Jews became Spanish citizens, some 450 years after their expulsion from Spain.

It was quite ironic that the descendants of exiles would want to go back to the land of the Inquisition but when you're being persecuted, any place was better than where you were. My family probably would have gone to Africa, Australia, Antarctica, or any other safe continent. The history of the Jews was that of a nomadic people escaping persecution and migrating to whatever countries would accept them. Obviously, a safe place in Europe, Israel, or the US was the most preferable destination. Almost all Jews in Bulgaria still spoke Ladino and could assimilate into Spanish society easier than in other countries. Spain might have allowed a few Jewish political refugees on a case by case basis but the predominately Catholic country did not embrace mass Jewish immigration in the 1940s and my family remained stuck in Bulgaria.

Seeco and Seli got lucky in a way because they suffered from a contagious illness. While my grandfather Isaac was on his work detail, the rest of the family received evacuation orders to leave Sofia and go a place called Razgrad. "Fortunately," Seeco developed Peritonitis, an infection of the abdominal lining, and the health authorities restricted him to a quarantine area in their home. Seli became infected with Mumps so the Bulgarian Red Cross put a warning on the front door that "Danger – Infectious Disease: No one allowed in, No one allowed out!" That ominous warning granted my family a temporary reprieve from being banished from their hometown.

It was yet another ironic moment of the times that a contagious illness was viewed as a positive development. They were able to spend

70

a little more time in their home city but it only delayed their inevitable relocation. The opportune illness also illustrated to my family the sheer insanity of the anti-Semitic laws that being ill sometimes saved you from a worse fate. The ludicrous policies of the fascist government were sympathetic to ailing Jews but hateful towards healthy Jews. It seemed to me to be an unresolved moral dilemma of the authorities similar to someone who was on death row, but cannot be executed until they are deeming mental and physically well enough to face death. Rather than a death sentence, it was a forced relocation order to an unfamiliar locale with the possibility of eventual deportation.

Early in 1943, the KEV started implementing the deportation process. The KEV made a list of all Jews who were considered "rich, prominent, and generally well known," and a collection of "subversive" Jews. The KEV top officials wanted to deport entire families over individuals, which made saving children from deportation very difficult. Excluded from these lists were Jews in mixed marriages, but the previously exempted Jewish war heroes were now condemned. My great grandfather, Samuel Leon, lost his status as a WWI honored veteran and was suddenly considered an enemy of Bulgaria.

When word of the secret deportations spread through Bulgarian society, many people were outraged. Bulgarian Orthodox Christian leaders such as the Holy Synod and the Bishop of Plovdiv protested the deportations on moral grounds. The president of the Writer's Union and other prominent labor organizations opposed the action for a variety of social and legal reasons. To find out the details of the deportation plan and how to counteract it, KEV officials were regularly bribed for information by Jews of the underground movement in Bulgaria.

The Jews of Sofia and Kuistendil were the most effective in mounting a protest to the government's secret actions. Haim Rehamin Behar of Kuistendil learned about the exact wording of the decree that mentioned the deportation of the Jews of the "new territories," but made no mention of the Jews of pre-1941 Bulgaria. Behar, a former classmate of Dimitri Peshev who was currently vice president of the Subranie, gave the influential political leader a strategy to save the Jews of Bulgaria.

In March of 1943, Gabrovski and Filov conferred and agreed not to deport any of the Jews in "old Bulgaria" at that time. Before the desist order could be conveyed through the proper channels, many Jewish families were rounded up for deportation, only to be released a few hours later.

The temporary reprieve by the government merely delayed an obvious policy of inevitable exile. Dimitri Peshev and forty-two members of the Subranie sent Prime Minister Filov a letter of protest regarding Bulgaria's Jewish policy. A week later, a fierce debate broke out on the floor of the Subranie chambers. Since most of the forty-two members that signed the protest were in the opposition parties, the majority party voted to withdraw the protest. Consequently, Peshev was asked to resign his position as Vice President of the majority party, but initially refused. Two days later, a vote of no confidence in the majority ruling party failed and Peshev was forced to tender his resignation. Peshev's protest as well as the not so public assistance of the other "righteous gentiles" showed my family that many fellow Bulgarians were willing to risk their own wellbeing to take a stand against the senselessness of the fascist state. The end result of Peshev's courageous action was an opening of public debate on the previously covert process of deciding Jewish policy.

Two weeks before Peshev's heroic protest occurred, deportations for the Jews of Thrace had begun. Every Jewish person living in Thrace was awakened in the middle of the night, evicted from their homes and told they were being transferred to the interior of Bulgaria. Most Jews knew that they would be sent to the extermination camps in Poland and claimed foreign citizenship as a last ditch attempt to survive. Jews in Thrace, who possessed foreign citizenship, including Bulgarians, were included in the initial round up but were later released and sent to forced labor crews in Southwestern Bulgaria.

The rest of the Jews of Thrace were placed in temporary camps awaiting deportation. The so called "departure centers" were mostly located in tobacco warehouses and empty schools which lacked sufficient supplies. The condemned Jews were sprayed with cold water and subjected to humiliating searches. The overcrowding and unsanitary conditions caused many illnesses. The lack of food, medication, and proper shelter in the camps resulted in several deaths per day.

Next, they boarded open railroad cars and endured a long journey where they received harsh treatments from mostly anti-Semitic guards. Some of the guards were just soldiers or police doing their job, they didn't hate Jews but they couldn't disobey orders either. A few of the guards treated the Jews as humanely as possible under the circumstances, but most were anti-Semitic and took sadistic pleasure in tormenting their Jewish detainees. They told the Jews that their destination had changed and that they were going to Palestine, but most knew this was a lie. On this cramped and freezing journey many fell ill and some died from hunger and exposure. While the Jews were imprisoned, their property was liquidated and the proceeds were put into the infamous frozen bank accounts or the Jewish Community Fund. Looting was common, perpetrated by every walk of life: policemen, judges, KEV officials, laborers, and other government employees.

In Pirot, a similar process was taking place but with even harsher implementation. Pirot was a small section of eastern Serbia forty miles northwest of Sofia that was transferred to Bulgaria in 1941. Jews of foreign citizenship, with the exception of Bulgarians, were not spared deportation. The guards were especially vicious at these deportation camps, where brutal beating of the men and raping of the women were widely reported. The awful journey by train mirrored what occurred in Thrace.

The Jews of Macedonia were the last group to be deported from the "newly liberated territories," and were well aware of their impending fate. Some individuals managed to escape into Italian controlled Albania, but most were confined in the converted tobacco warehouse of Monopol Cigarettes, which was utilized as a concentration camp in Skopje.

The entire deportation operation required the conspiring of several countries of the Axis powers, but Bulgaria was the main player. The departure centers were under the authority of the Bulgarian State

Railway and the KEV. From the regional camps, many Jews were transferred to Sofia which was the transportation hub of the nation and where many of the Jewish residents had already been relocated to a rural portion of the country. From the Bulgarian capital city, they would be moved to the border town of Lom. In Lom, some railway cars would wait for days with the overcrowded Jewish passengers screaming for help. From the port of Lom, the remaining Jews boarded ships up the Danube River on route to Vienna, Austria.

Once in the Reich, it was a fatalistic journey to Katowicz, Poland and eventually to Treblinka. The journey was supervised by German police but the security was done by Bulgarian officials. Meanwhile, my grandfather was busy laying rail road tracks and filled rail road beds with heavy gravel just a few miles east of where the deportations of Jews to Treblinka were routed. Whether he knew exactly what was going on at the time, we'll never quite know. Truthful information was scarce which further elevated the family's anxiety and uncertainty. Maybe their ignorance regarding factual accounts of the Bulgarian deportations spared them even more grief because they couldn't have imagined how horrific the truth really was.

According to Bulgarian and German transportation figures the total deportations per country were as follows: 4,075 Thrace, 158 Pirot, and 7,160 Macedonia, for a total of 11,393. The liquidated funds from Jewish properties far exceeded the deportation costs, making it a profitable venture for Bulgarian government. All but twelve of the deported Jews perished in the gas chambers of Treblinka. The shame of these Bulgarian atrocities was an overlooked chapter of history that even my father never mentioned to me.

When the Western powers started to learn about Nazi atrocities committed in Poland and elsewhere, world opinion began to affect the fate of the remaining Jews in Bulgaria proper. In March of 1943, Franklin D. Roosevelt, Secretary of State Cordell Hull, British Foreign Secretary Anthony Eden, and other prominent officials met in Washington to discuss the fate of the Jews of Bulgaria. Britain was now willing to accept 50,000 Jews into Palestine. Unfortunately, the US balked because they were unsure of the logistics and cautious against making a public statement. While America was tentative, millions of European Jews were perishing in the Nazi death camps and my family was desperately clinging to empty promises coupled with unsubstantiated rumors. A few weeks later, the Allies convinced neighboring Turkey to allow the Jews to stay there temporarily on their way to Palestine. This plan was never implemented because Romania and Bulgaria refused to provide the ships for transport, and the internal politics of Turkey broke down. A tepid effort by the American and British for emigration to Palestine never materialized for the hopeful and anxious Jews of Bulgaria.

By the spring of 1943, Bulgaria's policy towards Jews had shifted from slowly carrying out the Nazi final solution to halting any new deportation plans until the outcome of the war was clear. The Axis powers were no longer favored to prevail. Boris was trying to hedge while he explored other strategic options. Anti-Bulgarian Partisans were increasing their military pressure within the Bulgaria homeland while Jewish partisans managed to assassinate a small number of right wing politicians.

In April of 1943, Tsar Boris traveled to Germany to meet with Adolph Hitler to discuss crucial issues regarding the war effort. Boris conveyed his feelings about the necessity of the Bulgarian Jews for road labor and that he only intended to deport the Jews of the new territories. The RSHA felt that Boris was making excuses and wanted all the Jews deported in quick order. The consummate compromiser, Boris agreed to deport 25,000 "communist elements," while the rest of the Jews remained in camps and labor groups. That amount represented more than half of the surviving Jewish population in Bulgaria and the actual amount of communists among them was a tiny fraction.

While the country as a whole was moving away from anti-Semitic sentiment, KEV chief Belev was drafting new schemes for Jewish deportation. Plan A would immediately deport all Jews except foreign citizens, Jews married to non-Jews, persons the state needed, and those seriously ill. The actual process would mimic the deportation procedure in Thrace. Plan B stated that the Jews in the cities, including my family, would be transferred to the interior provinces while awaiting deportation arrangements. Boris accepted Plan B, not Plan A, and it was eventually implemented.

On May 21, 1943 all the remaining Jews in Sofia received orders to leave the city within three days. The Bulgarian Orthodox Church and political opposition leaders staged public protests. Belev and Filov defiantly insisted that the Jews would be deported. In the Danube River port towns, empty steamships began to ominously cluster around the docks. The rumors of mass deportations had reached the forced labor camps, and somehow my grandfather was able to go back to Sofia with the help of some of his Bulgarian friends to tend to his family. He made arrangements to transfer his wife and children to a small town near the Romanian border named Novi Pazar.

My urban father along with his mother and sister were going to be forcibly relocated to the countryside to live under primitive conditions amongst Turkish peasants. A daily routine in the fields was a drastic shock but at least there was food and they were still in Bulgaria. My grandparents secretly feared it was the first step to being deported and, in fact, if Belev and Dannecker's original proposal was implemented, they would have eventually been deported as the latter half of the two phase process. It's hard for me to imagine in today's context, being forced from your homes simply because of your religious affiliation, then required to live with people that you did not know and shared little commonality. When I was ten years old, I just wanted to play with my friends in my familiar neighborhood. I didn't want to leave my block, much less leave the city. As a young child, you generally become attached to your close friends and to have them ripped away was just one small tragedy of this entire appalling period of history.

On May 24, a national holiday commemorating Saints Cyril and Methodius for their contributions to Bulgarian education, culture, and the Slavic script coincided with large scale public protest over Jewish policies. The leaders of the Churches and the Synagogues joined forces with Communist Party activists and stole the spotlight from the lavish parades. The police quickly responded by suppressing any large protest through incredibly violent means. My family remembers this day as a pogrom in Sofia. Gangs of Nazi-affiliated youth leagues roamed throughout the streets and brutally beat any Jew they encountered. My grandmother Rachel spent that violent day visiting a friend and was still not home when the sun set. The entire family feared the worse, but a few hours later she returned and explained that she waited until the streets became quiet enough to proceed. The inhumanity of war time behavior made almost anything possible. Your mom could go out to visit a friend and be beaten to death by thugs on the street. Uncertainty, fear, distrust of neighbors, hatred of the government, and an overall feeling of helplessness made the honorable Bulgarians scared to stage any large scale public protest for fear of becoming a visible target.

Both the Jewish and Christian religious leaders devised a strategy to uphold the moral righteousness of Bulgaria. Metropolitan Stefan, after meeting with Rabbis Tsion and Hananel, sent a letter to Boris warning him "not to persecute the Jews lest he himself be persecuted," and "God would judge him by his own acts." Sympathetic church officials offered the Jews refuge and were willing to give them documents stating that they wanted to convert to Christianity. Belev responded to Stefan's protests by claiming that the deportations were politically necessary and basically ignoring his pleas. Boris and Filov were continuing to hedge and began to reconsider the political necessity of deportations. Although internal pressures had some effect on Boris, the main determinant on deportations was the outcome of German military actions.

Plan B was going forward but some Jews were not going to go without a fight. Street demonstrations turned violent and the Bulgarian authorities cracked down with arrests and deportations to Bulgarian concentration camps. Apprehended Jewish partisans, members of the BKP, and other political prisoners were placed in the largest concentration camps where they endured the physical abuse of beatings and depravation, as well as the mental abuse of being threatened with deportation. At the Samovit and Pleven short term camps, the Jewish prisoners spent anxiety ridden days peering over the guarded fences at the empty ships on the Danube while they dreadfully pondered their impending fate.

Most Jews were sent to the interior provinces where they lived in crowded houses with other Jewish families or peasants. Men of working age, including my grandfather, lived separate from their families with their assigned work detachment. The Varsano family went to Novi Pazar a few days after the May 24 riot. Novi Pazar was a small impoverished Turkish enclave left over from the Ottoman occupation. Jewish schoolchildren were not allowed to attend the local public schools, so every student received their instructions in only one humble room. They made the best of a bad situation with every bench in the classroom representing a different grade, Seeco was on the fourth and Seli was on the first bench. Even under these oppressive circumstances, Seeco still received some private lessons in English. Meanwhile in Sofia, Jewish property went up for auction, and an assortment of Bulgarians moved into Jewish homes.

Prior to the relocation order and the implementation of confiscation plans, my family tried to smuggle out as many heirlooms as possible. The only notable items that made it through the war were my grandfather's Swiss made chronograph watch with solid gold numbers and casing on a black leather band, a stainless steel Swiss

Army style knife, and assorted family photos. The solid gold back plate of the watch was missing, however, which was most likely used as a bribe. My grandparents tried to make arrangements for possessions to be safely stowed with their Christian neighbors, some successfully, some not.

My father knew that his family had to hide some of their valuables, but didn't realize the extent of the plundering. He naively hoped everything would, for the most part, remain the same when he returned home from his forced relocation. As a child, he was mostly confused about the entire episode of seemingly illogical events. As time passed and the restrictions became more severe, he became well aware of the reality of his persecution and his naivety turned into jaded resolve. Like any normal boy, he became attached to his neighborhood, as well as his few possessions, even more so than an adult. Nobody wants their toys taken away, especially all of them at once for no good reason.

The family was sent out to unfamiliar surroundings with barely any possessions. They could only imagine what was happening in their previous home as they tried to reestablish themselves in their new home. It was a nightmare that took many months to wake up from, but unfortunately, it was reality. They feared that burglars were breaking into their old home over and over again, and they were helpless to stop them. In fact, nobody needed to break in; they just moved in and legally appropriated the residence for themselves. While their fundamental rights of private ownership were being violated in Sofia, life on the fascist countryside was become more humiliating.

One day on a hot afternoon in Novi Pazar, my father was playing with a large group of neighborhood children in a field. Children of all religions and political affiliations would frequently play together in the multicultural Bulgarian society. However, the onslaught of war and fascism had robbed these children of their innocence. After working up a good sweat playing with the other boys, my father had taken his shirt off and was heading home with the rest of the shirtless kids. As the group came upon a bridge crossing, my father faced a dilemma. The most direct route home crossed a bridge that was forbidden for usage by Jews. There was another bridge that allowed Jewish passage but it was much further away. Being a naïve and carefree child, Seeco figured that since he had no shirt on and therefore no visible Jewish star, the bridge guards would not know he was Jewish. He took a chance and crossed with the rest of the children. Half way across the bridge, another boy betrayed my father's friendship and ran to a bridge guard to tell him that my father was a Jew.

My father was immediately arrested and detained in a KEV administered local jail. Little Seeco was a scared nine year old boy sitting in a jail cell, as KEV officers and Nazi SS officers decided his fate. Following a heated discussion, KEV officers administered a beating and a forceful interrogation to the scared child which included slaps across his face and threats of deportation of his family. After several lingering hours of detention, the tearful little boy was saved by the deep pockets of his loving father. My grandfather had made his way to the police station and bribed the proper officials to earn the release of his only son. It was the scariest moment of my father's young life, which made the evils of the war shockingly apparent to even a small child.

During the critical summer of 1943, German representatives again insisted on deportations. Boris and Filov continued to respond with the excuse of their imperative need for quality Jewish labor. The German ambassador to Bulgaria, Adolf Beckerle, tacitly accepted the excuse and recommended that Hitler should not continue to pressure Boris for deportations for fear of alienating the multicultural Bulgaria populace. Beckerle also recognized Germany's military vulnerability and suggested waiting for a change in the war to resume deportation pressures. The RSHA and SS insisted on deportations from a military standpoint because they feared that the Jews were spies for the West and communist partisans. Beckerle concluded that Bulgaria desperately wanted to avoid being bombed by the Allied forces, and sculpted their Jewish policy and other foreign policies to achieve that goal.

The tumultuous summer also brought several rescue attempts for the Jewish people of Bulgaria. As the outcome of the war became more predictable and Bulgaria's Jewish policy shifted, the government issued some Jews exit visas by the end of 1943. Many took unorthodox routes to Palestine in order to circumvent British authorities; a Jewish emigration technique used to great effect following the war.

As the summer progressed, the Axis powers had a major setback when the Allies invaded Sicily and Mussolini was forced to resign. Hitler now needed the Bulgarian forces to take over more of the military operations in the Balkans because Italy was ineffective.

Boris and Hitler met to discuss a new defense strategy that involved the utilization of two Bulgarian army divisions to hold the front in Northern Greece and Albania. Boris wavered and only pledged one division. Boris knew the Germans could not stop the Russians and the West could not stop the spread of communism in the Balkans. After the Americans entered the war and the Germans were unsuccessful in conquering Russia, Boris prophesized that "[two nations] would inherit the estate- the Russians and the Americans." With his vision of post war Europe in mind, he tried to position his country to minimize damage, no matter who won the war.

On August 23, after returning to Bulgaria from his meeting with Hitler, Boris retreated for some relaxation in the scenic Rila Mountains. After a hike on steep terrain, the forty-nine year old Tsar Boris III suffered a massive heart attack and died five days later. My family heard rumors that suggested that Bulgaria was ready to pull out of the war after the Italian collapse and that Filov's government would be replaced by communists. Some people suggested that Hitler secretly poisoned Boris because of his reluctance to sacrifice all the Jews of his country and his refusal to send troops to the Soviet Union. Although, these conspiracy theories make compelling stories, the historical facts suggest that Boris simply died of an untimely cardiac arrest.

The successor to Boris was chosen by a corrupt Bulgarian fascist infrastructure under significant German influence. Filov and his friends in the German government, citing special powers during a time of war, bypassed the Bulgarian constitution and nominated Boris' Brother Kiril as the chief successor, but Filov essentially still ran the country.

84

In October of 1943, Belev was asked to resign as head of the KEV when widespread corruption of the agency was revealed. Hristo Stomaniakov, an assistant prosecutor in the Sofia Appellate Court, replaced Belev and instituted a system based on a more objective legal adherence to the existing laws rather than a concerted effort to persecute Jews in any way possible. Many restrictions on Jews remained but did not worsen and deportations were out of the question. After years of deteriorating conditions for my family, the tide finally turned in favor of the surviving Jewish families of Bulgaria. In November of 1943, the Jews expelled from Sofia to the interior were allowed to return to their homes for ten days in order to "liquidate their movable property."

As the Allied Forces victory became a foregone conclusion, the internal politics in Bulgaria became even more turbulent. The Red Army of the Soviet Union advanced deeper into Western Europe, emboldening the Bulgarian communist partisans to incite a civil war that did not succeed but added to the existing instability. The USSR questioned Bulgarian motives because of German ships stationed in Varna and threatened to declare war on them in order to secure them as a strategic partner. In November of 1943, American and British war planes bombed strategic targets in Bulgaria – mostly railroad stations and rail lines, possibly the same ones that my grandfather had spent months of forced labor constructing. In January of 1944, the Allies proceeded with mass aerial bombardment of Sofia and other crucial Bulgarian cities, rendering the Subranie building (seat of Parliamentary proceedings) useless. Large sections of major cities had to be evacuated while panic gripped almost every Bulgarian. My family had mixed emotions. There was a fear of being killed by a bomb, but there was also the anticipation of being liberated from the years of suffering under the fascist regime. Many Jews were hopeful that the bombings would force Bulgaria out of the Axis. My father and many others actually cheered the American bombers as they flew overhead.

After years of trying to ride the fence with the Reich and the Allies, numerous factors contributed to the Bulgarian government's demise. The most dominant reason was the utter collapse and inevitable defeat of the Axis powers. Also the domestic policies of the fascist establishment had alienated and impoverished a majority of the Bulgarian population. Following Boris' death, the rulers of Bulgaria were slowly losing their grip on power and increasingly vulnerable to internal opposition groups ranging from communists to pro-Western sympathizers. By the spring thaw, a new cabinet, headed by Ivan Bagrianov, was sworn in that leaned towards Germany and sought to prevent the spread of communism after the war. Bagrianov's government also wanted to maintain the Saxe-Coburg dynasty and hold onto the annexed territories. To achieve these goals, the new administration would have to take a more moderate approach to the Allied nations. Some of the restrictions on Jews would be gradually lifted and the Bulgarians would not succumb to German pressure. The Soviets were also allowed to open a Consulate in Varna which represented a new chapter in the relationship. Life was slowly getting better for my family, but Bulgaria was still at war and the country's political crisis was getting more convoluted.

In August of 1944, Bagrianov addressed the Subranie and requested that Bulgarian pull out of the war and their alliance with Germany. A few days later, the German Embassy in Bulgaria was closed and soldiers of the Reich were evacuated. Negotiations in Egypt proceeded to lay out how post-war Bulgaria would be structured. Bulgaria would not retain Macedonia or Thrace, but kept Southern Dobruja which it had acquired from Romania because the residents were considered ethnically Bulgarian. The Allies wanted to march through Bulgaria and to institute a new cabinet with no fascist or pro-German elements. On August 31, 1944 the cabinet abrogated all of the remaining restrictive legislation affecting Jews both in the ZZN and the decree law of August 26, 1942. Finally, Jews were allowed the same freedoms as all other Bulgarian citizens and the government promised to return all the confiscated property.

Consequently, Bagrianov's government was replaced with a pro-Western administration led by the Agrarian Party's Konstantin Muraviev and other former opposition leaders. This government was unstable at the outset due to all the conflicting agendas among the new cabinet members. The Soviets were also not pleased with the pro-Western government and pushed for the ascension of the Fatherland Front, a coalition of left wing political parties dominated by the communists. My family had absolutely no say in the formation of the government nor did their opinion regarding foreign policy matter to the non-democratic rulers. They had to band together with the other Jewish community and pray for a way out of the mess. On September 5, the USSR declared war on Bulgaria, finally causing Filov to resign his powerful position on the royal regents. Finally, one of the prayers

87

of the Jewish community had been answered. To appease tremendous Soviet demands, Muraviev was forced to declare war on Germany. For a few ludicrous weeks, Bulgaria was officially at war with Germany, the Soviet Union, the United States, and Great Britain.

Four days after its declaration of war, the Red Army entered Bulgaria and the Fatherland Front seized control of key Bulgarian cities while arresting Muraviev's cabinet. The Allies and the USSR officially recognized the new government led by Kimon Geogiev and agreed—in principal—to an armistice. On October 28, Bulgaria signed an armistice in Moscow that placed its armed forces at the disposal of the UN under the Soviet command. Even though the UN charter of a world organization wouldn't be established until the following year, the United Nations that would administer post war Bulgaria was the Soviet part of a grand wartime alliance of powers allied against the Axis which was originally formed in 1941. Consequently, the USSR took control over industries, radio, transportation, and all other key components of Bulgaria society. The Bulgarians had to disband the Fascist Party and cooperate with the war crimes tribunal. Within a few weeks, the nation had been transformed from a fascist power in the Balkans to a satellite of the Soviet Union.

In November of 1944, the Varsano family finally returned to their home in Sofia. Unfortunately, their previous residence on Dragoman Boulevard was in the hands of wartime squatters, so they lived on Morava Street near the Jewish Quarter. Of course they were very bitter, but at that point they also felt a little lucky and just wanted to resume a normal life. The range of emotions was overwhelming: anger, resentment, frustration, relief, hope, vindictive, distrust,

88

disappointment, as well as being anxious for a new start. I imagine it being like returning home after a long vacation and assuming everything would be the same. Or waking up from a coma, hoping everything was alright but based on past experience, expecting the worst and having it materialize. That feeling of expecting the worse, so that you won't be disappointed, stuck with my dad throughout life. He also developed a burning desire to get back to work and problem solve which was exactly what his father did once the war ended.. There's nothing that can't be solved through hard work and perseverance, just block out discrimination and hatred as you go about your daily business. Everybody likes prosperity and a peaceful life, so striving towards that goal was an undisputed life ambition. I would have been mad as hell and probably would have wanted to beat up my neighbors. I would be suspicious of every one around me because they could have possibly been a thief or a former conspirator with the fascist authorities. That type of intense paranoia and mistrust would eventually eat you up inside and you would have to become more accepting and forgiving just to function within society and avoid mental illness. My family still had to live in this country while they tried to look for safe way out to a better place.

At the conclusion of the war, the Jews of Europe received some retribution as war crime tribunals judged a slew of people deemed criminals against humanity. In Bulgaria, a war tribunal tried and executed various KEV members as well as former high level political leaders, including Filov, Mihov, Bagrianov, Prince Kiril, and many others. The guiltiest culprit of genocide was Belev who fled the country and was sentenced to death despite not being in custody.

Dimitri Peshev, who was defended by a Jewish attorney in recognition of his protest for the Jewish people, was spared a death sentence but convicted of crimes punishable by fifteen years of hard labor for collaborating with the Nazis by being a member of the wartime parliament. He was also accused of saving the Jews for money. Even a righteous gentile like Peshev was punished, despite the pleas of some in the Jewish community. He was released after being imprisoned just one year and died in 1973, impoverished and largely forgotten, in his hometown of Kyustendil in western Bulgaria. Peshev's role in speaking up for the Jews only really came to light in the 1990s after the fall of communism. Before that the monarchy or the communists had been given full credit, depending on who was in power at the time. Recently, Bulgaria commemorated Tolerance Day on March 9 which corresponded to the day the Jews were spared from deportation. Unfortunately, it took over fifty years for Bulgaria to fully recognize the truth behind the events of WWII.

My family was more concerned with being compensated for their losses and the prospects for the future rather than bring politicians to justice. They viewed it as the new ruling party getting retribution on their former enemies and not necessarily a fair use of the corrupt legal system. Many of the judgments were politically motivated and would not be considered fair by traditional judicial standards. However, most of the top level perpetrators were punished.

In the years following the war, there was an historical debate about "who saved the Jews of Bulgaria" The Jews of "old Bulgaria" survived the war in better shape than any other Jews in Europe, with the possible exception of Denmark. Had Boris and the Bulgarian

90

people not tried to accommodate opposing factions, or if German military forces had been more successful in the summer of 1943, my family would have been exterminated. My father didn't talk about the possibility of death during the war years much at all. So many Jews were exterminated within the Reich and so many soldiers died fighting, the Jews of Bulgaria made it out of the war comparatively well. Complaining about almost being killed would have been considered an insult to all those who were actually killed, as well as those who survived the concentration camps within the Reich and emerged as mere shells of the human beings they once were. Suffering was a very subjective term to a Jew during WWII. Everyone suffered during the war; it was just a matter of how much. Life had to go on for the survivors. They simply picked up the pieces and moved forward. The prospect of death was not something they would dwell on, they were the survivors and there was much work to do in the coming years. I think they just blocked it out of their minds and focused on the anything positive

Later generations of Bulgarians have promoted King Boris as the "Savior of the Jews," but what about the slaughtered Jewish families within the new Bulgarian territories? What would have happened to all the Jews of Bulgaria if the Axis military forces would have been had a few more victories? What about the emotional and economic scars that the Jews suffered? For decades following the war, the survivors repressed their emotions and many eventual psychological ramifications would take years to properly diagnose. It's impossible for me to compare today's litigious and victims rights-oriented society to 1945 Europe. The survivors of these atrocities didn't have the sense of entitlement that a modern American plaintiff might have in a personal injury civil case. Many of the survivor's emotions were repressed and it would take decades for the true stories to come to light. They tried to forget, but they simply could not.

The war years were a horribly traumatic experience for the Varsano family, but they felt fortunate that they did not meet the same deadly fate as six million of their fellow European Jews. In the course of roughly five years, my father was transformed from a naive child to a mature teenager with an unquenched thirst for a better life.

CHAPTER 5

The Red Admiral versus the Zionist

Following Bulgaria's defeat in WWII, Russian troops and communist ideology rapidly took over the war torn nation. The Bulgarian people were subjected to yet another major change in their government and economy, mostly to their detriment. The Jews of Bulgaria, after narrowly escaping the perils of fascism with their lives, found a common bond with the rest of the persecuted European Jews. My family had their wealth robbed from them but their determination to build a better future was still intact. The Zionist movement gained momentum in almost every country with a Jewish population. Unfortunately, in Bulgaria the new forces of communism were often in conflict with the forces of Zionism.

Bulgaria was in ruins, the Russian Army controlled 75% of the country, and the Jews were an impoverished people. Jewish confiscated property that was supposed to be returned was either destroyed or lost in a confusing maze of a corrupt record keeping system. The property that was accounted for was usually undervalued or appropriated by the government without proper compensation. My grandfather never received compensation for his confiscated automobile, motorcycle, or any other stolen property. The family never regained possession of their pre-war apartment unit on Dragoman Boulevard. Even if the apartment was returned, the memory of their old home was forever tainted and it could no longer be a comfortable place to live. What was a status symbol and a proud financial milestone for my grandfather turned into a forgotten relic.

The hardware store, which was run by a well compensated Bulgarian friend during the war, was the only item that was actually returned to him, but it was in a complete state of disrepair. The servants and relatively affluent lifestyle that they enjoyed before the war did not return when the military battles and anti-Semitic legislation ended. The country, as well as the entire continent, was poor and war torn. Everyone had difficulties rebuilding, but it was especially hard for the Jews because they lost almost all of their possessions and livelihood during the war. My family was bitter and totally distrusting of government promises of any kind. They felt closer to their fellow Jews than ever because outsiders simply did not know what they were going through.

Their new residence on Morava Street was located near the Jewish quarter and the Zionist organizational network. After spending the war years unable to express his own free will or properly provide for his family in the way they were accustomed to, my grandfather looked forward to rebuilding his business and giving his family the best of all that was available. Even though the war was psychologically traumatic and a financial nightmare, he still had his health and the emotional support of his loved ones. He thought that all he needed to do was work hard and he would be able to regain the lifestyle and stature that he had held just a few years earlier. The government, however, interfered with his aspirations and rights of self determination once again. While my grandfather made a futile effort to rebuild his business, his wife spent her days arranging the new home

94

and cooking the best meals she could with limited ingredients. A few short months after reacquiring his dilapidated hardware store, the communist regime took state ownership of the store through the policy of nationalizing private business, and made my grandfather another cog in the communist machine.

Even though my grandfather was extremely upset about losing his hardware store again, it was expected once the Bulgarian Communist Party (BKP) took control of the Bulgarian government and closely aligned itself with the Soviet Union. The communist system of doing away with private enterprise meant that it was only a matter of time before the hardware store became the collective property of the people. An entire spectrum of emotional swings occurred within several short months, and nothing was expected or unexpected after the tyranny of Belev's KEV and Filov's fascist regime. Compared with the forced relocations and the fascist labor camps, the BKP measures were a relatively benign depravation. At least my grandfather still worked in a hardware store, albeit a government-run entity. The family was still able to live together peacefully in Sofia. Bulgaria simply represented a continuation of persecution to my family, instead of the overt anti-Semitism of the fascists it was the denial of economic freedom under the communists. My father forever retained a notion that material possessions were temporary and therefore not as meaningful as the ability to work hard and create something from nothing under any circumstances. He tried to teach me that a strong work ethic and loyalty to family was more important than flashy wealth and public fame. Status symbols are fleeting, whether by war, economic cyclical downturn, or by government intervention.

95

The Soviet Union had no Marshall Plan for its satellite nations which severely slowed any Bulgarian recovery from the economic ruins the war had brought. The Soviets exacerbated the problem by plundering the wealth and industries of its new communist bloc nations, and made a policy of relocating precious resources within Soviet borders. The Jews, like many Bulgarians, were impoverished and not happy with the communist government's notion of ending the ownership of private property. My grandfather was not a university educated economist, but he was a shrewd enough businessman to realize that the communist system would keep Bulgaria a poor nation for many years to come and it would take a painstakingly long time to rebuild the war damage.

The BKP also imposed educational requirements on the formerly independent Jewish schools. The Bulgarian language replaced Hebrew and Zionists ideals were suppressed. Zionist organizations were called bourgeois and chauvinist while facing continuous harassment from the authorities. Zionism and communism seemed incompatible within Bulgaria. If the Jews were to leave Bulgaria, then the Zionists could be used for the political benefit of Soviet-influenced foreign policy by thwarting British efforts in Palestine. Until they were ready to immigrate, the official government policy was to suppress their organizational abilities and to persuade them to realize the virtues of communist doctrine.

Since both my father and his sister had their education stunted during the war, they were required to take placement exams to reenter the school system. The two intelligent siblings were able to pass enough exams to attend classes corresponding to their age group. The

96

American College in Sofia, which was closed by the fascists during the war, was not reopened by the communists after the war. Seeco was unable to resume his advanced English language studies and Western liberal arts curriculum. He was relegated to attending the technician's school in Sofia because the communist government wanted to produce a country of workers, not thinkers, to fight the new cold war. Russian was imposed as an official second language to be taught to all school children in every educational institution. School children throughout the communist bloc memorized propaganda slogans such as "Long Live the Fighting Unity of Slavic Peoples; Long Live Freedom, the Independence of our Glorious Soviet Fatherland," except they were recited "Pa-Rooskey," in Russian. The communist reeducation schools also forced my father to join the Komsomol, which was the youth branch of the BKP.

The Jewish community within Bulgaria had broken up into two factions. The Zionists favored migration to Palestine with the help of the World Zionist Organization, while the communists favored staying in Bulgaria. Although there were some socialist theories embraced in the Jewish kibbutzim system of collective farming in Palestine, the communists were still clinging to the national pride of Bulgaria. Most Jews were not affiliated with any Bulgarian political party but did believe in the ideals of a Jewish homeland. The BKP courted Jewish involvement despite the resistance by most of the independently minded Jewish community. The few Jews within the Communist Party forced their agenda on their own people and helped displace the power of the Zionist leaders. The BKP proceeded to close every cultural and political institution related to Western countries.

97

In May of 1945, the Zionists staged a public demonstration to celebrate the Allied victory in WWII. The Zionists clearly had the support of the majority of the Jews of Bulgaria and eventually the government philosophically supported the concept of a Jewish homeland. Following the shattering of my family's life during the war and the forced indoctrination of Seeco and Seli by the new communist regime, the Varsano family made the material decision to embark on an Aliyah prompted by the nationalization of private industry and the start of the Palestine partition debate in the UN. Although going to Israel was the obvious choice for my family, my father and his sister were really at the mercy of what their parents decided. Immigrating to America, like many other European Jews, was never really considered. I suppose Israel was more geographically desirable and my family truly had Zionist aspirations. Also, Bulgaria profited from Jewish emigration to Palestine, so it was actively encouraged while going to the anti-communist US was forbidden. Ultimately, my family's goal was to make a socio-economic pilgrimage, as opposed to a religious one. However, there were still legal issues to be worked out and mass emigration would take several more impatient years.

As post-war Europe began to develop, the differences between the USSR and the rest of the Allied Forces became more divergent. By September of 1946, the Bulgarian monarchy of several hundred years ended and the country became a republic closely aligned with the rest of the communist bloc. The following month a Great Subranie met to form a new constitution and replace Prime Minister Georgiev with Georgi Dimitrov. While the Iron Curtain was being strung up throughout Europe, the Jewish people were trying to escape further persecution by finding a new home in the land of their ancestors.

The unanimous feeling amongst my family was that Zionism was the Jewish ticket to freedom. The modern Zionist vision had been developing over the previous fifty years and was about to come to fruition. Political Zionism was a direct reaction to Western European anti-Semitism. It sought to establish a Jewish homeland in any available territory including remote areas of Africa. The political Zionists believed that the "great powers" of Europe would help the Jews find a homeland because it was in their best interest to solve the "Jewish Problem." This false hope and reliance on the good will of anti-Semitic governments would be repeated in a much more dramatic manner during my father's childhood as the Nazis promised deportation to Palestine. It seems unfortunate that it takes a major tragedy for the conflicting sects of Judaism to unite for a common purpose. The Russian writer, Leo Pinsker, was able to spur an interest in Zionism with his accounts of the organized massacre of many helpless Jews in 1881. The following year the first Aliyah, or immigration to Palestine began. About 10,000 immigrants made the pilgrimage over a ten year span with the financial support of the wealthy Jewish families, such as the Rothchilds. Since they were not victims of a pogrom like the Russian Jews, my great grandparents felt secure in Bulgaria and felt no need to seek refuge elsewhere.

Theodor Herzl, a Vienna educated journalist and playwright, was a key player in early Zionist philosophy. He professed that the Jews of France were wrongly blamed for the problems resulting from industrialization and emancipation. Therefore, European society would

99

always consider them outsiders. In 1896, Herzl wrote Der Judenstaat (The Jewish State), where he offered Jewish statehood as the only viable solution to anti-Semitism. Herzl's urgency caused him to believe that any available territory worth living on was a suitable location for the Jewish state. Herzl's country would be primarily secular in nature with no special place for Hebrew or Judaism. He believed a secular Jewish State would be supported and recognized by the influential European nations.

The majority of Zionists disagreed with Herzl and favored a Jewish homeland in Palestine. My great grandparents and eventually their children wanted to establish a Jewish state but both the comforts and constraints of living in the relatively less vocal Jewish community of Bulgaria limited their participation. They attended Zionist organization gatherings and contributed some money, but didn't need or want revolutionary change because life at home was satisfactory. Most Zionists were skeptical about the European nations' support of a Jewish state in theory. However, Herzl was a prominent international figure who met with world leaders and gave the Zionist movement a recognizable legitimacy.

In 1897, the first Zionist Congress met and established the World Zionist Organization (WZO) which many of my family members, including myself, would eventually vote in their elections. The consensus opinion was that Palestine was the historic and rightful homeland of the Jewish people. The pre-state Jewish community in Palestine would be known as the Yishuv and the Jewish National Fund was established to buy land in Palestine. Several generations of my family have made contributions to the Jewish National Fund and felt a

100

strong commitment to further the Zionist cause through monetary donations if not active volunteering.

The Cultural Zionist movement sought to establish small settlements in Palestine that would revive Jewish spirit and culture in the modern world through a Hebrew renaissance. With a minuscule amount of funding and ambitious goals, the movement professed a Jewish self reliance and a general mistrust of the Gentile world, which were the same values that my father held for the most part. The self-reliance would be built up slowly in small steps that would eventually create a Zionist infrastructure in Palestine. At the Sixth Zionist Congress in 1903, Herzl, the political pragmatist, proposed a Jewish homeland in the African nation of Uganda. The concept of Jews escaping anti-Semitism to any location regardless of ancestral or theological relevance was also a strategy of desperation employed during the persecution of WWII. During the dim days of fascism, my family probably would have rejoiced about the possibility of a new Jewish homeland in Africa, but if they had their druthers, Israel was the eternal home of the Jewish people and should be the ultimate goal to achieve for any true Zionist. Thus, the Uganda plan was rejected by a majority of the Eastern European Zionists. The ideals of Cultural Zionism would become the true foundations of the Jewish state.

A few years later, Labor Zionism was founded by Nachman Syrkir and Ber Borochov, with the motto, "As long as the Jew is weak, anti-Semitism will exist." Labor Zionism was essentially Jewish socialism with the central theory of a Jewish homeland worked by exclusively Jewish labor. Marxism and Zionism were combined which attracted many Bolshevik Russian Jews. Aaron David Gordon was the

101

first Zionist to actually live in Palestine and practice what he preached. He established the first kibbutz and stressed the importance of physical labor in the land of Palestine which would was initial purpose of my mother's pilgrimage to Israel. The system of kibbutzim persists until today, but my father never participated. My father and grandfather were both entrepreneurs most of their lives, and they did not care for the socialist system in general.

From 1904 to 1914, following the Russian pogroms, 40,000 Jews immigrated to Palestine during what was known as the Second Aliyah. My great grandparents and their young children remained content in the non-communist and multi-ethic nation of Bulgaria. In November of 1917, the British government decided to endorse the establishment of a Jewish home in Palestine after discussions within the cabinet and consultations with Jewish leaders, which would be known as the Balfour Declaration. The new Zionists spoke Hebrew and were protected by the Hashomer, or the Watchmen. Years later, my father would become a member of the youth wing of the Hashomer. In fact, the majority of Jewish youth over the age of ten in post WWII Bulgaria were organized by He-Halutz ha-Za'ir for girls and Ha-shomer Ha-Za'ir for boys. It was similar to the Boy Scouts or Girl Scouts of America, but the children would learn about the history of Palestine and go on field trips to practice Jewish rituals in the great outdoors.

David Ben-Gurion arrived in Palestine with a driving conviction that economic power was the precursor to political power. Consequently, he helped create a framework for the institutions of Jewish labor. However, hard work alone would not create a Jewish

102

homeland. The rise of the Revisionist movement added a more aggressive approach to achieving ambitious objectives.

Revisionists believed that a strong military and political power would determine the fate of the nation. Founded by the Russian-born Vladmir Jabotinsky while living in Italy, he favored the drastic notion of mass immigration to Palestine and immediately claiming it as the Jewish state of Israel. Menachim Begin was a disciple of Jabotinsky and would be a historic rival of Ben Gurion as the history of Israel unfolded.

Agreeing upon the form and function of the Jewish state was not an easy task because there were many differences between the various factions of Judaism. Not all Jews were even Zionists; some were content with their assimilated lifestyle. Amongst the Zionist there were factions from American, Western Europe, Eastern Europe, and the Middle East, all with different customs and theories on a Jewish state. Within each region there were religious and secular. The religious considered themselves Orthodox, Reform, or a combination of both. Within the religious and regional subcategories, there were sociological subdivisions. The Content Jews were unwilling to sacrifice for Zionism. The Persecuted Jews were unable to help create a Jewish homeland. Apathetic Jews just didn't care and didn't want to be bothered. The fearful Jews didn't want to take any major risks because they had no military backing. The intermarried Jews had abandoned or watered down their traditions and just wanted to be like the majority. There were self hating Jews among all these categories who internalized the negative stereotypes about who they were and detested themselves, as well as the other categories of Jews. A

103

consensus among a diverse group of bickering Jews was as hard to come by then as it is today.

My family, like many Jewish families, could not be compartmentalized into one of these groups. They lived in Eastern Europe but were Sephardic like many of the Middle Eastern Jews. But they also lived a contemporary urban lifestyle similar to many Western European and American Jews. They were generally content but worried about no military backing. They did want they could in their little corner of the world. They made small contributions to the Zionist cause, but like Bulgarians in general, they were not the big players in the movements of greater Europe.

With the outbreak of WWII, progress towards the goals of Zionism was temporarily slowed because most of the Jews in Europe merely struggled to survive. In the early years of the war, the Nazis encouraged Jews to leave Germany and immigrate to Palestine. The Germans' intention was to offend the Arabs; thereby creating an unstable environment for British controlled Palestine. Great Britain would be forced to dedicate resources away from Europe and into preserving security in the Middle East. In May of 1939, the British White Papers were issued which expanded the colonial mandate for ten more years and further limited Jewish immigration to Palestine. It also eliminated any realistic chance, regardless of their intentions, for my family to make a safe and legal Aliyah until after the war.

Although mass immigration of Jews from Germany never occurred, Britain stopped land sales to Jews in Palestine on the last day of February of 1940. The sinking of the SS Salvator which resulted in the tragic deaths of hundreds of Jews from Bulgaria shed even more doubt on my family's thoughts of make the harrowing journey to Palestine.

Despite a few attempts at illegal immigration, the goal of establishing a Jewish homeland was delayed during WWII as the Jewish Brigade, consisting of Jewish soldiers from Palestine, fought alongside British forces to defeat the Italian fascists. The Haganah, which was a modest Zionist military organization from Palestine, orchestrated the Bricha, or escape for persecuted European Jews.

After WWII, Europe was divided into zones controlled by Britain, France, the USSR, and the US which resulted in four borders where there was formerly only one. Throughout the European continent, Holocaust survivors were waiting in Displaced Persons camps for a safe place to permanently live. Many Holocaust survivors were ashamed and astonished that they even survived while their loved ones did not. Thousands of Jews were wandering aimlessly with all of their worldly possessions in hand. The lingering anti-Semitism of many non-Jews remained as they openly questioned why the Jews were still around. Jewish families had been decimated and their synagogues had been destroyed. The returning Jews felt inferior and had no legal claim to their former residences that non-Jews now occupied which was the case with my family. Many Bulgarian ethnic minorities, especially Jews, were legally inferior to the Bulgarian Eastern Orthodox majority even though they didn't experience the virulent Jew hating that plagued many other countries in Europe.

Most of the survivors felt more Jewish than European, which made them want to leave Europe more than ever. Many found refuge in America while others scattered to various corners of the globe far

105

away from their memories of the Holocaust. The Jewish Brigade came to Europe from Palestine to tell the survivors about Eretz-Yisrael (Land of Israel). The Jewish Brigade spoke Hebrew and had a professional appearance with a proud uniform. The tattered survivors were reassured by their presence and slowly gained the courage to help create a Jewish homeland. They would need as many willing Jews as possible because a difficult struggle lay ahead of them.

Great Britain was considered pro-Arab in the late 1940s because it was increasingly dependent on petroleum. The British still controlled Palestine and actively forbade mass Jewish immigration. For a time, they would only allow married couples with no children to immigrate, causing many phony marriages to occur followed by a swift divorce in Palestine. My grandparents were certainly not going to abandon their children to go to Palestine. They would continue to be patient and wait for an opportunity to have the whole family immigrate. They had a strong sense that it was just a matter of time until Jewish victims of the Holocaust would make their own final solution to solving the problem of creating a viable Jewish homeland. The main goal of the Displaced Persons (DP) was to leave the "cursed land," which resulted in virtually no Jews living in Poland, Czechoslovakia, Germany, Austria, and most of previously Reich-controlled Europe.

In Bulgaria, the Aliyah grew more popular as the communists exerted their control over the Zionists. During the four year period following the war and before the creation of Israel, approximately 7,000 Jews from Bulgaria made the illegal journey to British controlled Palestine. Secret Mossad agents such as Ephraim Shilo, would bribe officials and ship supplies would be purchased from receptive Bulgarian businesses with US dollars. In 1947, converted cargo ships such as the Paducah, Redemption, Pan York and Pan Crescent sailed from the port of Burgas, Bulgaria, destined for Israel carrying both Romanian and Bulgarian illegal immigrants

Almost all of the wandering immigrants had to lie about their destinations and pretend they were from different cities. Some wandered for many years with "an entire house stuffed into a suitcase." Some border guards were sympathetic to the cause while others were bribed, which was essential to the success of the network of illegal immigration operatives. Stolen cars, trucks, and gas were also indispensable components of the secret transport of the Jews eastward. Even US Army Chaplain Rabbis helped transport Jewish DP's with US Army trucks to Jewish Brigade vehicles bound for Palestine. Increased British pressure on the Allies to stop illegal border crossings soon made the Aliyahs virtually impossible. The most desperate resorted to crossing the snow covered Alps on foot. Most of these Jewish DP's, however, were headed for Mediterranean ports.

The methods and persistence of the Jewish illegal immigrants reminds me in some respects to the Latin American immigrants that illegally cross through Mexico into the US. Both impoverished people sought economic opportunities, must evade a dominant power, use unorthodox methods and utilize an underground network of assistance. Some of the Latinos were victims of civil wars, like the Jews were WWII refugees. Both feel a sense of historical entitlement because the southwest US was part of Mexico, just as British mandate of Palestine was the biblical country of Israel. However, most of the Latinos were not religiously persecuted or significantly discriminated against in their former countries. The Jews were trying to establish a homeland for their people and a sovereign nation, while the Latinos just want a better life. Perhaps, it was their identification with the underdog that makes so many of today's Jews, liberal Democrats. The Jewish people felt suffering and could empathize. Not so long ago, we were the ones clinging to hope and trying to make it to brighter shores.

The ships that carried the Jews towards Palestine were mostly freighters converted for passenger travel which was a practice that continued even after the state of Israel declared her independence. They were routinely overloaded and passengers secretly boarded the vessels under the cover of night. Most made an approximately twelve day journey in a hot, overcrowded, and foul smelling boat suffering from bouts of sea sickness. Although the conditions were deplorable, most Jews had been through much worse during the war and cooperated with the often youthful captains.

The Sabras, or native Jews of Palestine, saw the European Jewish Aliyah as a blessing and assisted as much as they could. Volunteers on the ground in Palestine contacted the approaching ships through wireless Morse code communications to coordinate the landing.

Back in Bulgaria, my family heard stories about the Royal Navy of Great Britain flying planes off the coast of Palestine to spot incoming Aliyah ships. The passengers would quickly hide under the deck, but the British had no trouble spotting an overloaded ship of immigrants. The British officers said the shabbily converted ships usually had excrement running down the hull because of the lack of proper toilet facilities. British destroyers would surround the Aliyah

108

ships and tell the crew that they were going to board the ship when it entered the territorial waters of Palestine. The Jewish hopefuls were in sight of the coastal towns of Palestine which seemed vibrant compared to the war torn ruins of Europe.

As the Aliyah ships closed in on Palestine, the British Navy boarded the ships and detained the passengers. Some of the frustrated Jews chose to fight the British with many injuries and some deaths being suffered on the Jewish side. When my family heard about such losses and frustration, they chose to persevere with the Bulgarian communists a bit longer. The BKP limited their economic opportunities but at least they weren't being killed or detained like the failed Aliyah passengers. After the futile fighting subsided, the Jews caught in the blockade were medically attended to and deloused by British representatives. The Jewish detainees were then placed on well stocked British ships and sent to camps on the island of Cypress. Only about one in ten Haganah ships slipped through the British blockade. My family felt that lending external support through a united Jewish community from within Bulgaria gave them better odds at reaching Israel than gambling on a Bricha.

On December 2, 1946 – my father's 14th birthday – the Bulgarian government's gift to him was a declaration by Prime Minister Georgi Dimitrov confirming that all Jews of Bulgaria were free to immigrate to Palestine. However, there was still significant resistance on the British end, so mass immigration did not occur until the UN officially partitioned Palestine about a year later.

Throughout 1946 and 1947, European Jews -- some with Bulgarian citizenship -- continued to trickle into Palestine despite tight

109

British immigration regulations. In response, Britain changed its policy of sending the Jews caught in the blockade to Cypress and instead sent them back to Europe. This was done to further discourage illegal immigration and humiliate the offending nations, namely France. Land and sea routes became increasingly cut off. American planes did manage to make some airlifts successfully, but it was becoming more difficult and costly to enter Palestine.

Meanwhile, the Varsano family was on the move, but not to Israel. My grandfather purchased an apartment at Carnigratzka 6 in the center of Sofia for his sister Vicki who lived in the new apartment with her family. Their neighbor was a family physician who had to perform a life saving appendectomy for my father when he was only thirteen years old. Lacking modern surgical procedures, a nasty scar remained on his belly for the rest of his life. When I was a little boy, I thought the scar was a war wound because it was rather large and grotesque, but it was it was just a caused by old medical techniques where appearance wasn't that important. My dad could have easily conjured up a grand tale about a glorious war wound but he did not exaggerate or lie. He was the type of person that would just give you the cold hard facts if you bothered to ask him. He also had some gold fillings in his teeth that were a relic of Old World dental work. With a golden smile and healed scar tissue on his ample belly, my father received a good dose of inspiration from the Zionist leadership. One of the founding fathers of Israel brightened the Jews of Bulgaria's spirits with a motivational address in the heart of Sofia.

David Ben Gurion's speech in the fall of 1947 was an important moment for the Zionist movement of Bulgaria. Although

110

most Bulgarians and Ben Gurion spoke Russia, he refused to speak the Slavic tongue despite their pleas, and spoke in Hebrew, the language of the Jewish state and the Bible. On another occasion, Ben Gurion stated that "we're ready to be killed and to die, but not to give up fighting for three things: freedom of Jewish Immigration, the right to build our homeland, and the political independence of our people in its own land." My family was invigorated and would begin to make arrangements for their Aliyah shortly thereafter.

On October 13, 1947, the USSR and her satellite nations on the UN Palestine Committee voted in favor of the UNSCOP Partition Plan. The Soviet Union was not historically an advocate for the Jewish people, but creating a Jewish state in the Middle East had strategic implications that the communist bloc believed favored them. The Jews were more likely to be an independent and sovereign nation than were the Arabs. The Arab nations would never accept a Jewish state neighboring them and wars would result. The unstable environment would eventually give the communists' opportunities to set a foothold in the region. Throughout my father's life, he never trusted or particularity liked Russians for a variety of reasons including their misleading support for the creation of Israel.

The USSR and Bulgaria wanted to politically embarrass Great Britain and their imperialistic policies. Bulgaria also had economic and nationalistic reasons for voting for the formation of Israel. Jews that left Bulgaria had to renounce claims for confiscated property. Many years later in 1997, the Bulgarian Ministry of Justice announced that Israelis of Bulgarian origin will be able to reclaim their Bulgarian citizenship which the communist authorities had taken away from them. One of the BKP's original objectives was to crush dissent by creating a more homogeneous society which was further reinforced when it coerced the minority Turks leave the country in 1950. Greeks and Armenians were also actively encouraged to leave.

Prior to the UN vote, only a few countries openly favored partition namely the US, USSR, Norway, Canada, and Guatemala. Any country with a high Arab or Moslem population was against partition including countries such as India, Yugoslavia, and Greece. The French were undecided because of the Arab influence from their North African colonies.

The General Assembly resolution vote was thirty-three for and thirteen against, constituting more than the two thirds majority necessary to pass. France, in the end, did vote in favor of partition. With the exception of Cuba and Greece, all the nations that voted against the resolution were Moslem or Asian. These same nations continue to stymie Israel's international legitimacy to this day under the rules of the multilateral UN. Most Latin American countries voted in favor of the partition which became the deciding factor. It was widely speculated that many Western nations had a sense of guilt regarding their lack of intervention in the Holocaust and voted with that in mind. Although intent has been debated for decades, the Jewish people finally had a UN sanctioned homeland. Unfortunately, the limited ability of the UN lacked the strength and resolve to make peace between all of people of Palestine.

When the legal restrictions on immigration to Palestine were lifted, a tidal wave of Jewish families from around the globe swept onto the shores of Israel. Concerned with the welfare of the next

112

generation, some children arrived ahead of their families, accompanied by the members of the Zionist youth organizations. Seeco and Seli remained with their family in Bulgaria, because they realized everyone would be going together within months not years. Boatloads arrived daily at the ports of Haifa and Jaffa. My family had been preparing to depart for some time, but it was not as simple as buying a ticket and flying into Tel Aviv like it is today.

Israeli and Jewish philanthropic organizations – mainly from the US – paid hard currency for the exit visas of Eastern European Jews. Every Jewish individual leaving Bulgaria cost fifty to one hundred dollars. Bulgarian businesses made a profit from Israeli "nation building" while the politicians earned points by sticking it to the British. The Varsano family had to secure enough money to pay for their transport then make a reservation on an overbooked ship. Secret routes were drawn up to bypass the volatile military situations that still existed around Bulgaria. Greece had reacquired the territory Thrace on the Aegean Sea, so Bulgaria had no direct water route to the ports of Israel. Greece did not have good relations with Bulgaria and was in the midst of civil unrest, so my family needed to find a less direct route. A long and circuitous path up through Yugoslavia then down the Mediterranean Sea to Israel was determined to have the greatest likelihood of success.

Shortly after the UN vote, the camps in Cypress were shut down, which symbolized the true end of WWII and barbed wire captivity for many of the Jewish detainees. It also marked the beginning of their future life in Israel for many imprisoned Jews. The tenacity of the illegal immigrants exemplified the spirit of the Zionists

113

and was an inspiration to all those captive souls that were still stranded in the "cursed lands."

Even though they felt lucky to survive in Bulgaria while six million other European Jews perished, they were not willing to take another chance with an experimental form of government that possessed authoritarian leanings. What had been a fringe movement in Judaism for several years became the overriding concern of millions of Diaspora Jews. The will of the Jewish people with the crucial help of sympathetic Gentiles propelled a political, cultural, and economic movement that was just able to pass a UN vote in favor of establishing Israel. Although much work lay ahead, the nomadic Diaspora Jews were finally coming home after several hundred years and were willing to make whatever sacrifices that were necessary to build a future in Israel. My family had been persecuted in France, Spain, and Bulgaria and was finally ready to make their Aliyah to begin their new life in Israel.

The ways of the Old World were behind them. Fascism was relegated to the dust bin of history, while communist totalitarianism replaced it throughout most of Eastern Europe. The bulk of the European Jews, including my family, recognized that the communist ideals of a classless society and communal ownership of property were unrealistic and would result in the continued poverty for the subjects of this defective ethos of governing. The 20th Century was nearly half completed and it was time for more progressive and pragmatic thinking. Just like the pilgrims to the New World who escaped the religious persecution from the Old World monarchies, the Jews of the Aliyah escaped the Old World anti-Semitism and embarked on the

114

building of a modern Jewish state. My family would represent one small brick in the foundation of the new great temple in the Holy Land, which would be built in the form of the state of Israel.

PART II
Israel

CHAPTER 6

The Port of Haifa

My family was optimistic about starting a new life in Israel and anxious to start working diligently to secure a peaceful and prosperous home. They hoped that the evils of fascism and communism in their life were vanquished forever. However, there was a new evil that would terrorize them in the Middle East. Fascism and communism were replaced by a shaky socialist society encircled by hostile Arab neighbors.

The problems of Palestine intensified when the UN voted to partition the country with a small portion for the Israeli Jews and the remainder for the Palestinian Arabs. After the Partition Plan became official, Britain offered little help to make a smooth transition for the UN commission. The British mostly despised the Israelis because Jewish "terrorist" groups had been harassing them for years. The Irgun Zvi Leumi, (National Military Organization) attacked British police stations, offices, and headquarters. They seized weapons and replenished their arsenals. The Irgun and later the Stern Gang—led by Avraham Stern—employed paramilitary tactics against the Arabs, which provided relief for the settlers, but also hampered the political creditability of the Jewish Agency. The British responded by making mass arrests and many Irgun fighters were driven into hiding. The

Hagannah kidnapped several of the Irgun's members and handed them over to the British.

After the tragedy of the Holocaust, Jewish unity was strengthened as the Irgun, the Hagannah, and the Stern Group combined to fight the British who were unwilling to combat Arab terrorism against Jews—which is a support that Israelis still lack today. The Irgun in a sensational attack blew up the wing of the King David hotel in Jerusalem which housed the British Palestine Command. Warnings went unheeded and ninety-one lives were lost. The British carried out mass arrests and the fighting intensified with the British authorities resorting to public floggings, deportations, arrests and hangings. When the British hung three Irgun members, the Irgun captured three British soldiers and hung them in retaliation.

Despite the bloodshed, the British authorities were trying to posture themselves as neutral. However, they did not want to appear publicly sympathetic to the Jews in any way and thus anger the Arab nations. The British believed that the Arabs would be victorious in a military confrontation with the Jews because of a superior number of soldiers. If the Arabs did win, the British believed that the former colonial power would still play an important role in Palestine. To achieve this goal, the British aided the Arab militaries and restricted the Jews in every legal way possible with intentional bureaucratic delays and totally ignoring the necessities of the new settlers. When news of the British treatment of the Jewish immigrants spread to Bulgaria, my father began to develop a certain level of resentment towards the British, even though they weren't officially enemies.

Arab nations responded to the Partition Plan by persecuting Jewish citizens within their own borders and voting for a military intervention with an Arab Liberation Army. On May 14, 1948, the nation of Israel declared its independence and was invaded by Egypt, Transjordan, Lebanon, Iraq, and Syria. A cycle of violence began in Palestine that still exists today. The country became divided into war fronts and battle zones. While the battles raged, my family was trying to liquidate what little possessions they still had in Bulgaria in order to afford the uncertain Aliyah to the troubled land of Israel.

During the British mandate, the various Jewish military factions were independently operated with often conflicting agendas. The Irgun were determined to use military force to clear the Arabs and the British out of Israel while the Jewish Agency tried to appeal to the world's political forces to be sympathetic towards the Zionist cause. For the War of Independence to be successful, it was crucial that the separate military factions unify into a cohesive and powerful unit. Two weeks after independence was declared, the Israeli Defense Forces (IDF), or Zvah Haganah Le Yisrael (Zahal) in Hebrew, was formed by Ben Gurion. The Jewish opposition group Irgun—led by Menachim Begin who had been follower of Jabotinsky and Revisionist Zionism that stressed the need for a strong military—challenged Ben Gurion's proclamation. Although there was a brief confrontation between the two military units, the common cause of establishing a viable Jewish state trumped any other opposing philosophies and the IDF became the only military power representing the Jewish people. Rather than resort to violent resistance, Begin eventually turned his opposition into the political realm with the formation of the Herut

119

Party, or Freedom Movement while most of the Irgun leaders eventually ended up in the Likud party The Jewish Agency and its followers splinter into other groups that ultimately morphed into the Labor Party. Unfortunately, the Palestinian leaders have yet been unable to make the transition from freedom fighter to legitimate political rulers.

The Haganah, the underground military organization of pre-state Israel and the Palmach, an elite Jewish army unit of post WWII Palestine, were replaced by the IDF. By July of 1948, Israel had set up an Air Force, Navy, and Tank Battalion. A couple of years later, my father would be conscripted into their recently formed ranks. The newly unified IDF acquired most of the weapons from Czechoslovakia and the US black market. Israel received WWII surplus weapons broken down into pieces and shipped separately disguised as official import products such as textile and agricultural machinery.

After several months of warfare, Israel defeated the invading Arab nations and expanded its borders beyond the UN partition plan. Israel had lost 6,000 lives representing 1% of the total Jewish population. The Arabs suffered far more causalities, but they represented a much smaller percentage of the total Arab population. In February of 1949, Egypt signed an armistice with Israel but refused to recognize it as a nation. Similar agreements followed with Lebanon in March, Transjordan in April, and Syria in July. Iraqi forces simply withdrew and did not sign any agreement.

Well before the peace accords were agreed upon, the displaced Jews were flooding into Israel. Once a military victory appeared imminent, the top priority of the Israeli government shifted to

120

emptying the Displaced Persons Camps in Europe, as well as the Cyprus and Atlit Detention Camps. During this initial period of massive European immigration, the Bulgarians along with the Yugoslavians and Turks, were swept onto Israel's shores in the first wave of nation building.

Once immigration became legal, 45,000 of Bulgaria's 50,000 Jews relocated to Israel within two years. The 5,000 that remained were mostly high ranking communists or persons married to non-Jews. My grandfather, with a strong conviction to establish a secure Jewish homeland, joined the Zionist Liberal Party that would later merge with the Likud Political Party in Israel. As my father and my aunt learned more about the political dynamics in Israel, they considered themselves idealists. They didn't pledge allegiance to one party or another because thier main objective was to survive in a hostile land. The political platforms were untested in a new country, so it was hard to find a basis to form a strong opinion either way. They agreed with the party whose system was effective and ensured them the best quality of life in a secure homeland.

On November 5, 1948, my father, grandfather, grandmother, and aunt, boarded a freight train in Sofia and embarked on the long journey to Israel. After an almost 500 year presence in Bulgaria, the Varsano family left the region in as unorthodox manner as they had arrived there so many years ago. They came as victims of the Spanish Inquisition and departed as survivors of fascism and unwilling subjects of communism. From all of their days on the Iberian Peninsula to their last moment in Sofia, they were always outsiders, the Jewish minority.

121

Finally, they were going to live in a country that would fully accept them as a mainstream member of society, but it would be no easy task.

Although the Bulgarian government allowed Jews to go to Israel, a brewing civil war in Greece and antagonistic Arab neighbors accounted for the circuitous route my family dared to venture. The train was not designed for passenger travel, but it would get them where they needed to go. The train had no facilities and was reminiscent of the cattle trains that transported concentration camp victims. Shortly after the beginning of the journey, my family stopped in Pirot, where just five years earlier Jews under the control of the Bulgarian authorities were sent to the death camps in Poland.

For nine long days, my family suffered through an uncomfortable exodus through almost the entire country of Yugoslavia. Finally, they arrived at the port of Bakar in northwestern Yugoslavia, near Rijeka. Unfortunately, the accommodations would get even worse when they boarded the ship to Israel. An old Greek boat named "Kefalos" would be their home for another nine days. The boat, like the train, was not built to carry passengers. The desperate Jews—anxious to immigrate to Israel—improvised to create makeshift seating. My family sat on wooden stools on the lowest level. The boat was rickety and the seas were choppy, which resulted in rampant sea sickness amongst the travelers. For nine days, they bathed with salt water and drank strictly rationed purified water. They were constantly nauseous from the choppy waters and terribly nervous about what to expect once they landed in the unstable environment of Israel, but they possessed a war hardened resolve that gave them the strength to manage a situation that I would have found unbearable.

122

On November 23, 1948, the Varsano family arrived in Haifa, Israel where it was cold and raining. With queasy stomachs and a cold wet heads, the Promised Land was not what they had imagined in their Zionist dreams, but their goal had been achieved. Their fantasy was almost always better than their reality because their vivid imagination as hopeful immigrants constructed an image of their destination that was wishful rather plausible. The staff of the Jewish Agency, or Sochnout, that orchestrated the journey with the consent of the Bulgarian authorities, took them to the immigrant's camp in "Pardess-Hana", and placed them in a big tent with a few more families. The first night they heard what they thought was a baby crying, but in reality it was jackals around the tent looking for food.

The next day, my grandfather took a trip to Jaffa, where he had relatives that helped him look for a house. Jaffa—a largely Arab inhabited port town—was considered disputed land under the UN Partition Agreement of 1947. The Arabs had protested that they wanted Jaffa under a Palestine Committee. After the War of Independence started, most of the Arab families fled the town and the ancient port became the new capital for Bulgarian immigrants. The new bright eyed settlers lived in abandoned Arab dwellings, primitive shacks, and tents.

When the new immigrants arrived in Jaffa, the Israeli authorities told them to inhabit any dwelling they found vacant. Officially, the Tel Aviv Absorption Department and IDF army units were in charge of accounting for the goods confiscated and apartments acquired from the Arab homes. Housing in Jaffa was supposed to be selected by a committee determining the qualifications for residents.

123

However, the reality was that the massive influx of Israeli Jews caused the displacement of many Arab families. It was an unfortunate byproduct of the political reshuffling that occurred around the globe in the aftermath of WWII. There were millions of people displaced around the globe during the 1940s. Many were Jews and many were Arabs. If a Jewish family could occupy an apartment by having their bed in a room it was considered to be in their possession. Some Arabs were removed at gun point to accommodate the tens of thousands of new immigrants that settled in Jaffa. Some Israelis looted abandoned Arab homes and boarded up shops in Jaffa.

Although in today's context the treatment of the Arab families seemed cruel, I think that every group of people looks out for their own good, especially when they have been recently oppressed and forcibly impoverished. If achieving a better life for my family means that someone else was going to be demoralized, then it should be recognized as unfair and an effort should be made to compromise. However, human nature was such that every man does what's in their best interests. If the shoe were on the other foot, how would my family have been treated? Perhaps they would be treated in the same ghastly manner that the Jews in Arab countries were when the UN Partition plan was implemented.

The first Israelis were not Saints on a humanitarian mission; they were pioneers and refugees fighting for the survival of an experimental nation. Many Arab families living in Palestine were victims of unfair treatment and illegal confiscation of property, but this was a case of unfortunate circumstances and not a threat to the existence of the Arab people or the survival of Arab nations. Oil rich

Arab nations with tens of millions of citizens could have easily absorbed their displaced Palestinian Arab brethren into their friendly confines and sought to negotiate a political solution with Israel under the auspices of the UN. Instead, the 1.3 million Palestinian Arabs supplemented by armies of five great Arab nations chose to engage the 650,000 Jews in a prolonged military confrontation starting in 1948. Rather than seeking an immediate post-conflict solution the Arab forces retreated and left their fellow Palestinian Arabs in refugee camps as sacrificial lamb for decades. After the initial round of fighting ceased and borders were established, you would have thought there would have been a negotiated settlement involving restitution to the victims and a lasting peace for all. However, as the years passed without resolution, the conflict became bloodier and the extremists on both sides became more vindictive which made the early actions of the conflict seem moderate compared with the inhumanity that ensued. The political leaders allowed the wounds to stay open and the animosity to fester, while average families on both sides just yearned for a normal peaceful life.

My grandfather did not have to force anyone out and felt lucky to quickly find a vacant Arab house near the Jaffa harbor. When the rest of the Varsano family arrived at their newly claimed home, they found it to be so recently vacated that the cupboards were still filled with food and Turkish coffee was recently brewed on the stove.

My family was certainly not thieves. The property that they occupied was abandoned because of the circumstances beyond their control. They certainly did not want the Arab family's forsaken possessions and probably would have returned their belongings if it

125

were possible, but that was simply not logistically viable under those volatile circumstances. It was extremely difficult to understand their actions without putting myself in the context of those times. They didn't have the luxury to contemplate moral dilemmas; they just acted out of instinct and a survival of the fittest mentality. By today's standards, some of the things the first Israelis did were abhorrent and downright criminal, but in a war zone if property was abandoned and you were homeless, it was an understandable breech of peace time etiquette.

Trying to rationalize the situation, I would certainly feel the need to reconcile with the particular Arab family that my family displaced. I would also feel a general guilt about all the displaced Arab families, but unfortunately war has many victims and those who instigated the fighting weren't the ones who usually suffered the most. Once the dust settled there was always a lot of blame to go around but ultimately to the victor goes the spoils. What would have happened to the Jews if Arabs had won the war? Based on the way Jewish citizens of Arab countries were treated following the Israeli Declaration of Independence and the persecution of other minority groups within most Arab nations, I believe the surviving Jews in a an Arab-governed Palestine would have been treated far worse than the Arabs who chose to live in the Jewish state of Israel. I am sure that many of the Jews could empathize with the Arabs that remained in Israel and were now legally considered a minority group.

It was quite ironic that my family was forced out of their apartment in Sofia just a few years earlier, and now they were doing the same to an unknown Arab family. The minority group that was once oppressed by the European Christian majority was now oppressing—albeit in a much different way—the former Moslem majority in a small corner of the Middle East. On a slightly positive note, I saw it as a testament to the strength of the Jewish people that they were able to politically and militarily turn the tables on their own predicament in such a short time period.

Following the urban-centric pattern of Jews throughout the world, two thirds of Israelis lived in cities, including my family. The Jews living in Israel were considered a community of people calling themselves Edot, while the non-Jews were the minority groups consisting of Christians, Moslem, Druze Arabs, Circassians, Armenians, and smaller groups known as Mi'utim. While the Edot did maintain distinct cultural traditions from their place of origin, there was a much greater degree of commonality and unity among the various sections of the Israeli Jewish population than in other immigrant societies. A unique Israeli ethnicity was primarily associated with immigrant groups from the Middle East and North Africa, but native-born Israelis of European parents expanded the notion of the typical Israeli. The generation of my parents and grandparents that originated from Europe formed various organizations, but these were usually designed to provide mutual aid and memorialize particular European communities, especially during the difficult early stages of integration into Israeli society.

At this time in Israel's history, the average Bulgarian's life was much more difficult than even the post war years in their previous country. Temporary government settlements, known as ma'abarot, housed the most destitute. The Bulgarian value system that stressed self reliance and hard work made it difficult for any of them to accept welfare or live in ma'aborot for very long.

After the War of Independence ended, the new nation faced several major hurdles to overcome. The absorption of immigrants, a refugee problem at the borders, defense against the hostile Arab neighbors, an economy ravaged by war, and managing foreign policy were the most predominant obstacles to improving the quality of life.

To cope with the myriad of problems, David Ben Gurion and the leaders of the Zionist movement announced the formation of the Provisional Council of State with Ben Gurion as Prime Minister. The first statute the Provisional Council of State made legal was the Law of Administrative Ordinance of 1948 which allowed for the free immigration of all Jewish people. The new citizens of Israel quickly elected a Constituent Assembly (CA) to draft a formal constitution. On February 16, 1949, the CA became Israel's first parliament with 120 members elected for four year terms.

A short time later, the Knesset—which was the single-chamber parliament of Israel—passed the Law of Return for every Jew as an olah, or new immigrant. The Nationality Law of 1952 granted Israeli citizenship to people (including non-Jews) who lived in the country prior to 1948. The population of the infant nation tripled in the first three years of existence with immigrants from over seventy countries. Some say that the liberal immigration policies exacerbated the domestic stress within Israel, while others say that it was necessary for the Jewish state to form its identity. Generally, the Ashkenazi's held most of the political offices and tended to support the left wing secular socialist parties, while the Sephardic, particularly the Orientals (Jews

128

who lived in the Middle East and North Africa, but later spread to Cental Asia and South Asia), held less power and sided with the right wing parties. My grandfather was more conservative than the average Ashkenazi which was a political tendency that was passed down to my father. Conservative or liberal were relative terms in Israeli politics, and could not be compared with the two party system in the US. There were many political factions with overlapping and conflicting agendas that had a substantial say in national policy. Despite their differences on some issues, there were universal values that became the cornerstones of the Jewish state.

The basic ideologies of the Israeli immigrants were Kibbutz Galuyot meaning "ingathering of the exiles" from the lands of Diaspora and Mizug Galuyot meaning a "merging of the exiles." The new immigrants from Europe or Northern Africa/Middle East arrived in Israel terribly impoverished and psychologically traumatized. The Bulgarian Jews, although impoverished, were fairly well suited to cope with the challenges of a new nation compared to other European Jews.

The Jews from Bulgaria did not neatly fit into a typical Israeli ethnic category. My family was Sephardic like many of the Middle Eastern Jews but they were of European descent. The Varsanos truly had more in common with the bulk of the Ashkenazi community being that they were urban, educated, and westernized. Over half of the Bulgarian immigrants came from Sofia where they had a long history of Zionist activism. After hundreds of years of prospering under the multi-ethnic Ottoman system, the Bulgarian people had a unique ability to fit into many groups within the diverse population of immigrants. Although my family lived in a predominately Bulgarian community, they had friends and colleagues from Eastern and Western Europe, as well as North Africa and the Middle East. My father would eat an Iraqi sandwich for lunch and have Hungarian Goulash for dinner then top it off with a Turkish coffee and a Bavarian chocolate dessert. His eating habits mimicked the multi-ethnic way he lived his daily life in a country full of new immigrants. The Bulgarians were well adjusted and very adaptive compared to the more severely persecuted immigrants.

Many of the Bulgarian immigrants did not harbor much animosity to their former homeland of Bulgaria despite their maltreatment. Compared to the other European Jews, they suffered far less during the war. Time and the enthusiasm over the success of establishing Israel healed their wounds much quicker than most. My family placed more blame on the Germans because they forced fascism upon the opportunistic Bulgarians.

The Jews of Eastern Europe, including the Bulgarians, were the largest group of immigrants during the first years of the nation. From 1948 to 1952, the immigration of 300,000 Sephardic immigrants changed the ethnic make up of the mostly European and Ashkenazi Israeli populace. The small country was inundated with a significant amount of well educated Iraqis and Egyptians, as well as impoverished Iranians, Yemenites, Turks, Moroccans, and other Jews from Moslem nations.

The main concerns of Northern African and Middle Eastern Jews were securing food and shelter upon arrival to Israel. Many lived in abandoned Arab settlements because there was a lack of investment capital in the new country to build housing units. Most of these new immigrants arrived a few years later than the European immigrants and had little knowledge of the Zionist movement. Their countries of origin lagged behind the European nations in regards to technological advances and cultural progression. The rise of Arab Nationalism and the Declaration of Independence in Israel made living conditions for these Jews unbearable. After escaping the tyranny of their homelands, they sought the most basic needs of proper housing, running water, electricity, and a decent supply of food. Immigrants from cosmopolitan areas like Baghdad or Cairo already were accustomed to most modern conveniences and quite educated while the refugees from the poorer areas of the Arab World were practically illiterate and had lots of trouble assimilating into the European-dominated culture of Israel.

About one-third of the new immigrants went to Moshavim and Kibbutzim. Moshavim were small cooperative agricultural settlements consisting of individual ownership of land combined with communal services and mutual aid. Unlike the Kibbutz, the basic social unit was the nuclear family which resulted in a cultural continuity with the new inhabitant's original country of origin. The Kibbutz was a diverse collective farming organization. My urban centric family steered well clear of agricultural settlements, just like their parents had rejected the concept of making an Aliyah in the early 20th Century to Palestine to work the land and establish a Zionist foothold in the region. Communal farming was necessary to help start the fledgling state of Israel and it was better to work with fellow Jews than non-Jews, but both my father and my grandfather sought to become independent businessmen. My father viewed the "kibbutzniks" as idealistic farmers, and he was a life-long city dwelling merchant and shop owner. My family continued to live adjacent to the large city of Tel Aviv, and patiently waited for the administrative chaos to subside.

The fate of all immigrants depended largely on the policies of the national authorities. Family connections and other personal resources helped improve certain people's lives, but fundamentally, people were at the mercy of the new government, the Jewish Agency, and the donations of Diaspora Jews. Despite how hard my family worked, they were vulnerable to the fluctuations of the shaky economy and the uncertainty of insecure borders. After unsuccessfully attempting a military takeover of Israel, Arab nations resorted to terrorist tactics and international political pressure to achieve their goal of overthrowing their Zionist enemies. Foreign investment was muted by the economic leverage of the hostile oil-rich Arab neighbors, while domestic tranquility was constantly disrupted by their violent attacks. Under these conditions, there were thousands of Arabs who were Israeli citizens that just wanted a normal life. Inevitably, there were problems with maintaining equal rights for the Arabs living in the Jewish state.

A primary argument since the establishment of the modern Jewish state had been the interpretation of how and why the Arabs were displaced. Israel contends that at the outbreak of fighting in 1948, most Arabs fled Palestine to avoid the perils of war. The Arabs insisted that the Israeli military and Jewish "terrorist" groups forced them out. In 1947, there were 1.3 million Arabs in Palestine, but by 1949 the Arab population of Israel had dropped to 170,000.

The remaining Arabs were legally granted equal voting rights and social status. However, in practice they had their freedom of movement restricted and their lands were confiscated for the influx of Jewish immigrants. The Islamic faith and the Arabic language were overshadowed by the predominance of the Jewish religion and the Hebrew dialect. The regions in which Arab families dwelled were ruled by military governors whose decisions were not subject to civil court review and had the power to seal the Arab neighborhoods whenever they deemed it necessary.

The Arabic community was further hindered by Israeli land sale policies. During the second Aliyah of 1904-1914, a policy was adopted that land acquired by a Jew could never be sold, leased, or rented to a non-Jew. The old policy was carried forward to the new state of Israel which resulted in 95% of Israeli land being off limits to non-Jews.

From an American perspective, I feel this was clearly a discriminatory policy for a purely pluralistic society, but Israel was officially a Jewish state. Since a relatively small numbers of Jews lived in a fairly undersized area and were surrounded by millions of Arabs who would have quickly purchased and moved into vast amounts of Israeli land, the Jews would have rapidly became a minority and lost control over the democratic country that they started. Some safeguard measures—unfair as they may appear—had to be instituted for the ever-present reason of survival.

The idea that Zionism was the equivalent of racism was a theory pushed forward by many UN General Assembly nations including Moslem, Arab, and even some European countries. I believe

133

that in any society, certain groups of people will have preferential treatment over others based on a variety of issues such as religion, race, educational background, wealth, sex, sexual orientation, political affiliations, and a whole slew of potentially discriminatory characteristics. I am not excusing these prejudices as acceptable, but being a Jewish state implies that there will be preferential treatment for Jews. How to minimize discrimination and produce a harmonious society were challenges that all nations faced, and Israel was no exception. If Israel was such a racist state then why have so many non-Jews from Eastern Europe and Asia immigrated there recently?

The concept of a Zionist nation was founded on socialist and somewhat idealistic principles, but in reality Israel was not a classless society even for Jews. Sephardim did not enjoy all the power and privilege of the Ashkenazi community. Most of the government officials were Ashkenazi who typically originated from the "cultured" European nations, while Sephardim were the darker skinned inhabitants of mostly "less sophisticated" Arab countries. Even within the Sephardic community, Northern African immigrants from countries like Morocco were looked down upon socially by the fairer skinned Eastern European Sephardim like my Bulgarian family.

Arabs legally had many of the same rights as Jews and realistically had a chance to prosper like never before in a peaceful Jewish state. If they were unhappy with their predicament and sought more human rights, the Israeli government allowed them to mount valid legal challenges within the court system and political campaigns to gain elected representation in the Knesset. In the same way the oppressed peoples of the US such as women, people of color, and gays took the opportunity to wage a civil rights struggle, the oppressed minorities of Israel were allowed to struggle for their rights within the established framework of the Zionist government. Compared to the rights of ordinary Arabs within Arab countries both secular and religious, Israeli Arabs enjoyed more civil liberties, despite their inherit discrimination as a minority group.

The Israeli system and the principles of Zionism were not perfect and continued to evolve, but the Zionists most certainly did not aspire to be "Jewish Nazis," as some extremist ideology contends. For the most part, Zionists sought a fair and pluralistic society that was subject to change based on the will of people. Unlike most Arab and Moslem nations, all the policies of Israel were subjected to open and honest public debate, which was a unique concept in the Middle East. Being a democratic society with a market based economy was a key reason Israel gained relative prosperity, as well as a enduring international legitimacy with the US and many other Western nations.

The people of Israel had few skills and meager financing, while the land that inhabited had virtually no natural resources. Funds were raised by a high level of domestic savings, capital imports such as foreign loans or grants, and foreign private sector financing such as State of Israel Bonds. Many American Jews—including my mother's family—purchased these bonds through their temple congregations. The bonds were sold in a variety of denominations ranging from as little as eighteen dollars up into the thousands, and were marketed as a financial investment, as well as support for the Israeli cause. Domestic infrastructure projects in agriculture and housing were funded by public funds. Regardless of the help of Diaspora Jews and the hard

135

work of Israelis, the economy was terribly in need of regulation and substantial foreign assistance. To combat an unstable economy and unforeseen shortages, the Israeli government imposed strict price controls and rationing. Obtaining foreign assistance would take more time and a bit of savvy in the world of international politics. While every Israeli struggled, my grandfather tried to adapt his job skills as a proprietor of a hardware store to an economy where adequate supplies and tidy shops were at a premium. He would most likely have to find a new career in this land of uncertainty.

The triumph of Zionism did not produce paradise in Israel for the Jewish immigrants that hoped a new homeland was a recompense for all their suffering. A military victory did not ensure security for the Israeli people. The tenuous peace allowed the infant nation to crawl out of the womb but it was born into an unfriendly world surrounded by enemies. The battle weary people of Israel, including the Varsano family, were excited to start a new life despite the seemingly insurmountable obstacles. The Varsanos were overjoyed at the achievement of the Zionist objective and content to live in Jaffa. In a few short years, my family had gone from a luxury apartment in frigid European city to forced relocation in the Bulgarian countryside to an abandoned Arab stone house on the balmy shores of the Mediterranean. My family was indeed able to adapt to their surroundings, no matter what the circumstances.

CHAPTER 7

The Burden of Being Captain

In a few short years of living in Israel, my father would experience the problems of a fledgling nation first hand and be transformed from a struggling boy to a leader among men. After briefly celebrating their victory in the War of Independence, the first Israelis faced the reality of managing a country inundated with impoverished immigrants that lacked basic infrastructure. In the midst of this feverish nation building, unsafe and sometimes chaotic conditions existed in the metamorphosing nation.

In the years immediately following the war, Jewish immigrants from around the world flooded into Israel at a staggering rate. The Law of Return welcomed all Jews to "come home" with an open door policy. The infant nation was in dire need of massive population growth for several reasons. The most obvious was that more citizens meant more soldiers and greater security. There were large areas of uninhabited land that needed to be filled in as a buffer against invading enemies. These remote areas were mostly developed into agricultural communities that required an influx of Jewish hands to work the fields, as well as to defend the residents and property. A large and dedicated work force was needed to modernize the economy so a higher standard of living could eventually be enjoyed by all citizens.

The mass immigration had idealistic intentions, but in reality the early years were filled with virtual chaos. The Israeli authorities inherited an inadequate infrastructure from British administered

Palestine. Law and order was difficult to maintain. Transportation systems were particularly lacking and incapable of moving the nation's new residents. Railroad crossings did not have traffic lights or guard gates.

One of the first major projects to improve infrastructure was the construction of the government-run railroad lines between Tel Aviv and Haifa. On Thursday, February 3, 1949, my grandfather and another recent immigrant—who was in need of work—loaded his truck in search of a new livelihood. Both of the ambitious Bulgarians left Jaffa headed north towards Haifa to look for business opportunities outside of the Tel Aviv metropolis. At an incomplete and unregulated railroad crossing in Benimina—north of Tel Aviv—the truck was broadsided by an oncoming train. Both the driver and the passenger were killed instantly. No one in the family knew anything for several days, and then my grandmother heard the bitter message. On the fourth day of the Jewish month of Shevat in the year 5709, Isaac Varsano—patriarch of the family—tragically perished.

My dad was very tightlipped about his father's untimely passing, and only made mention to me if I specifically asked questions. For years, I thought the story was fabricated because it just didn't seem plausible to me. How could someone that was so resilent and hearty, die in such a senseless and random matter so soon after surviving the horrors of WWII? I thought that he told the train accident story to cover up the true reason he died. I thought there might have been something that he was ashamed of, but in fact that was the true story and it was just too painful for him to recount the graphic details that would have made it seem more believable to me. Also, no one in our family was an actual eyewitness to the accident. They just heard second hand accounts a couple of days after the fact. One day, my grandfather simply went off to look for work and never came back.

My father was overcome with a wave of strong emotions: shock, disbelief, angry, and frustration. Why him? Why now? How could this happen? He questioned his values and possibly lost some of his faith in God. Why would a just God do this to his family after the years of suffering in Bulgaria? Since my father only gave me the cold hard facts about the tragedy, the feelings and emotions were simply conjecture on my part. However, what was not spoken was conveyed through the look in his eyes and his actions.

I don't think my father ever truly came to grips with that tragic loss in his life, so telling the story of Isaac's accident didn't seem real to him. My mom told me that my dad had confided in her that his imagination would play tricks on him when he would look at the back of some stranger's head and believe that it was his father. From a certain angle, if the lighting was right, it looked like his father. Could it be? He thought maybe there was some horrible mix up and his father might return. He was still clinging to his last remnants of an irrational sense of hope.

Just prior to his father dying, little Seeco craved a pet donkey. As silly as it sounds, it was actually a possibility in the hectic days of redeveloping Jaffa. After settling in their new home, both siblings requested gifts from their parents. Seli wanted a sparkling red dress and Seeco wanted a donkey. It seems unimaginable to me that my father would want a seemingly frivolous farm animal in the middle of a port city. I guess that in those final days of having the security of two

139

parents and a happy home, my father was a regular carefree kid that asked for outlandish things. This would all change after his dad was no longer there.

The loss of his father represented the discarding of what little remnants remained of little Seeco's youthful spirit. At age fifteen, he had become an adult with a serious nature that characterized his personality for the rest of his life. The toxic combination of fascism, communism, and the accidental death of a parent stifled the jovial spirit of the otherwise normal teenage boy. It set the tone for my dad being the man of the house at a very young age. For the next fifty years he would feel the burden of being the breadwinner. Never again would he have the luxury of relying on someone else for financial or paternal support. Even though he had loving uncles and other older men in his family, no true father figure ever emerged in his life. My adolescent father was to assume the role himself.

Immediately following the passing of his father, Seeco was forced to work to help support his family from age fifteen until he was conscripted into the army three years later. My grandmother was compelled to work at Shekam, the soldiers' only store, and a few years later my aunt would also become an employee when she turned fifteen years old. My father chose to take an apprenticeship with a local machine shop. After a hard day of labor in the dusty and greasy alleys of Jaffa, my father would study at Organization for Rehabilitation through Training (ORT) during the evening hours.

The technical training at the privately funded ORT was an immediate necessity that replaced a traditional high school education. The students were mostly ambitious young men concerned with nation building, helping their families, and simply earning a living. At ORT, my father met a fellow Bulgarian student named Simontov Zarfati, who eventually became his business partner.

In the aftermath of WWII, more than 80,000 displaced persons were trained in ORT schools that prepared them for their new lives in Israel, Europe and the United States. ORT began operations by creating workshops in Jaffa to rehabilitate and train demobilized or wounded soldiers. The first ORT school in Israel was founded in Jaffa in 1949. The school's pupils and teachers were all from the olim (new immigrants) which originated in Bulgaria, and classes were offered in tool manufacturing, electro-mechanics, and radio technology. It eventually moved to Tel-Aviv and is now the famous ORT Syngalovsky School.

ORT prepared students for technological, scientific, and vocational careers which enabled them to live secure and productive lives and played a crucial role in developing the future high-tech industries that would fuel Israel's modern economic growth. The school maintained close ties with the IDF and high-tech industry while constantly adapting its courses of study to the ever-changing needs of the economy and society. My father would use the skills acquired at ORT for the remainder of his life while he worked in various machine shops and in the commercial laundry business. Whether it was fabricating household items, medical supplies, aerospace parts, or servicing laundry equipment, his ORT skills were being put to use. Frying pans, landing gear, stethoscopes, and washing machines, all became his fields of expertise thanks to the technical background he received at ORT. Even though he never really had the option to attend public school and receive a liberal arts education, his technical training gave him a base of practical knowledge, as well as helping to reap impressive financial rewards for him later in life.

Along with the other problems of the developing nation, the public schools of Israel were under funded and lacked qualified teachers which was ironically similar to the conditions of US public education institutions today. The government paid for public education and received its funding from a progressive and somewhat onerous income tax. Primary school was free to all children, but parents had to foot the bill for high school. Once his father died, attending ORT was the only logical choice for Seeco. Also, regular public schools were not available to the new immigrants because most did not have sufficient knowledge of the Hebrew language.

On December 2, 1950, my father turned eighteen years old, and was required to serve in the military despite his obligations to his family. Israel had developed a three tier military system based largely on the Swiss Reservist model. The forces consisted of a small standing officer corps, universal conscription, and a large pool of well trained reservists. Conscription was mandatory for all able bodied Jewish male and female citizens, as well as resident aliens over age eighteen. Males were required to serve at least three years of duty while females—including my aunt—were required to serve for two years. Christians and Muslims were not required to serve but could volunteer. Exemptions were rare, conscientious objectors were not excused, and over 90% of Jews were drafted. The orthodox Jews— who had devoted their lives to theological study at the Yeshiva—were some of the rare exemptions from military service. The protected status of the Orthodox young adults still remains a controversial political issue in the entrenched camps of the Israeli domestic factions. However, in the early 1950s it was simply a new and experimental policy among a government looking to define itself.

The military served kosher food and adhered to the laws of the Jewish Sabbath and holidays. However, the majority of soldiers were not strict observers of the religious laws, so many were indifferent to forced ceremonies. My father, who was a relatively secular young man, sat through many orthodox Jewish ceremonies in the military. Rather than enlighten him, it mostly annoyed him. He found it ridiculous to force a diverse group of independent thinking young men to participate in antiquated ceremonies in a highly structured military environment. Every Jew practiced his religion differently; to homogenize everyone into the strictest form of Judaism, he believed, was inappropriate. It also gave him his first taste of the disproportionate power that the orthodox lobby possessed. For every year of IDF duty, he attended Passover Seders where the presiding rabbi would recite several hours of prayers before anyone could their meal. After sitting through many of these highly formalized meals, he vowed that he would never subject his family to the burdens of orthodox observance.

The discipline in the military was informal with little attention paid to military drills and ceremony—instead focusing on being ready for combat. Saluting an officer was not an obligation especially when the unconventional Moshe Dyan was the Chief of Staff of the Israeli Defense Forces. Dyan was unpredictable and known to pull off political stunts such as surprise attacks on the Arabs. He sought to draw the Arab militaries into open battle to minimize the terrorist attacks within Israel. On the other hand, Dyan was a member of the dovish Labor party and had a decent relationship with Arabs from his early days living in Palestine. Moshe Dayan's daughter was stationed at the same base as my dad, which gave him a more personal connection to the military and political leader who he generally supported throughout the years. With the exception of the religious students, every walk of life enlisted in the IDF, from pauper to the children of the country's leaders.

Conscripts were thoroughly tested before assignment, so the better educated and physically fit persons could be placed into combat units. The Air Force got the first pick of the elite units which were mostly volunteers. Basic training was separated into the brigade of infantry troops and the corps of non-infantry conscripts such as armor or artillery. After the first month of orientation the corps trained for an additional three to four months while the brigade endured a more strenuous four to five months. Assimilation of new immigrants and teaching young adults the country's history were two goals of the initial training programs. After the first five months of service, recruits were evaluated for leadership potential. About half of the conscripts qualified for further training as squad leaders, tank commanders, and other types of non-commissioned officers (NCO).

The further training included three months of a Junior Command course. At the completion of the course, the Junior NCO returned to his original unit where he finished his three years of mandatory service. The lowest career rank of an NCO was samal, or sergeant, which was the highest rank my father achieved. After completion of the compulsory duty, the NCO's were evaluated for potential as officers. Ratings were made by fellow soldiers, recommendations by commanders, and screening by a military psychologist. If chosen to be an officer and accepted, the recruit served an additional year – minimum. Israel has no military academy for officer hopefuls. All officers are taken from among the conscripts.

My father served in the artillery section of the army. He wore a black beret and an olive green uniform with an IDF pin on the left collar. Eventually, he earned the right to wear a white owl in a black circle on his left shoulder tag which represented wisdom and teaching. The owl on a shoulder tag is still used today for training bases and schools. He also wore a green braided rope which showed he was an Army instructor belonging to the training command, or Pikud Hahadracha.

Shalom Eitan, a Romanian born Second Lieutenant and author of *Survive and Tell,* was his instructor for the RADAR technician's course. In 1951, Lieutenant Eitan was appointed head of the Anti Aircraft RADAR School and shortly after received two recruits to train as RADAR operators and eventually instructors. Mordecai Varsano, known as "Verasano" to his fellow soldiers, was one of the initial recruits in the new RADAR program. According to Lieutenant Eitan, my father was "a very intelligent and skilled person who became my right hand and an excellent instructor. I choose Mordecai because I liked him as a person." The RADAR used for training was the only RADAR that the IDF had at that time. It was a prototype of a WWII RADAR AN-SCR 545, which was built by cannibalizing two RADARS that had been smuggled out of the US as combines for agriculture in Israel during the time of the arms embargo.

145

The first RADAR technician's courses were filled by artillery soldiers and fresh faced high school graduates. The courses were conducted in Hebrew and in English. All the books and technical material were in English. The main book, which became the bible for many generations of radar engineers and technicians, was the "The Principles of Radar," published by MIT during WWII.

Actual training consisted of tracking simulated enemy aircraft. In 1948, the Israeli Air Force was supplied planes and training by Czechoslovakia. Propeller driven Messerschmitt's and reconditioned Spitfires from WWII constituted their entire fleet. The Israeli Air Force was later equipped with mostly Meteors and French Mysteres, and had some P-51 Mustangs as well. The soldiers were numerically inferior to their Arab enemies but better trained. The Arab nations were supplied by several countries, including the Soviet Union, which provided them low flying MiGs and Vampires for their air forces.

After graduating form RADAR school, my father was stationed at the Number 9 Artillery School as an instructor in the Anti Aircraft wing. His assignment was being a RADAR operator and instructor involved in tracking and destroying enemy aircraft. He was eventually offered and declined an invitation to become an officer because he did not particularly enjoy the regimented life of the military or the rough outdoor experience of field patrols. During his service, he learned to never volunteer, especially if he didn't know what it entailed. Sometimes his commanding officer would involuntarily station him in remote areas of the desert wher he feared Feyadin terrorist attacks during watch duty and woke up in the morning to frequently find scorpions in his boots.

146

I loved to hear stories about his days in the army, even though he did not really put a positive spin on his time in military service. My dad would always watch war movies, though, and I would ask him questions like "Did you ever kill any Arabs?" "Were you or your comrades ever wounded?" His answers were very tight lipped. He would usually responded with words to the effect of "sometimes we would shoot but not know if we hit anything or anybody" He didn't like to brag or glorify the military for fear that I might want to join. When watching a war movie, he would be entertained but he always tried to impart the fact that the valiant portrayals of soldiers on screen were a far cry from the grim reality of war and the restricted life in the military.

One story that he did tell me was that his IDF unit would hunt wild boar with their machine guns in the forest while killing time on patrols. In the evening his unit would cook the non-Kosher boar meat. His helmet was used to boil water and doubled as a soup bowl. He used to say that the Bulgarians were the musicians and the Hungarians were the cooks in the army, wild boar goulash with Slavic folk music anyone? Later in life, he never liked to go camping because he said that he had too much of "roughing it" in the wilderness as a soldier. Being a scout master wasn't in his character and I was never a boy scout. He didn't really enjoy hiking, shooting, hunting, off road vehicle driving, or any outdoorsman activities.

When I was a child and got really sleepy, I would ask my dad to "carry me like a wounded soldier." He would then proceed to slump me over his soldier with my feet tangling in the air while gently carrying me to bed. A practical skill acquired during basic training in

147

the IDF translated to a loving interaction between a father and a small boy. I knew it was a sign that I was no longer a little boy when my father said that I was much too heavy to do the wounded soldier routine anymore. As an adult, my father spoke about the military even less and I felt that he saw his army duty mostly as a disruption to his career in business.

When his three mandatory years were up at age twenty-one, he had seen enough armed conflict in his life and sought to go back to civilian life in order to help his family. From the bombing and artillery battles of WWII to the Israeli War of Independence, he had seen enough mechanized battle. He knew that he still faced many years of service in the reserve and the constant threat of a terrorist attack, but desperately wanted to maintain a peaceful and prosperous city dweller life. What little income he earned in the IDF went to family or was saved for a future business venture. The tragedies of his life had stripped him of a desire for material indulgence, while the necessity to make prudent financial decisions gave him a lifelong frugality that pervading his spending habits no matter how monetarily secure he became in later years.

During his compulsory IDF service and in the years that immediately followed, his impoverished nation continued to struggle. Foreign investment was lacking despite Israeli legislation that encouraged it. Invasive government regulations and high taxes resulted in a thriving black market. There was rationing of clothing, food, and other essentials, as well as a lack of raw materials and electric power for businesses.

148

The Zionist dream versus the reality of living in Israel had taken shape. The Zionist dream was to live in a land of plenty as prophesized in the Bible. All Jews would be working together against any common enemy. Israeli society would be a melting pot for all of the various sects and ethnicities of the ingathered Diaspora. Every citizen would sacrifice for the common good of the state. Some religious zealots believed the establishment of the state of Israel was fulfilling Biblical prophesy and it was the first signal in the coming of the messiah.

The reality of the first years of the Jewish State was of conflicting agendas, prejudices of all types, a multitude of infrastructure problems, unresolved political debate of the right wing versus the left wing, as well as the secular versus the religious. The Jews fought against their common enemy, the Arabs, out of the necessity to merely survive and not because of a unified and calculated vision of how the country should evolve. Jews were constantly fighting with Arabs while arguing with fellow Jews. The lack of consensus and the inability to sustain a long term coalition government in Israel continues today. The absence of harmony in the Israeli political process has helped stymie efforts to achieve a lasting peace.

Of course, these are some of the pitfalls of being the only legitimate democracy in the Middle East. Political harmony and ideological consensus were rarely achieved in a society with open public debate and free press. The dictatorships of the Arab nations did not allow the same freedoms for their citizens as the Israeli democracy did, so if public dissent from the stated national agenda became a political problem it was legally suppressed. Israelis enjoyed the

149

freedoms of democracy and an open society, but suffered the double punch of being a new nation surrounded by enemies and a political body that lacked substantial consensus. As a result, Israel continued to economically stagger while my family came to grips with losing their patriarch and earning enough income to live a decent life.

By 1952, a "New Economic Policy" was instituted by Ben Gurion that sought to end the inflationary credit expansion that had existed in the first years of economic development. The currency was devalued, rationing ceased, and the black market curtailed. Immigration of Jews was even slightly restricted. The Shilumin Agreement in the fall of 1952 outlined the reparations treaty between Germany and Israel. $820 million worth of German goods would be paid to Israel over a twelve year span. Although the value would decline over the following years, in 1955, 47% of the Israeli government's budget was supplied by the Shilumin Agreement. The country would still struggle, but with the help of several new and significant friends, survival and even a relative peace seemed obtainable.

My father and my aunt had mixed feelings about the reparations. From a negotiation standpoint, it was best to try to acquire as much as possible, but they didn't want to appear greedy or vindictive. The goal was not to punish the Germans. It was to try to regain the feeling and financial position that the persecuted Jews held before the Holocaust.

Receiving substantial foreign aid from the nation that spawned the Nazis was a controversial decision at the time, but I feel it was a necessary part of reconciliation for the Germans. Israel was fighting

150

for its very survival both militarily and economically. They were in no position to take the so called moral high ground and reject the German offer, or be greedy and hold out for more. By the 1950s, it was clear that the Nazi party or any similar incarnation would not reemerge any time soon in Europe. Events like the Nuremburg trials and the strategy of the Marshall Plan had effectively transformed West Germany into a new country that could establish cautious relations with a skeptical Israeli populace.

If Israel was going to survive, it needed the help of not only the Germans, but a consistent and substantial flow of foreign investment from a variety of sources. Diaspora Jews, especially American Zionists, played a critical role in furthering the viability of the Jewish state. My mother and I are both Americans who strongly support the State of Israel. I was born in the US and believe in the principles of this country. Unless the principles and ideals of America change dramatically and Israel becomes an enemy of the US, I will remain here.

I feel that Diaspora Jews can help Israel in their own countries, perhaps even more so than actually living in the mother country of Israel. Millions of Diaspora Jews help the Israeli economy by investing in State of Israel Bonds and purchasing Israeli-made imports. Political support was expressed and still is expressed by funding of Israeli charities and pro-Israel lobbying groups, as well as direct pressure on local politicians to influence foreign policy. Religiously, Diaspora Jews furthered the evolution of Judaism by teaching in the country's native tongue and not restricting the religion to Hebrew only. In America, new forms of Judaism that appeal to liberal American

151

Jews have sprung up and have been countered by an American brand of ultra-orthodoxy.

I feel that the Jews that don't support Israel have a similar attitude to the mostly passive population of Jews before the Holocaust: We were citizens of the country that we lived in and have safely integrated into this community, intermarriage with non-Jews made us even more integrated, we can still observe Jewish traditions if we wish but Israel was for the more extreme Jews. I believe those Jews are short sighted, somewhat selfish, and slightly delusional about the way vast numbers of non-Jews will treat Jews in a crisis situation. When you are a minority group and the majority group begins to suffer, history shows that you will get blamed, no matter how integrated or patriotic that you think you are. You must be true to your heritage, your values, and your country. It's not a choice of one or the other, you must do all.

The Jewish people, with the assistance of their former tormentors, had risen from the ashes to create a land of tenuous opportunity. By the time my father completed his compulsory service in the IDF, he had seen more death, destruction, and forced servitude than most people had seen in a lifetime. From the anti-Semitism of the Bulgarian fascists to the forced indoctrination of the communists to the War of Independence to the untimely death of his father to the constant fear of an attack by Arabs and the mandatory enlistment in the army, he just wanted to live in peace. He had been severely challenged in the previous few years, but rather than crumble under the pressure, he rose to the challenge. In reality, he had no choice. His family was depending on him. He was a natural leader who acquired valuable military experience and practical technical skills. It was now time to build the business that his father had set out to start on that tragic day five years earlier. He certainly had the ability and the ambition, but would Israel offer him the economic opportunity and personal freedom to satisfy his aspirations?

CHAPTER 8

All Hands on Deck

After three compulsory years of full time enlisted service in the Israeli Army, my father returned to his home in Jaffa. He re-entered the work force of the greater Tel Aviv area with the technical skills that he acquired at ORT and the leadership qualities he gained in the IDF. Even though he went through a great deal of hardship in his first twenty-one years, he still possessed a fair amount of youthful enthusiasm and was eager to start earning a substantial income.

Jaffa in the 1950s was primarily a Bulgarian community. Bulgarian was spoken everywhere and Bulgarian food was served along the main street of Shderot Yerushalayim. The Maccabi Youth Sports Organization from Bulgaria had produced an adult soccer team that competed nationally in Israel. The Maccabi Jaffa Soccer Team, which was mostly comprised of players of Bulgarian descent, was one of my father's passions as a young man. With his Bulgarian soccer hoodlum comrades, he would wait for hours after a game just for the opportunity to pelt the referee's armored car with rocks as he departed the stadium. He pledged fierce loyalty to his team.

Years later when he lived in Los Angeles, he was a devoted fan of the Lakers basketball team. He rarely even watched other teams play and was mostly indifferent to other televised sports. Loyalty was a strong characteristic of my father and he expected the same from family, friends, and business associates. No matter how much money he made, he always took care of his family first. He routinely deferred large purchases for himself in order to help support his mother and sister. Later in life, he spent a lot more on my mother than he would ever dream about spending on himself. I was deprived of very little and my father made sure that I was able to have all the things that he could never have. In addition to financial support, my father was also very loyal regarding his marriage. He was never unfaithful in over thirty years of being with my mother.

In business, he expected employees to stay for the long term and took it personally when they left for a better job. Starting in late 1970s, he would sell the Wascomat line of laundry equipment for twenty years, despite being lured with enticing offers from other manufacturers. He also lived in the same house on Crespi Street in Woodland Hills for over twenty-five years. Once he was comfortable with something, he stuck with it. After a childhood of not being able to latch onto something permanent, Maccabi Jaffa became a source of passion and pride.

Perhaps he had displaced some of the anger and frustration of his earlier life and channeled it into sports. The quality of life had improved in Israel and the average person was now concerned with matters other than mere survival. "The spontaneous emotional commitment of the independence movement" had been replaced by a more conventional life. Many kibbutzniks abandoned the rigors of farm life, and moved to Tel Aviv to indulge in the prosperity of the city.

My father started searching for his fortune in the rugged industrial alleys of Jaffa. After working as an apprentice and saving his earnings, he was able to open his own machine shop on 330th Street in Jaffa. He managed to simultaneously help his family and gradually increase his standard of living. To enable his business to grow, a fellow ORT graduate and Bulgarian named Simotov Zarfati was taken on as a business partner. My father was the leader of the fledgling company with his business savvy, product ideas, and precise technical ability. Simotov helped to increase output and shoulder some of the burden from my father. They manufactured a variety of small metal goods such as kitchenware items including pots and pans, as well as military parts such as air craft carrier launching equipment. The Mordecai/Simontov partnership was a tiny building block of a burgeoning Israeli arms industry which specialized in the upgrading and overhauling imports of WWII surplus weapons.

By the 1950s, it was apparent that populating and irrigating remote farmland and deserts was not an economically efficient domestic policy. The national authorities began to see the opportunities of developing light industry instead of agriculture. Israel's economy was rapidly evolving and military-related production was quickly becoming a profitable sector. The largest defense firm was the government-owned conglomerate, Israel Aircraft Industries (IAI), which had its beginnings as a small machine shop. As it expanded, IAI worked with subcontractors to upgrade and maintain the WWII surplus stock. Young and ambitious Seeco dreamed that his machine shop would someday blossom into a larger firm like IAI that could help Israel's economy and security.

Conditions prevailed such that my father was able to earn a comfortable living and take advantage of the Israeli version of modernist culture. With a little bit of money in his pocket and some leisure time, he was able to indulge in the rock 'n roll culture of the 1950s. He had been tooting around town in an Italian-made Lambretta scooter, but was ready for an upgrade. His first step at being "cool" was buying himself a fat motorcycle like his father had in Bulgaria. As he rolled through town on his English-built BSA 550, he could hear his favorite tunes by Chubby Checker and Elvis Presley playing in the cafes throughout Tel Aviv. My dad was always fascinated with American culture from the epic war movies to the twisting dance moves of rhythm and blues music, to the blue jeans and the leather jacket of the pop icons. The super high pompadour hairstyle of James Dean and Elvis Presley were the looks to emulate in the US as well as Israel. From his American school in Bulgaria to his "Made in the USA" tools in his machine shop, he respected the quality of what the US had to offer.

American "Negros" were a fascinating spectacle to him because he never saw one in person until being in Israel. He told me that he thinks that he might have seen a Black man in the circus in Bulgaria as a small child. Even in Israel, Black people were few and far between. He once mentioned that he went to a Harlem Globetrotters game and might saw some R & B musicians who were Black, but that was the extent of his interaction with the entire race of people.

Since moving to Israel, he had never been outside the country so his cultural influences were limited to what was within the country.

157

He didn't have the time or money to go abroad yet. His vacation time was spent exclusively within the diminutive area that was pre-1967 Israel. He yearned for more out of life, but liked his community, friends, and the challenge of running his own business.

His moderate affluence and Sephardic good looks brought him plenty of girlfriends and a degree of happiness that he hadn't experienced since being a small child in the 1930s. It's hard for me to imagine my father with a woman other than my mother because that was never a reality during my lifetime. My mother, as well as girlfriends of mine, always said that my dad was good looking but I never thought of him in those terms. I could see my father as a very confident young man which was a trait that many women were attracted to, but imagining his life as a bachelor in Israel was hard to fathom. His agreeable routine of working and dating was often disrupted by obligations of national duty because Israel was surrounded by enemies that constantly sought to destroy her.

All adult males were required to be reservists in the military until age fifty. My father was in the anti aircraft unit of the army and was required to serve up to thirty days per year. Getting an ominous "call up" notice in the mail marked with a distinctive triangle on the envelope was a traumatic experience for the all the loved ones of every male reservist in the country. His mother and sister feared that Seeco would be a victim of a terrorist or be killed in combat each and every time that he was called up to Miluim duty.

In the aftermath of the War of Independence, approximately one million Arab refugees sat in "temporary" camps in Jordan, Lebanon, Syria, and the Egyptian-controlled Gaza Strip. Less Jews

158

lived in Israel than Arab refugees in the camps, and the Israeli government was unwilling to allow hostile displaced people to return to their former homes for security reasons. In turn, Arab nations deported their Jewish citizens and pledged to destroy Israel, which if successful would thereby allow all the refugees to return. Many of the "temporary" camps still exist today and several generations of Arabs have continued efforts to destroy Israel through both conventional and unconventional means. Half of my family still resides in Israel today and is vulnerable to the danger posed by Arab terrorist attacks that have persisted since the establishment of Israel.

Spurred on by the concept of fedayeen (Arabic for self-sacrifice), terrorist militia groups began systematic raids against the Israeli civilian population. Several thousand raids were conducted primarily by Palestinian-born refugees financed by the Egyptian military. Cash bonuses for "trophies," such as the ear or finger of an Israeli Jew were rewards. Approximately 1,300 Israelis were killed and wounded by Arab terrorists between 1949 and 1956. The Fedayeen guerilla detachments operated from bases located in and controlled by Egypt, Lebanon and Jordan. My father had avoided Fedayeen attacks while serving in his reservist unit for several years, but the danger of falling victim to their attacks was unrelenting. Whenever he was on night watch he was vulnerable to an ambush. When his unit was on a patrol, the terrorist engaged in unscrupulous tactics that put the lives of innocent civilians at risk, as well the IDF soldiers. Taking cover in homes and mosques, as well as sniper attacks from residential apartment windows were common operations by these paramilitary groups and unfortunately the same inhumane

159

activities are still implemented today. The nations that supported these actions may have slightly shifted, but terrorist attacks by Arabs continue to threaten my family today. In the belligerent days of the 1950s in the Middle East, the build up in tensions inevitably resulted in another war.

In 1954, Gamal Abdel Nasser named himself Prime Minister of Egypt, resulting in a marked increase in violence against the Jewish state. Within his first year in office, Egyptian sponsored raids by Arab commandos originating from the Sinai Peninsula, Gaza Strip, and Jordan, into Israel began escalating. By February of 1955, Ben Gurion returned to the Ministry of Defense and proceeded to conduct raids against Egyptian held territories for the protection of Jewish settlers. This show of force helped to restore the leadership of the Mapai party, which was later combined with other left wing movements to form the Labor Party. However, Israel's strong handed response in Gaza and the West Bank resulted in much civilian causality, eliciting complaints by humanitarian organizations and public relations problems for Israel that still exists today. Both domestic Israeli and international public pressure forced the IDF to focus their counter attacks on strictly military related targets. The recent US-led War on Terror has shed light on the legitimacy of many of Israel's "controversial" defense tactics, but other nations in the international community continue to cling to the old notions of restricting an armed response to conventional military targets. Unfortunately, terrorists never have presented many viable military targets, but the Arabs of the 1950s had not yet given up on conventional warfare to achieve their objectives.

Arab leaders still felt that that it was logistically and practically possible to destroy Israel with an invasion of uniformed troops.

In October of 1955, Nasser of Egypt purchased new weapons systems from the USSR and other arms from Czechoslovakia. In response, Israel brokered an arms deal with France because President Eisenhower stubbornly refused to sell any armaments to the fledgling Jewish state, because he did not want to upset the balance of power in the region. Many hawks within Israeli society favored a preventive war against an Egyptian nation that was clearly preparing for a confrontation, while my father remained focused on his business.

The Middle East conflict began to morph into a struggle between the Western World and Arab Nationalism. Nasser viewed the Suez Canal as an extension of Western imperialism, while the proposed Aswan High Dam was to be the modern day pyramid of the Arabs. After Egypt officially recognized communist China and struck an arms deal with the Soviets, the United States—in the midst of the Cold War—refused to help finance the Aswan Dam project. An upset and disappointed Nasser responded by nationalizing the Suez Canal zone.

In response to US isolationism, Ben Gurion entered secret talks with Great Britain and France regarding a joint military action against Egypt. The IDF would attack the Sinai Peninsula while French and British forces would move into the Suez Canal area. Since Nasser's provocative actions threatened the interests of all Western nations in the Suez Canal, the joint operation seemed logical. Similar reasoning helped form the coalition that removed Iraqi forces from oil-rich Kuwait during the Gulf War of early 1990s. However, US foreign policy was obsessed with the Cold War during the 1950s and chose to let the Europeans primarily handle the Suez Canal crisis.

On October 24, 1956 a military pact between Egypt, Jordan, and Syria known as the "Arab Entente Militaire," was formed with General Amer as the supreme commander. After the three powerful Arab nations publicly announced an armed alliance to combat Israel, the majority of Israeli society was willing to accept the need for preemptive military action. Israelis knew that French and British forces were planning to occupy the Canal Zone and reclaim the Suez for the international community. Such a military maneuver would split the Egyptian forces and isolate a vulnerable army in the Sinai Peninsula.

In the early morning of Friday, October 26, 1956, a secret call up of IDF forces was conducted. Sergeant Varsano received his orders along with approximately 50,000 conscripts and regular troops, as well as an additional 100,000 reservists. The anxiety ridden soldiers were to assembly at secret strategic points and prepare to commence Operation Kadesh (Kadesh refers to the Biblical story of the children of Israel wandering through the Sinai Desert). On Monday, October 29 at 1600 hours the operation commenced. The Advance Guard of Colonel Ariel Sharon's Airborne Brigade crossed the frontier into the Sinai. The goals of the initial assault were to capture Gaza thereby eliminating the Fedayeen bases and to capture the city of Sharm-El-Sheikh in order to open the Gulf of Aqaba to Israeli shipping. The IDF easily defeated Egyptian troops at Gaza and at the Gidid and Mitla passes.

The Chief of Staff of the IDF, Moshe Dayan, characterized the Israeli strategy as a campaign of "speed and risk." The role of the

162

reservists was to bring brigades up to war establishment, strengthen the line of frontier posts, fortify the settlements which were Israel's first line of defense, and to form additional brigades. Reservist Sergeant Varsano was reunited with active duty Lieutenant Eitan at the 883 Heavy AAA Battalion. The RADAR specialists' mission was to defend Tel-Aviv from enemy air attacks. They were positioned at the site of the famous Hilton Hotel for the duration of the campaign where they spent the majority of their time waiting and staring at a round green lit monitor with flashing icons. At least he was in comfortable surroundings, although it must have been an awesome burden to know that he was the last line of defense to protect against an assault on the urban jewel of Israel.

Dayan's overall deployment strategy included the notion that fighting should take place on Arab lands to ensure that the small area of Jewish territory not become a war zone. The Arab militaries were so swiftly defeated that Tel Aviv never received any enemy fire. Therefore, my father kept close watch over the skies above the city but never saw action. Thankfully, Israeli civilians were safe and my dad didn't have a bomb dropped on him. He was relieved that he didn't have to shoot down any enemy aircraft or receive an enemy fire. He didn't want to be a war hero or be awarded medals. He simply did his duty to protect his nation and wanted to return to his family, as well as his friends and machine shop.

By Tuesday the Sinai Peninsula was effectively cut off from the Egyptian command. Israeli troops massed along the east bank of the Suez Canal. The Egyptian Air Force responded with a limited number of planes but never attempted to bomb Israeli cities. In the air

163

battle of the Sinai, Israel lost two Mustangs while shooting down four MiGs and three Vampires. By Friday, Israel had announced the capture of the "bulk of the Sinai," and the Governor-General of Gaza formally surrendered. Within exactly one week from the operations commencement, the Island of Sinafar was captured and Israeli shipping was opened through the Gulf of Aqaba.

French and British troops landed at Port Said and sought to internationalize the zone. France and Britain took control over the Suez Canal zone after only one day of fighting. By Tuesday, November 6, the campaign for the Sinai was over with minimal Israeli casualties and only four IDF prisoners of war captured. Fortunately for my father and Lieutenant Eitan, the war ended after approximately 100 hours and they were never at serious risk for being killed. Egypt had its Air Force destroyed and one-third of its Army defeated. The Egyptian forces did put up a better showing than in 1948, but were no match for the superior military force of Israel, Britain, and France.

The Americans feared Soviet involvement in the conflict and forced the European powers to enter into a cease fire. France and Britain quickly departed and left control to the UN. In March of 1957, Israeli troops—due to significant international pressure—were also forced to withdraw forces to the Armistice line of 1949. Abba Eban – Israeli Ambassador – said, "Withdrawal from the Occupied Territories was demoralizing to Israel. Israelis felt abandoned and alone in foreign policy. US-Israel relations reached a low point." The "us against them" world mentality of Israel and the Jewish people was further solidified. My father certainly didn't hate America, but had a similar feeling to his days in Bulgaria when all the Jews had to look out for themselves and didn't trust outsiders because everyone else had ulterior motives.

The United Nations Emergency Forces (UNEF) took control of the captured territories with the objective of preventing raids from Gaza and allowing Israeli shipping to proceed. The operation was ultimately considered an Israeli victory because the fighting ended with only 170 Israeli causalities, the IDF had established itself as an international military threat, and the Arab raids from Gaza ceased. In addition, international cooperation helped stabilize the region with UN peacekeepers separating Egypt and Israel.

Unfortunately, stabilization and peacekeeping were very subjective terms in regards to the Middle East. After several years of relative peace following the War of Independence, the Arab world conspired to vanquish Israel with a coordinated militant effort, but the Jewish people endured another challenge to their legitimacy in the region. My father rode the emotional rollercoaster of being an Israeli citizen with duty, diligence, and determination.

On the up side, he was proud of the military victories in the War of Independence and the Sinai Campaign. Jews—like my family—who made an Aliyah were viewed as pioneers, heroes, and patriots of their people. Even though he was still considered a Bulgarian, there was a relatively low level of discrimination for any ethnicity of Jews in Israel compared to Europe. He was young, healthy, and earned a decent income that enabled him to acquire the toys that a young man enjoys such as a fast motorcycle, quality tools, and a stylish wardrobe. There was also an abundance of young eligible women and he had many male friends from his neighborhood. He never had to be pressured by his mother about dating Jewish girls like me, because there were basically only Jewish girls in the pool of single Israeli women in his social circles.

On the down side, there was a constant tension in the air and nervousness in the pit of his stomach about the large numbers of hostile Arabs that surrounded his tiny country. Attacks by sworn enemy nation's threatened Israel's survival, and that grim reality posed a clear and present danger. Terrorist attacks were a constant worry and made my dad somewhat uneasy in remote areas. Milium duty was a long term obligation that was distracting from business and dangerous to his well being. Virtual every Israeli citizen would come to a near stand still when the regular radio broadcasts would be interrupted by ominous security warnings and reports of any recent casualties. The unstable economy relied heavily on foreign aid and small business owners like my dad had to work long and hard hours to earn a decent living. Political disharmony caused many heated arguments among the vocal and passionate Israelis which added to the general anxiety in the air. Jews from different parts of the world expressed their prejudices against each other while the secular battled the religious for political power.

Life in Israel had its ups and downs, but my father was terrifically resilient and impassioned to make the best of his current situation. He yearned for a stable, prosperous, and peaceful existence that would break the cycle of violence that had characterized his first quarter century on this uneasy planet. Following his honorable service in the Sinai Campaign, he had once again fulfilled an important obligation to his country. In the next few years, a relative peace would return to Israel and give Seeco the opportunity to build on his past success and experience, to create a better life for the future. He had once again triumphed over a major test in his struggle for survival and he was ready to move forward in life as a shrewd businessman and an eligible bachelor.

CHAPTER 9

Global Crossings and Love

L ife in the late 1950s and early 1960s in Israel was a mixed bag. On one hand the economy and quality of life were steadily improving but on the other hand there was the ever-present threat posed by the bothersome Arabs. My father began spending more of his hard earned income on himself because his sister and mother had been fortunate enough to find new men in their lives.

My father and his partner Simontov adapted their manufacturing process to suit the market demands for their region. The industrial based economy in Israel continued to shift from relying on natural resources and farming to new technologies and brainpower. After the Sinai Campaign, Israel's hodge-podge of military equipment needed to be updated and overhauled. One-half of Israeli vehicles needed base workshop repairs after only five days of fighting. Incorporating military parts production into the assembly line was profitable, as well as patriotic. My father was constantly inventing new ways to manufacture small parts and would profit accordingly. He was driven to reinvest in his business with bigger and better tools and machinery. After he paid his business expenses, he even had enough disposable income to purchase more prestigious luxuries for himself such as his first car and another motorcycle. The majority of his scarce indulgences centered on mechanical devices. It was his hobby, as well as his livelihood. He developed a love affair with all things mechanical and became quite proficient at fixing whatever was broken throughout his entire lifetime.

When he was a young man, everyone would fix their own car. The more you did it, the better you got at it. My dad would always try to fix his own car, as well as my car and the company trucks later in life. At home, he would feel the need to fix all household appliances such as vacuum cleaners, chainsaws, lawnmowers, and cordless phones. I remember spending many hours talking on a cordless with homemade antenna consisting of nuts, bolts, and some wire from his workshop. I also recall helping my dad install certain mechanical device at home such as a garage door opener and a gas range in the kitchen. We were not professionals and we usually made some errors with the job because we didn't read the manual, but in the end it was functional. He was a real do-it-yourselfer and his workshop at his eventual laundry business was his playground. Later in life he really felt at ease when doing work in his the shop area with his service technicians.

He adapted conventional front load washers to be steam injected for dying clothing. He always insisted upon delicately threading the brass nipple on the steam input himself. He did not trust his technicians to undertake this process because it needed the special touch of someone who had worked in a machine shop for many years and if the procedure was done incorrectly the machine would have to be sent back to the outsourced arc welder. This variation was known as a sample machine in the industry because small batches could be test dyed to get the coloring correct before a entire production run could be made. There was a lot of Israelis in the garment industry in Los

Angeles and he was able to develop a tight relationship with these clients that other non- Israeli competitors could not.

My dad rarely, if ever, hired an installer or assembly person for any item he purchased. If my dad—the boss—didn't want to fix, assemble, or install something, rather than hire a professional, he would just have one of his service technicians do it. Automobiles and fork lifts were two very frustrating items that I wished he would have just hired a real mechanic to fix. He tried to keep everything in house – within his small trusted circle. He took any sign of disloyalty personally. He expected hard work, loyalty, and obedience, but wasn't prepared to compensate lavishly and wasn't particularly complimentary or polite. He felt that his teaching and mentoring gave his employees a valuable skill and that coupled with a fair wage was adequate

As a kid, I let my dad do all the fixing because he seemed to enjoy it while I was much more into sports and other youthful activities. As I grew older—probably shortly after college graduation—I began to tinker with fixing various things. After repairing a tape deck or a washing machine, I realized that I had inherited my father's ability to be a problem solver and I got better at it the more I practiced. After a while, instead of asking my dad for advice or help, I had the confidence to figure it out on my own. There were certain things that just were not worth my time, and my dad was the same way.

When newer cars started being built with computers and loads of microelectronic components, my father stopped trying to fix it himself and paid the experts to do the job. The same can be said about home appliances or commercial laundry equipment, computer boards with micro circuitry were where he drew the line. Although computer circuitry was not his forte, he did fiddle with other types of electronics such as relays, capacitors, motors, and other conventional electrical components of a washer or dryer control panel. In fact, he even invented a control panel testing board that simulated the functions of the entire machine, complete with indicator lights to diagnose a problem in the electrical system of the laundry equipment. When he was at ORT in Israel, he learned the basic skills of electronics and simply adapted them for use in the laundry industry. However, his technical instructions ended in youth and he became self taught for the remainder of his life. He never was interested in expanding his technical knowledge to include computers. He was a rugged machine shop owner and not a white smocked computer technician. His friends in Jaffa were just like him. They labored with their hands all day and chased women at night. After work, they would change out of their dirty grease stained clothing, and threw on a spiffy outfit in search of their Israeli dream girl.

My father was becoming somewhat of a ladies man. With his best friend Marcel Bracha and other friends who were mostly Bulgarian, they would cruise the popular streets—such as Dizengoff—prowling for women. A favorite luring technique was to tap lightly on the car horn in order to get the lady to turn and look. Once they grew bored of cruising the boulevards, the Israeli "rat pack" would step out of their cars with their thin lapelled black suits complimented by extra-skinny ties and saunter into a local café to approach a table of girls.

The brash Bulgarian boys even resorted to crashing wedding receptions to meet women.

Unfortunately, lots of dates with young ladies did not translate into love. Many of the women that he dated were Bulgarian and didn't offer him anything out of the ordinary. In a country with so many cultures, the prejudices of each group sometimes hindered open relationships between all peoples. Rather than subjecting himself to bringing an outsider into his community, my father chose the convenient option of establishing a long term relationship with a woman within the Bulgarian community. She was supposedly very pretty, but my grandmother didn't particularly care for her family. Despite Rachel's feelings, my father continued a tepid relationship with her for about seven years. They finally succumbed to the pressure of other family members, as well as friends, and decided to get married. They didn't marry each other because of love or passion, but simply because they felt it was time. The marriage was doomed from the outset and resulted in a rapid divorce. The marriage produced no children. Strangely enough, the entire relationship was kept secret from me until after my father's death. This covert footnote of his life still remains somewhat of a mystery to me. My father was probably ashamed of being divorced and failing at marriage, so he just covered it up. He didn't fail at too many things and rarely admitted failure even when it did occurr. His secret marriage was not his proudest moment, so he must have felt that it didn't set a good example for me to follow.

Following his bad experiences with the available women of Bulgarian descent, he sought to break the traditional Sephardic mold and look for something outside his family's centuries old customs. Furthermore, a more confident Seeco became more selective the older he got. He also had a bit of a temper. He once left a woman on a date because she slammed his car door too hard.

I saw his foul temper manifest itself in a variety of ways. He would threaten me with intimidating words and possibly a beating, and then chase me around the house. I would usually hide in the bathroom where I could lock the door to escape him. When I was a smaller child and did something extraordinarily bad, I would get a spanking, sometimes with his belt, other times with just his hand. I never saw him hit my mother, although she claims that he was more physically aggressive towards her before I was born. If I was making too much noise with my friends, he would belligerently yell at me as well as my friends in his crude accented manner. If you disturbed him while he was on the phone, especially if he was speaking to business associates on a long distance call, he would often throw small and accessible objects—such as a pen or a scratch pad—to shut me up.

He was also very protective over certain material possessions especially his automobiles. He didn't like me being "too rough" with them. Slamming of doors and playing the stereo loud were definitely verboten. Putting the hood down too hard, stomping your feet, tapping on the dashboard, dinging the door in the parking lot, revving up the engine unnecessarily, screeching of the brakes, and extended honking of the horn made him rather perturbed. Machine shop owner Mordecai was very protective over any and all mechanical equipment.

My father and Simontov kept a close watch on their precious assets which eventually paid off for them. For the first few years, the business was harmonious and each partner would cover for the other one while they served their yearly reservist duty. Mordecai Varsano had finally reached a place in life where he was his own man. For several years, he had been living at a single residence with his sister and mother. On September 13, 1960, his sister married Shimon Gerecht—a Polish-born concentration camp survivor—and with my father's assistance moved to a middle class apartment in the Tel Aviv suburb of Holon.

My gregarious grandmother had also found a new man to take care of her following the tragic passing of her first husband. My father was very protective over his mother at first and absolutely did not want her to remarry. After some time passed, he realized that his mom's happiness was the most important thing and learned to accept his mom with man other than his father. In 1963, she married a Bulgarian man of modest means named Nissim that she had been friends with for a few years. Nissim was not as rich as Isaac and my father felt that he was not classy enough for his mother. He didn't look at Nissim as a father figure, but was respectful to him. My dad had his own life and was a grown man by the time Nissim entered the picture. Nissim never was involved with any of my dad's business matters and mostly provided much needed companionship for my grandmother. The marriage lasted a little more than a year and the two separated amiably for the vague reason that they both felt that the relationship didn't work.

During a small window of opportunity in 1964, however, Rachel and Sarah were settled down with their new men, and my father was truly independent for the very first time. He was free to

174

choose his own destiny and finally had the financial capacity to really do so. After several years of hard work and deliberate savings, he was able to afford to take the first real vacation of his lifetime.

In the early fall of 1964, an enthusiastic Seeco embarked on a world tour that would take him to Western Europe and North America. As an inquisitive and ambitious machine shop owner, one of his goals was to establish his own factory, therefore expanding his current operations of metal items production. Although the vacation was primarily for relaxing, he was also trying to promote his factory proposal. His best friend Marcel had a brother living in Sweden which would be my father's first stop on his globetrotting excursion. Upon stepping foot on the streets of Stockholm, the Bulgarian-Israeli was shocked at the high level of cleanliness in the public areas. He remarked that "you could practically eat off the street here." He spent most of his time consuming salted fish products and staring at the breathtaking Scandinavian women.

Even though Sweden was on the same continent, it was a far cry from the Eastern European nations that he was exposed to as a child. It certainly wasn't anything like Bulgaria. It might as well been Australia for all he was concerned, because it was so different from the Balkans. He might have had a tiny bit of reservations about returning to the continent that hosted the Holocaust, but he was determined to see the world as a tourist and not a refugee.

After a few relatively boring days patronizing the hygienic avenues of Sweden, he boarded a plane to visit the US for the very first time. His brother-in-law Shimon had relatives in New York City, so that would be the first destination of his swing through the eastern

175

part of North America. My father was rather overwhelmed by the magnitude and diversity of New York City. Up until this point in his life, he had come in contact with very few non-Caucasian people. He was a jaded Israeli and not an open minded liberal ready to embrace the cultural differences and freedom of expression in the US. New York City with all of its diversity was just too much for him to digest. He was largely left to his own devices while in New York and made a few poor choices as a naive tourist. His hosts didn't really give him much of a tour of the city or warn him about dangerous areas. During the heart of the civil rights battle in the US, an oblivious White foreigner with a heavy accent cluelessly headed towards Harlem and had a culturally shocking experience that he would not soon forget.

Armed with very little knowledge of New York City and a curiosity to explore new lands, my dad hopped on a subway destined for Harlem under the darkness of night. Whether he thought there was great nightlife there or was searching for the Harlem Globetrotters, it was not the best decision. At the time, there were not too many White people milling about Harlem at night and my father stuck out like a sore thumb. Many people stared and one man pointing his finger in the shape of a gun at him, then made shooting sounds directed at him. My dad might have not understood the ghetto jive talk behind his back, but he knew that fake gunshots were not good and got the hell out of there.

After an eye-opening adventure in New York, he journeyed north to Canada. Shimon's relatives knew a family in Toronto with an eligible single daughter. My father was open to the idea of finding a new bride and starting his own family, but craved something other than a Bulgarian-Israeli. Upon arrival in Toronto, my father met a plump rich girl that was not to his liking. Just like in New York, he explored the Toronto area largely on his own. Not overly impressed with what he saw in a few of the eastern regions of North America, my father—who was somewhat disappointed—boarded the Israeli cruise ship named Shalom back across the Atlantic Ocean to Europe.

Reservations for the voyage by ship were made well in advance. This was no commuter boat. My father took a ship rather than fly because it was more fun and glamorous. He received three good meals per day and it was a new experience for him. The only other large ship that he had been on during his life was the converted freighter from Yugoslavia to Israel.

While the Shalom was pulling out of the New York harbor, a young American lady approached my father who was standing pensively on the deck, and uttered the words that would open the gates to a new chapter in his evolution, "I didn't know the Statue of Liberty was green." It seemed so appropriate that a naïve young woman would ask a question about something being green. After all, she was a native New Yorker and didn't know the color of one of the city's and the nation's most important landmarks. My father, on the hand, was definitely the right person to ask because he was familiar with the properties of various metals from his machine shop. He knew that the Statue was copper and the green patina was a result of oxidation. Of course, neither of them cared about the appearance of the monument, it was just a pick up line to break the ice. My parents, Elaine and Mordecai met on October 9, 1964 in front of the global symbol of freedom and the American way of life. A new journey had begun.

177

Throughout the cruise, the two love birds were inseparable. It was a classic case of love at first sight. Both parties found what they needed from each other at the same time and space. My mother craved adventure and a man who would take care of her. He was an older man that was able to be the mature boyfriend/father figure to the scared girl away from the nest of her parents for the very first time in her life. My father needed a woman to heal his emotional wounds and help raise a family. He was looking for something different from what he was used to. She was perfect for him at that time in his life because she was good looking, Jewish, American, Junior College Educated which was a higher level of education than most women at the time received, and all of these qualities added up to her being a very good potential mother.

Whether it was destiny or luck, it appeared to everyone as a storybook romance from the outset. Since their cabins happened to be close to each other, the other passengers just assumed they were a married couple. I am glad that they did not hide their true feelings and quickly progressed in their level of intimacy. Neither of my parents was prude and after all it was the 1960s.

Upon arrival in La Havre, France the new couple temporarily went their separate ways because of previously booked travel plans. My father boarded a train to Paris, while my mother took a train to Marseilles where she embarked on a journey by boat across the Mediterranean Sea to Haifa, Israel. My dad made sure my mom would be taken care of for her journey to Israel. He had some old Polish ladies from the ship escort her by train to the ship destined for Israel.

The idealistic young woman just might have found the adventure and a new way of life that she dreamed about.

My mother's new life in Israel began at Ein Hashfat Kibbutz in the remote Galilee Desert in northeastern Israel. She would spend approximately three months immersed in the Ulpan Program which consisted of foreign youths and young adults working four hours per day tending to the fields and learning Hebrew for another four hours. This rigid work schedule was not easy for the dainty suburbanite that had just finished a story book romance on the cruise across the Atlantic.

Just as things began to look grim, her Bulgarian savior came to the rescue. My father—upon returning from his European travels—hopped into his modest car and drove from his apartment in Jaffa for several hours to the Galilee. Seeco and Elana—as they were called by the Israelis—resumed their relationship where it had left off, only this time my father was on his home turf. When they were on the ship, they were more in my mother's comfort zone. It was a luxury cruise liner that was Israeli-owned but tried to mimic American and European style. Many of the passengers were American Jews and the staff catered to the luxurious desires of the affluent clientele. Leaving the friendly hospitality of a dream cruise and being thrust into the hard labor of the kibbutz, as well as the pushy streets of Tel Aviv was an abrupt change for my mom.

My dad was already accustomed to the Israeli lifestyle and determined to acclimate his precious companion to his environment. The popular young business owner would bring his bright eyed American girlfriend to all the hot spots of Tel Aviv. Every weekend

179

became an opportunity for the couple to put aside the drudgery of everyday life and bask in the glow of new found love. My mother has fond memories of sitting on the back of my father's motorcycle with her arms shamelessly wrapped around his waist as they toured around the country simply enjoying the sensation of speeding through the landscape.

Elaine's female Israeli friends at the kibbutz told her that Bulgarian men were known for being hard working, successful at business, and having good family values. My father certainly looked the part with his strong muscular forearms and rough thick sausage-like fingers. His work clothes were stained with muck and grim from working with the machine shop tools where it was hard to stay clean even if you tried. Later in life, my father would always have at least one grease stain on his clothing from working in the shop. He was indeed a hard worker, but he was smart enough not to do unnecessary chores. After a few weeks, the long commute between Jaffa and Galiea became burdensome, so my father arranged a transfer for my mother to a kibbutz in Netzer Sereni which was near Tel Aviv.

Following a two month stint at this kibbutz, she was exhausted with the demanding schedule of communal farm work. She began to toy with the idea of returning to the comforts of home, which helped spur my father to make a monumental commitment. After only four months of dating, my father proposed. At age thirty-two, he truly fell in love for the first time in his life and was ready to quickly turn this infatuation into a marriage.

Both were madly in love, yet a little nervous about making rash decisions. My mom was overjoyed at finally getting hitched because

180

the early 1960s were still a time where most women were married at a young age. If she was still single in her late twenties, she would have been considered an old maid. She was completely head over heals with her dark handsome older man. My dad was excited about making a change in his life with a new American bride at his side. He was also determined to rise to the challenge of making this marriage work better than the first marriage.

One of the implied conditions of their marriage imposed by my father was that the couple would continue to live in Israel. Mainly, he wanted to remain in Israel because he loved his country and loved his life there. He felt a strong connection to friends, family, and business. He had no real reason to leave Israel in 1965. He most certainly didn't like what he saw when he was in Toronto and New York. My father had done very little traveling at that point in his life and had not yet been to my mother's home in California, and thought America was not for him. Even though he loved his country, a Zionist passion was not the reason for staying in Israel; it was simply the high quality of life that he enjoyed.

Unlike the custom in the US, a traditional diamond engagement ring was not presented at the proposal. Instead, my father went to his favorite jeweler in Jaffa and was given an assortment of the finest wrist watches. On his honor, he was allowed to present this assortment of watches to his bride-to-be and have her choose her favorite.

With new watch in hand and new fiancé at her side, Elaine moved into Seeco's cooperative apartment in Jaffa. The new couple lived in relative style in a modern building at 12 Yejuda Hayamit with a view of the main stretch of the town of Jaffa, Yerushalium Street.

Mordecai and Elaine Varsano were married on March 2, 1965 at the Great Sephardic Synagogue in Tel Aviv, Israel. The sizable wedding ceremony had about two hundred guests; the vast majority were Bulgarian-Israelis from Jaffa and a few of Elaine's friends from the kibbutz. Elaine's parents were unable to attend the wedding because her mother Gertrude was in the hospital for an emergency surgery. My father's Aunt Jinka and Uncle Jack stood in as Elaine's ceremonial parents.

The wedding ceremony and reception were clearly a traditional Sephardic event. My father's family exclusively planned the entire function and Elaine's dress was rented which typified the modest nature of the Israeli affair. The entire ceremony was conducted in Biblical Hebrew with some Ladino mixed in, so my mother understood very little and simply smiled throughout much of the service. At the conclusion of the ceremony, there was little in the way of a formal reception. A small gathering at an apartment followed the ceremony. Harkening back to the pre-war days in Bulgaria, a traditional Sephardic meal was served to compliment the Old World theme of the wedding. Heart shaped marzipan and other traditional Sephardic wedding treats were handed out to departing guests.

The next morning, the newlyweds embarked on a week long honeymoon across practically the entire country of Israel. Traveling across Israel was dangerous, exciting, multifaceted, and yes, even romantic. The jubilant couple drove their car through one tourist site after another, and they were careful to avoid the Arab villages that peppered the countryside. The honeymoon culminated in the resort city of Eilat, where my parents basked in the sun and surf of the Gulf of Aqaba portion of the Red Sea. My father tried to provide the best honeymoon that he could, given his financial ability and geographic position. It was not as luxurious as an American honeymoon. There was no honeymoon suite at a luxurious resort, no heart shaped bed or complimentary bottles of champagne. Their life—including their honeymoon—would all be done Israeli style. The polite and clean suburban life of my mom's youth had merged with the gritty Israeli immigrant of my dad.

In a life filled with much tragedy, my father had finally found true love and financial security giving him a taste of the happiness that he had longed for his whole life. It seemed as though years of hard work and a struggling existence had at last paid off. Whether it was through his personal drive to succeed or a divine intervention that brought the two kindred souls together, a life changing milestone had occurred. My father was not content to rest on his laurels, a new chapter in his life needed to be written. He was now tied to America by way of marriage even though he still lived in Israel. In the coming years, he would explore every option available to him in order to provide the best quality of life for his family and would no longer be constrained by the obligations of age-old tradition.

CHAPTER 10

Paddling Upstream

"Mazel Tov!" the congratulations poured in from the moment the newlyweds returned from their honeymoon. The giddy couple began their new married life in Israel with my mother remaining the cautious foreigner, and my father maintaining his role as the bread-winner and tour guide. Seeco was approaching his mid thirties and was far more experienced in the ways of the world than his carefree twenty-something wife. Both were at a point in their lives where they were ready to have children, but just like everything in my father's life, conception was not going to be easy.

After my parents returned from their honeymoon, they continued to live in my father's old apartment. My grandmother would come over frequently and deposit a variety prepared dishes and cakes in the refrigerator. She realized that my mom couldn't cook very well and didn't want to deprive the young couple of the culinary delights that they had already grown accustomed to. She also hired a Moroccan-born assistant to help clean the newlywed's apartment because my mom had trouble mastering the rag-on-a-stick mop contraptions that were prevalent in Israel at the time. My grandmother was trying to teach my mom the ways a wife acted during her generation. However, my mom was going to do things her way as an American living in Israel.

Following the end of the Sinai Campaign until about 1966 was the most tranquil period of modern Israeli history. The United States government's relationship with Israel started to steadily improve during this period of relative calm which considerably benefited Israeli citizens. The President Kennedy administration had slightly better relations with Israel than his predecessor President Eisenhower. JFK began the warming trend between the two nations and his successor President Lyndon B. Johnson continued in a similar vein.

My father was able to capitalize on the relative peace and prosperity which was an unusual occurrence in his turbulent life. During the lull in the trauma, he managed to fall in love and build a prosperous business. Only a precious few Israeli's were very wealthy by American standards, but he was at least able to enjoy an above average income. He was still young, healthy, and energetic enough to easily deal with his exceedingly heavy work load. He had a great sense of community and a wealth of friends. His popularity combined with his large family, meant that that he was never alone and almost always had a special occasion to attend. After living there for almost twenty years, he was completely comfortable in Israel despite the hectic atmosphere. He had the security of marriage, but not yet the responsibilities of fatherhood. The promise of Zionism and the dream of a viable Jewish state were actually being realized to a certain extent. Looking back in time, he once confided that those years were the golden days of his waning youth.

Unfortunately, good times are usually fleeting and are only easily recognized looking into the mirror of the past. Troubles—both minor and major—began to creep into the storybook romance. The relative tranquility in Israel translated to only minor skirmishes along the borders of Jordan and the Golan Heights with Syria. The growing intensity of Arab terrorism was answered by the constant vigilance of the IDF supplemented by the continuous service of the reserves. Yearly milium notifications sent the women in my father's life into a nervous but familiar panic. My mother was afraid to live alone during the seemingly endless month of reserve duty. Her sister-in-law Sarah spent time comforting her and let the worrisome American girl stay with her family to stem her anxiety. Sometimes my father would be stationed as far away as the southern city of BeerSheva in the Negev Desert, but other times he would be located close to Tel Aviv. If time permitted, he would go home for part of the weekend to reconnect with his family, but all the while carrying his Uzi submachine gun in the truck of his car.

My mom found it a bit odd that he was a civilian with a gun, but it also excited her. She definitely felt protected and vicariously empowered around my armed father. In America, only a lunatic would drive around town with a loaded machine gun in their trunk, but Israelis had a different sense of security and normal behavior. She was not afraid of it because it a common practice for teenage soldiers to have guns as well as older reservists on weekend leave like my father. After the initial shock of seeing young adults walking around with firearms, it just becomes another accessory. Despite the shock and the apparent lawlessness of so many young men with guns, there was actually much less street violence in Israel than the US.

On returning back to everyday life as a married couple, the pressure to conceive children began to loom from all angles. My

186

grandmother wanted more grandchildren and the rest of the traditional Bulgarian extended family believed that my father being in his mid thirties was long overdue to be a father. Conceiving a child would be a long and difficult process.

Initially, it was thought that my father had fertility problems, but after several tests it was determined that my mother had blocked fallopian tubes. The doctors at Dejani Hospital in Jaffa told the anxious couple that Elaine would need a specialized surgery that had a very low success rate in Israeli hospitals. In fact, there were only two surgeons in the world that were experts in this delicate procedure, Dr. Palmer in Paris, France, and another skilled surgeon in the United States. Upon receiving the prognosis, the couple decided that adoption was not an option and would eventually find a way to make time and money for the risky surgery abroad.

My dad had made up his mind that he didn't want to adopt a child, unless he had no other choice. My mom had brought up the issue of adoption only after having such a difficult time trying to conceive naturally. She was somewhat open to exploring the possibility of adoption, but my dad's stubborn determination pushed for a baby that was his own flesh and blood. He wanted to explore every medical avenue for restoring fertility in my mom. Until that was done, he was dead set against adoption.

While contemplating their limited options regarding having a baby, they relentlessly practiced the impregnation process in vain. Test tube babies and artificial insemination were not common fertility techniques in the 1960s, so my parents engaged in lots of traditional sexual intercourse and prayed for the best. Ultimately, their valiant

187

efforts were in vein, but at least they had fun trying. Perhaps, a vacation would be a pleasant distraction from their infertility problems.

In the summer of 1966, my parents took a vacation to the West Coast of the United States to visit the Schneider family. My father had never been to the West Coast, nor had he met his in-laws yet. The dark complexioned man took an immediate liking to sunny Southern California. Unlike the cold and gray east coast that he had visited two years earlier, California reminded him of Israel but with less tension. My grandparents Jack and Gertrude Schneider gave the newlyweds a grand tour of the region. After being wooed by the great urban life and natural wonders of Los Angeles, San Francisco, Yosemite, and the Grand Canyon, my parents actually contemplated the eventuality of moving to the West Coast of the US.

My father said that "California was like a beautiful Israel." My mother had grown homesick living in Israel. She missed her friends, family, and the American way of life. The positive experience of my father's first trip to the West Coast of the US gave him the first inkling that a move to California was a possibility. In all practicality though, my father still had a business, a family, and other obligations back in Israel that would prevent them from immigrating to the US in the near future.

Upon returning to Israel, he bought an apartment that was under construction in a fashionable district of Tel Aviv. While waiting for this apartment to be completed, the young couple rented a stylish apartment with a sea view in Bat Yam. Attempts to conceive continued to be unsuccessful, so they took a pet dachshund named Gila as a temporary surrogate child.

188

A dog was not going to replace a child, so my parents decided that it was finally time for my mom to undergo fertility surgery. They had spent countless hours contemplating whether it was the right thing to do, but after several years of frustration, they felt it was there last option for conceiving naturally. In order to afford first class medical care, my father had to work diligently, make smart investments, and save a fair amount of money. Even though there was an American doctor in NY and a French doctor in Paris that could perform the innovative microsurgery, France was much closer to Israel.

My parents flew to visit the Clinic de Passey in Paris where the delicate surgery to solve the fertility problems would be performed. They stayed together in a small family run hotel in Paris for the about one month. Dr. Palmer explained that a microscope was going to be used to examine the fallopian tubes and perform the surgical procedure because the effected area was so tiny. The success of the lengthy surgery was surely not guaranteed and my mom would have to spend a month resting in bed to recuperate. Six months after the initial procedure, they would need to return to Paris for a two week follow-up.

My mother was nervous before and after the procedure. She had never been under the knife before and was uncertain of what the outcome would be. During her month-long convalescent period, my father lived in the hotel room along with my mother and sharpened his French speaking skills during the many idle hours of waiting. He had learned to speak a little French from watching movies and listening to his relatives that spoke the language. After spending some time in Paris, phrases such as le miracle de la vie (the miracle of life), and

189

realisez la grossesse (achieve pregnancy) were wishful thoughts that gave the struggle a purpose.

Seeco—the native European—tried to make the most out of his extended stay in Paris—the city of romance. While roaming the avenues he soaked up the best and worst culture the city had to offer. From the delectable food and the bohemian 1960s artist community, to the typical tourist sightseeing and the occasional run-in with a nasty Parisian, he freely roamed the great metropolis. Every morning—without fail—he would bring my mother croissants and chocolate to her bed.

After completing the first thirty day phase of the fertility surgery, my parents returned to Tel Aviv to resume their usual life. The relative calm in the Middle East that existed for several years was rapidly deteriorating because of Arab terrorist attacks. Those aggressions were followed by Israeli reprisals and an escalating arms race in the region with weapons pouring in from all the world's major powers. The Soviet Union supplied Egypt and Syria while West Germany, Great Britain, and mostly France equipped Israel's military with limited sales of coveted US-manufactured anti-aircraft missiles. Jordan bought arms from the US and Great Britain. It's difficult for me to imagine the French as Israel's greatest military backer given the current condition of relations between Israel and France. The coming years would see the US come to the forefront in arming the sole democracy in the region, while France would primarily back the Arab dictatorships. The large weapon suppliers profited from the hatred and revenge that festered in the Middle East, no matter who was supplying who. A combination of economic incentive and cold war strategy exacerbated the pre-existing tensions to make the conflict more deadly and prolonged than the Arabs and Jews could have possibly created by themselves.

In 1964, Israel had nearly completed building a major irrigation project which diverted water from the Jordan River to the Negev Desert. Thwarting this development was Syria, which started building a similar project that would dry up the Israeli irrigation efforts. Israel responded to this provocative action by launching air and artillery attacks on the Syrian installation. Terrorist guerilla attacks by different Arab factions persisted over the next few years while the full militaries of the Arab nations built up their arsenals and plotted their next move.

By May of 1967, President Nasser—his prestige much eroded through his inaction in the face of Israeli reprisals—requested the withdrawal of UN forces from Egyptian territory, mobilized units in the Sinai, and closed the Gulf of Aqaba to Israel. The UN Emergency Force stationed on the border between Egypt and Israel at Sharm el-Sheikh in 1957 – which had provided an actual separation between the countries – was evacuated in response to Nasser's "request." A few days later, Jordan joined the Egyptian-Syrian military alliance of 1966 and placed its army on both sides of the Jordan River under Egyptian command. Iraq, Algeria, Kuwait and other Arab nations also aided the coalition. The much smaller Israeli military was confronted by an Arab force of some 465,000 troops, over 2,880 tanks and 810 aircraft.

To combat the overwhelming number of enemy forces, Israel increased its reserve forces call-up which had already been underway, and established a National Unity government to solve the crisis through political channels. The government of Israel approached the

191

British and the French to keep their promise to ensure the security of shipping, but they reneged. President Johnson proposed a plan for breaking the blockade by an international armada but he was preoccupied with the war in Vietnam. It soon became clear that the political efforts had failed to resolve the crisis, so the Israeli Government gave approval to the IDF to undertake a military offensive to eliminate the ominous threat posed by the Arab provocations.

My mother had never lived in a country facing attack by a larger hostile force. She only knew a relative peace that had existed in Israel during the three years that she lived there. The anxieties over the impending war only added to her growing sense of being uncomfortable in Israeli society. My father—on the other hand—was accustomed to the ever present tension and insecurity, but had even less interest in taking part in the conflict as a reservists than he did ten years earlier during the Sinai Campaign.

Just days before the June 5, 1967 launch of pre-emptive air strikes by Israel and the ensuing war, my mother received devastating news from home. Her father—who had defeated a bout with cancer years earlier—had a reoccurrence of the disease which the doctors diagnosed as terminal. They couldn't just hop on a plane and leave right away; many arrangements still had to be made. My father had to go to Jerusalem to arrange for the proper Visa. At age thirty-four, he was still in a reserve unit of the IDF and would possibly be needed if the potential for a prolonged war was realized. After receiving emergency clearance from his reserve unit commanding officer, my grieving parents boarded the last passenger ship to leave Israel before the outbreak of war. The waters of the Mediterranean Sea were dangerous with a war looming, so they ended up departing in the nick of time. They packed lots of large packages that needed to be transported by ship to New York because they knew that they would be staying in the US for an extended period of time.

A tense journey on the high seas from Haifa to New York was followed by a cross-country flight to LAX. Most of their belongings had been packed in boxes and arrived several days later by truck. My parents stayed at my grandparent's house on Goodland Avenue in North Hollywood under very difficult circumstances. Jack was fighting for his life while the rest of the family was understandably upset and nervous.

My father split his time helping the Schneider family and speaking to his family in Israel to find out about the outcome of the war. Israel had launched a pre-emptive air assault that crippled Egypt, and then issued an appeal for Jordan to stay out of the war. But King Hussein refused and opened a heavy artillery barrage on both West Jerusalem and the Tel-Aviv area which forced Israel to counterattack. Within six days, Israel had captured the entire Sinai Peninsula, the Gaza Strip, Judea and Samaria (commonly referred to as the West Bank), and the Golan Heights. Since international guarantees of the past had proved meaningless, Israel did not withdrawal to the 1949 armistice lines. Some regions were annexed while others were deemed "occupied territories" which continues to be a lingering issue today.

The IDF granted a release to Sergeant Varsano prior to the 1967 War on the grounds of a family emergency. Personally, my dad felt that being in America to support his wife and her ailing father was

193

more important than defending his country once again. He had already served his duty in the IDF for many years and felt the younger troops with the reserve units were more than capable of solving the current crisis. He was also thirty-five years old and absolutely sick of war. At his age, he wouldn't have been on the front lines or played a very active role anyway. Just like his role in the Sinai Campaign, he probably wouldn't have seen any action and didn't want to hero. He still had no aspirations earn medals or awards. He simply did what his country asked him to do. At this point in his life, he was much more a mature business man than a young soldier.

Israel's military dominance in the Six Day War showed the world community that it was an emerging and formidable global power. Preserving Israel's democratic existence also became a more popular cause in the US. Unlike the Sinai Campaign, the US did not pressure Israel to withdraw from the territories that it captured and occupied in the 1967 War. In response, France cut off arms sales to Israel and the US became its chief supplier. France wanted to be the European friend of the Arabs because of financial reasons and a sense that they were tolerate and understanding of Islamic culture because of their experience with colonies in Algeria and other Moslem lands. French support for belligerent Arab nations coupled with the ultimate powerlessness of the UN continues today, and contributes to the inability of achieving a lasting peace in the Middle East. Economic incentive for the arms producers prolongs the bloodshed while keeping a tenuous balance of power that masquerades as Middle Eastern stability.

A military victory for the Jewish people and Israeli popularity in the US did not help to numb the pain of the Schneider family's struggle with cancer or the inability of my parents to have children. Even though my grandfather's health was steadily deteriorating, my parent's needed to fly back to Paris to complete the second phase of the fertility operation. Going from California to France was not only a longer distance than traveling from Israel, but there was added fear about my mom leaving her father when he had a terminal disease. My mom was bed-ridden in a hospital in a foreign land, worried about her chances at becoming fertile, and distressed about her father's condition back home. Meanwhile, my dad was gallivanting around "gay Pari" having fun and constantly munching on his latest favorite snack— crusty French bread sandwiches with non-kosher sausage. To say my mom resented him a bit at this point, was an understatement. My dad was simply having a good time while he had the opportunity. He still brought my mom chocolate and croissants and comforted her in her time of need, but the days were long and Paris was an exciting city. The procedure was seemingly successful and upon returning back to North Hollywood, my father's attentions would be turned to the sobering pursuits of building a career and consoling an emotionally fragile family.

My dad mainly tried to lend moral support to Elaine, Gert, and Gene who were coping with the slow and painful demise of their patriarch. They didn't need his financial support, but after a while my parents did make a token payment of rent. My dad also fixed some minor problems around the house and helped purchase groceries. My mom would wander around at night worried about her father. When death became imminent, my father empathized with her. He told her that with time, it gets better. The pain of the loss will eventually subside but it will take a fair amount of emotional healing. He reasoned that at least my mother had the opportunity to say goodbye and make her peace with her father. My father never had that sense of closure. In addition to helping his wife get through this emotional time, he was also trying to establish a new life in California.

Even though my parents moved lots of their possessions, living in California was only supposed to be temporary. While my grandfather was still alive, they would live in California and see if they truly liked it as much as they thought they did. My dad would research his economic opportunities and test the feasibility of relocating permanently. It was impossible to move his machine shop to the US, because it was too costly and not practical to move the heavy machinery. In addition, he still had a partner that lived in Israel and had no intention of moving to the US. My father would most likely have to get a job working for someone else, initially.

While he weighed his options, he tried to transfer as much of his assets from Israel as possible. Although my dad did not have any savings in US banks, he was able to illegally transfer funds out of Israel. Israeli law had restrictions on domestic currency leaving the country, so my dad arranged for his Israeli Shekels to be converted to US dollars and smuggled out the country. The smugglers nickname was Cucarico, which roughly translates to cockroach in Ladino. He was quite an unsavory character, but sometimes dealing with those people was necessary, just as his father "made arrangements" to have his Bulgarian money sent to Swiss Bank accounts during WWII. My

196

father managed to have enough Israeli money smuggled into the US to live and was making progress in establishing a steady income in the Los Angeles area. While my father was his typical hard working self and a rock of stability, the Schneider family was an emotional wreck.

After several grueling months of fighting for his life, on December 19, 1967, Jack Schneider at the age of fifty-nine lost his battle with cancer. My mother's life was on a rollercoaster ride, from the high of falling in love on an international adventure to the low of having her father die at a young age and not being able to bear children. My father offered a comforting shoulder and an optimistic outlook to his distraught wife.

The immediate situations called for him to console and stabilize a family which had just lost its figurehead. He tried to be the surrogate man of the house, but realized that he was not going to replace Jack. Gert missed her husband deeply and would never remarry or even date another man. Elaine and Gene lost their father while they were both only in their twenties. There was no way my dad could step into the role of husband or father, even though he was now the oldest and most mature man in the household. He did what he could and tried to be optimistic about the future.

The burden of lending a helping hand to the Schneider family following the tragic death of his father in-law sped up his plans to make the transition to living in America. Since the enjoyable vacation the previous year with the Schneider family, my father had been contemplating moving to California in a slow and deliberate manner. He was not the type of person who made rash decisions based purely on emotion. Although the immediate crisis clouded his vision, the

197

sunshine of Los Angeles offered hope and the prospect of yet another phase in my father's life.

The main reasons that they decided to permanently relocate to America were my mom's desire to move back home and my dad's love of Southern California. My mom wasn't that happy living in Israeli society because the people were too pushy for her taste and not orderly like Americans. Every time she went to the market, she had people cut in front of her in line and she just got sick of that kind of attitude after a while. There was constant pushing, shoving, yelling in a variety of languages, always haggling; no matter where you went. After a while, it was too much for a suburban American young woman to take. She also missed her family back home tremendously.

Perhaps even more than she missed her family, she craved the plush American way of life again. Israel was a nice place to visit, meet a husband, learn some Hebrew, and even live a little while, but she certainly didn't want to spend the rest of her life there. The country was simply not as wealthy or well established as America and she feared her husband serving in the milium. Although attacks from Arabs were a constant worry for Israelis, surprisingly my mom said that the Arabs did not make her want to leave Israel; it was more the Israelis themselves.

Just as living in Israel was culturally shocking for my mom, the American way of life was an enormous change for my dad. There were many differences between the customs of the Varsano family in Israel and the Schneider family in the US. For instance, it was commonplace for newly married couples that were establishing themselves in a new place to live with their relatives for an indeterminate amount of time. It

198

was all part of the family support structure where every family member contributed to the good of the whole. In America, boarding a young married couple was considered a temporary accommodation. Gert expected them to get their own place sooner rather than later. My father felt insulted by this and didn't quite understand the way of thinking. It would be the first of many adjustments that he would have to make in America.

In Israel, Shabbat dinner on Friday night occurred every single week and was something that everyone looked forward to. It signaled the end of the work week and brought the family together for a special meal. On Friday afternoon, all the businesses would close early so that people could prepare for Shabbat. My dad's ritual was to leave the machine shop in the mid afternoon, and then go home to shower. Next, he would dress himself in one of his finest outfits which most often consisted of a white cotton button down dress shirt and black virgin wool slacks. He rarely wore a sports jacket or tie, and his shirt sleeves would usually get rolled up early in the evening due to the balmy Mediterranean climate.

While the men finished up their work day and changed into their Friday night attire, the women were slaving away in the markets and the kitchen all day preparing the festive meal. My mom enjoyed the celebratory tone of the Shabbat dinner, but rarely did much of the cooking. My grandmother Rachel was the greatest chef of the family and she would cook mouthwatering delicacies that I can still remember today. Shabbat dinner favorites were sliced steak tomato, onion, and cucumber appetizers, followed by a buffet of Moussaka (a casserole dish with eggplant, beef, eggs, tomato, and spices), delectably stuffed

199

vegetables, fried zucchini and eggplant, as well as an assortment of homemade puff pastries. The dinner was always at my grandmother's apartment, and the guest list would vary from just my parents to larger groups with the entire extended family and friends.

When my parents moved to North Hollywood, the Schneider family did not have many Shabbat dinners nor were they as extravagant. In America, Friday night was just another meal to be eaten and not a celebration of the Sabbath. Even though, both families were relatively secular, secular in Israel was much different than secular in the US. In Israel, Jewish holidays were a very big deal. During the high holy days, the entire country basically shut down. During Purim, every child was dressed in a costume much like Halloween in the US. During Passover, the Seder was much longer and of course recited entirely in Hebrew. Since the Varsanos were a Sephardic family, rice dishes were permitted to be eaten on Passover unlike Ashkenazi families like the Schneiders. Generally, Israelis have more feasts and more family celebrations than do American Jews.

The only big family dinners relating to Jewish Holidays in the US were Passover and Rosh Hashanah. My grandfather Jack was the most observant Jew of the American family. He was a member of the choir at Beth Hillel in North Hollywood and considered himself a Reform Jew. He encouraged his family to attend services and was an active member of the congregation. Once he passed away, any affiliation to an organized Jewish congregation for Schneider family ended forever. My father was a rather secular Jew, anyhow, so the watered down version of formal Judaism in America was not a big disappointment to him, but the loss of Shabbat dinners and Sephardic feasts was.

On the bright side, the United States offered him much more economic opportunity than Israel and did not require him to serve in the military reserve which had grown more inconvenient not to mention dangerous. Age thirty-five, he still had yearly miluim service for fifteen more years if he had remained in Israel. Furthermore, he and my mother did not wish to expose their eventual children to the stressful life in Israel.

Immigrating to America seemed to be a ripe idea at the time, but leaving Israel was a complicated decision for him. Although he never considered himself a hardcore Zionist, he still loved Israel. He once had a dream to live a free life without discrimination and have a maximum amount of economic opportunity for his family. Israel partially made that dream come true and compared to Bulgaria, his family had a great life there. The biggest apprehension about leaving Israel was not being able to see as much of his mother and sister. He would also miss the lifestyle of a close-knit community of friends that shared the common bond of being Jews that survived WWII and the Aliyahs. He had grown accustomed to the European immigrant lifestyle of sitting in outdoor cafes and eating traditional meals with the extended family.

In America—for better or for worse—the lifestyle would be much different. If given the opportunity to go to the US in 1948— instead of Israel—I don't know what our family would have decided. They definitely would have gone to the US over staying in Bulgaria, but who knows about US instead of Israel. After the scare of WWII, many survivors were probably inclined to make the "safe" choice and go to the US instead of fighting Arabs and economic uncertainty in Israel. The Jews of Bulgaria didn't have the option of going to the US, so their Aliyah to Israel was as much a practical decision as a philosophical one. I suppose any Jew who lived in Israel in 1948 was considered a Zionist, but there were certainly varying degrees of commitment. My father wasn't a Zionist zealot, and did not necessarily want to live in Israel for the rest of his life. Even though he loved his country, events beyond his control had determined the direction of his life once again. Going to the US represented an incredible opportunity and a family obligation rather than a betrayal of Israel or Zionist objectives. By the late 1960s, the state of Israel was much more mature and solidified than it was in 1948 thanks to the courage and hard work of Israelis like my father.

Despite hard work, the opportunities in Israel were still limited compared to many other Western countries, especially the US. The socialist nation had, and still does have, an onerous income tax. High taxes along with political uncertainty continue to stymie economic opportunities for every Israeli. Even though my father had decided to escape the tangled web of the Israeli economy, he still had significant business interests in Israel, and would eventually have to dissolve his partnership in the machine shop.

Besides selling his Israeli assets, everything else back home was in good shape. His sister was married, his mother was financially secure, and neither was dependent on him in any substantial manner. Finally, my father felt that after three years of active duty in the IDF, fourteen years in the reserves, and twenty years of living as an Israeli citizen, he had fulfilled his role in achieving the goals of Zionism that were so pressing in post-WWII Bulgaria.

Israel was established country both militarily and economically. Relative to 1948 there was security and prosperity. My father helped establish the pillars of a stable Jewish state with his machine shop which directly contributed to incremental growth in the economy while his service in the IDF strengthened the military. He continued to support Israel in general with cash donations and his family in particular after he moved to the US. Perhaps he was even more effective at bringing economic stimulus to Israel from the US than he was ever able to as an Israeli because he took advantage of the unlimited economic opportunity in the US to give money back.

He also instilled the ethos of the importance of foreign support of Israel in me. He taught me that every Jew must do their part. The collectivity concept of the kibbutz was an example for Diaspora because they could use their own personal skill for the benefit of the common good. Human nature was such that you will fight collectively to battle a common enemy but when there was no immediate threat everyone goes about their own business and looks out for themselves As Israel grew stronger, the enthusiastic idealism of early years was no longer necessary. The pains and struggle of the first time set up in the building of a new nation were behind them. Their survival seemed more secure than ever, and the average Israeli was now free to pursue more selfish goals. My father felt liberated enough to move to America without guilt.

Since he was married to a US Citizen, he was able to visit America with permanent resident status. Despite a rushed temporary move to the US, my father never worked illegally because he was able to go to the American embassy in Tel Aviv before departing and register the proper documents for legal employment in the US. After making the decision to stay in America for an extended period of time, he applied for US citizenship.

While making this transition, my parents continued to live in my grandmother's house in North Hollywood. Living in cramped quarters during a time of mourning and recovery proved to be too difficult to sustain for a long period of time. Although it was the custom for Israeli young couples to live with their parents for extended periods, this system did not work in California in the late 1960s. Jack and Gert had put my parents up in the den because it was the farthest point from their bedroom in the modest track house.

My mother and her brother Gene were always—and still are— at odds about a myriad of issues. A typical sibling rivalry increased tensions further, while my dad gained some insights into his brother-in-law's way of life. My father sometimes made comments like "If Gene had served in the Israeli Army, he would have been more of a man." Yes, possibly a physically strongest and perhaps mental tougher man, but there was also a greater likelihood that he would have become a dead man. It's a bit curious that someone who didn't particularly care for the military life could draw some positive after effects from it years later. The notion of praising military service of any kind to my uncle—who was against the Vietnam War—did not make the point that my father had intended. Overall, there was a lack of harmony between my parents and the rest of the Schneider family because of both personality and circumstantial reasons.

A few weeks after my grandfather passed away, my grandmother told my folks that they had over stayed their welcome and they proceeded to find their own apartment. My mom didn't work at the time, so my father had to foot the bill for the new place.

He was a very proud man and did not want to impose on his in-laws, but my mother wanted to remain close to home where she raised. Therefore, the young couple rented an apartment close-by on Whitsett Avenue in North Hollywood. The building was typical 1960s boxy complex with modern amenities and most of the residents were young adults.

My father took a job at Pharmaseal Industries—a medical supply and drug company—in nearby Glendale. The young Israeli immigrant worked as a tool and die maker, earning a decent salary for that time period. One of my father's biggest adjustments to living in Southern California was working for someone else after being his own boss for so many years. To go from employer to employee was a blow to his ego, but he realized that he must pay his dues in order to reach greater heights. He still technically owned a business in Israel, but establishing a new life in America was a higher priority then tying up the loose ends with Simontov.

Throughout my father's life, major changes were always precipitated by unpredictable occurrences. A chance meeting on a cruise ship led to a quick marriage, then the inability to build a family in Israel and the tragedy of a terminal illness caused my parents to move to America. Perhaps as a boy in the American College in Sofia, living in the US was a life long dream of my father. Whether it was by destiny or by chance, he never thought it would be through such

205

circumstances. The tragedy of death and the frustration of infertility could have broken my parents' commitment, but instead it strengthened the bond between them. With love and courage, they both stepped forward to start a new life in California with the hope of peace, prosperity, and fertility.

CHAPTER 11

Sailing towards the American Dream

During the tumultuous late 1960s in California, my parents both lived and worked in the Los Angeles area, but still had loose ends to tie up abroad. They were continuing to have difficulty conceiving a child even though the medical procedure was an apparent success.

While problems beyond their immediate control were bothersome, they focused on taking advantage of their current opportunities.

Seeco—once again a new immigrant—quickly learned that the path to economic success in the US involved landing a better job than the position he currently held at Pharmaseal. While the salary was sufficient and the opportunity was adequate for somebody new to the country, my ambitious father wanted to achieve the consummate American dream.

My father had watched many American movies and television shows with Hebrew subtitles while living in Israel. The idealized suburban life of "Ozzie and Harriet" helped form his vision of what this country was supposed to be. The quintessential symbol of the American dream was to own a house with a white picket fence in a pleasant neighborhood. Owning a house was not an option for most Israelis because the densely populated urban environment was dominated by multi-family housing. My father began to slowly put away money, so he could eventually afford a decent sized house which would give him a higher degree of comfort in America and something to brag about to his Israeli friends.

My father was patient and relatively conservative regarding how he spent his money. Purchasing a house would take a few years of saving and careful research, but in the meantime he still embraced the "buy American" ethos even as war protesters burned the flag. He drove a Ford Mustang and used American-made tools because they were the best quality. In Israel, it was important that consumers bought Israeli-made products in order to support the local economy of the small country. When my father moved to the US, he applied a similar philosophy to the American economy especially regarding large purchases such as a car. He would tell me that in Sweden everyone drives a Volvo and in Germany everyone drives a Mercedes, so Americans should support the autoworkers of Michigan and drive American cars. He had only lived in the country a short time and was already more patriotic than the average citizen. He realized that he could combine his nationalism and desire to earn more money by working for a defense contractor.

After some research and several interviews, he landed a position at P & J Engineering on Raymer Street in North Hollywood. P& J was a subcontractor for the aerospace industry which had a tremendous amount of orders due to the urgency of the Vietnam War and the steady build up of Cold War arsenals. He took his experience manufacturing military parts in his own machine shop in Israel and transferred that knowledge to the American Military Industrial Complex.

My father thought that the Nixon Administration was good for Israel, so he was more forgiving about other controversial foreign policy decisions such as the Vietnam War. He liked Henry Kissinger because he was very intelligent and also of Jewish heritage. Nixon had appointed Kissinger and listened to him very closely, so my father concluded that "tricky Dick"—who was purportedly anti-Semitic— was good for the Jews. He definitely did not participate in any war protests, but did have some reservations about the mounting causalities being suffered by American boys overseas. My mom—on the hand— was a liberal Democrat at the time who had marched in Civil Rights protests. She was very much against the War in Vietnam, but avoided the protests because of my father's indifference. He was focused on creating a better life for his family in his new country, and was most certainly not going to be mounting public protests against the government.

My father often worked ten or more hours per day in order to earn overtime and advance within the ranks of P&J Engineering. He possessed valuable machinist skills and was well compensated for his hard work. Overtime pay was a perk that he never enjoyed when he owned his own shop. However, he did monotonous work for long hours with co-workers that he had very little in common with. The average worker at P&J was less educated and less worldly than my father. There were few—if any—Jews who worked there and certainly no Israelis. Generally, it was an ego-deflating transition to be an expendable employee of a corporation, after being accustomed to being his own boss in Israel.

My father would have to pay his dues in order to once again enjoy the autonomy of being successfully self employed. He did contemplate whether the stress of running his own business was better than just working for someone else and collecting a weekly paycheck. It would take several more years of working at P& J and living in the San Fernando Valley before he was able to understand what his American dream was.

Was it about freedom or money? How much was enough? Would he make the best of his opportunities? I don't know if my father—or anyone else for that matter—truly answers these questions. One thing was for certain; my father did not like taking orders from people. He had an entrepreneurial spirit, but also was a conservative investor. He would always choose an industry that was relatively stable and provided something that everyone needed. His work also helped identify who he was. I think his hard working mentality was a byproduct of starting his career in the early 1950s during the post WWII rebuilding years. As that generation grew older, many men felt that if they lost their job—either by retirement, lay off, firing, disability, or going out of business—that they lost who they were. If you weren't successful and hard working, then you were simply a good-for-nothing or an old man on the way out. So my father spent the majority of his waking hours at his job and tried to be the best that he could be at it. Being successful in his career was paramount to just about everything with the exception of his family.

As 1968 ended and 1969 began, Elaine was still having problems getting pregnant. It had been a year since the second phase of the fertility surgery had been completed and they still did not have

210

the result that they had hoped for. They wondered whether the long and expensive surgery had been successful. My mother went for X-Rays in an American hospital to see if the surgical wound has healed properly. The X-Rays revealed no abnormalities and the doctors concluded that she was capable of having a baby. The doctors further deduced that the couple was just trying too hard and the problem was more mental than physical. They simply advised them to relax and take a "real vacation."

On the eve of the summer of love—in the springtime of 1969—my father with my mother in hand jumped into his metallic green 1967 Ford Mustang destined for the elusive heart of America. Both my parents sped away from the freeways of LA and headed across the heartland of the US. They decided to take a route through the southern states over a two week span with Miami, Florida as their final destination. They were determined to experience Americana at it finest. My mom was relaxed and my dad learned a lot about what it was to be an American.

A long road trip was the stereotypical American vacation. In Europe or most other places in the world, the driving distance from California to Florida would take you through several countries and might not even be logistically possible. Unlike Europe or Israel, English was the only language spoken for thousands of miles. America's great expanse gave him a great feeling of empowerment and freedom to explore the open space of a diverse landscape.

Financially, the trip was inexpensive relative to driving or traveling by train elsewhere in the world. Gas was about thirty cents per gallon which much cheaper than the petrol in Israel or Europe.

America was also internally secure and virtually immune from attack from any foreign enemies. Unlike their honeymoon in Israel where there was a physical threat of attack from Arab terrorists, the only obstacles on American roads were the verbal prejudices of our own homegrown rednecks.

My father had never traveled to the so called heartland of America. He had only been to the East and West Coast mainly staying the urban areas. Dangerously low on gas, my parents pulled into a gas station at late night in Oklahoma and my father—in his heavily accented voice—requested a fill up. The station attendant gave him a strange look and proceeded to moo liked a cow and "bahaha" like sheep. He wasn't sure if the person was crazy, on drugs, or simply didn't like foreigners.

It was the era of "Easy Rider," where the country was divided between those clinging to the conservatism of 1950s, and those who wanted to change to a more liberal society. Open hatred of people who were different was still entrenched in a large parts of the country, while other parts saw the emergence of hippies, new age spiritualists, bohemians, and beatniks. My parents belonged to none of these categories, but were exposed to a panorama of ideas and slogans. Give Peace a Chance. Burn your draft card. Make Love not War. "Sit ins", "love ins", Tune In, Turn On, Drop out. Nobody Colored Me, I was Born this Way. Say it Loud, I'm Black and I'm Proud.

My father had a hard time relating to most of these slogans except for "It's a free country" and "You can do your own thing." For the first time, he saw the whole country and realized where he fit in. He experienced the simple and pure people of the rural areas. He saw

212

the good and the bad of cities across the nation. He met people that were both wholesome and ignorant. It made him appreciate Southern California and gave him a glimpse of the various degrees of the American way of life.

While he observed and learned, he also had a good time being a tourist with his more tranquil wife. There were able to spend many romantic nights and they sensed that my mom was finally pregnant. Somewhere around Las Cruces, New Mexico, I was most likely conceived. My entire extended family was overjoyed at hearing the news that my mother was finally pregnant. Unlike the trouble-ridden conception process, the nine months of pregnancy were completely normal.

On January 7, 1970, Mordecai and Elaine Varsano's first and only child was born at Valley Presbyterian Hospital in Van Nuys, California. My father was thirty-seven and my mother was twenty-seven years old. It was a little counter intuitive that two Jewish parents would have their baby delivered in a Christian-affiliated hospital but that was the closest hospital to their apartment. Furthermore, having quality medical care at a convenient location was more important than having a Jewish hospital on my birth certificate. Typical of the way my father ran his life, the decision was more practical rather than theological.

My existence in the world was a testament to my parent's persistence in conceiving their own child and the effectiveness of modern medical research. If my mother had the same problems with infertility just a few years earlier, giving birth to me would have never been possible. It would have been much easier to just adopt a child, but it was important to them to have their own. Whether the reason was to perpetuate the Varsano name or to pass on their genes to the next generation or a combination of other reasons, I am grateful for their resolve.

Conceiving me was difficult, but raising me was going to be even harder. The virulent property manager at the apartment complex on Whitsett Avenue where the we resided, promptly served our three person family with a vacate notice. Although it is illegal today, in 1970 having a child in an apartment designated as "adults only," was grounds for removal. Still wanting to stay close to their in-laws and my father's employer, my family rented a modest apartment nearby on Fulton Avenue in North Hollywood.

Both Mordecai and Elaine were first time parents, so every aspect of taking care of a baby had to be learned from scratch. My grandmother helped them by babysitting and preparing some meals, but most of the baby rearing was done by my mother. She subscribed to a diapers service that delivered fresh cloth diapers, but she hated the messy process of changing them. While my mom stayed in the apartment and acted as a homemaker, my dad continued to work long hours in order to pay for the new expenses of a baby. After a short stint living on Fulton Avenue, the family was compelled to resolve some unfinished business in Israel.

On the flight from LAX to Ben Gurion Airport in Tel Aviv, I supposedly spent a good portion of the long journey pulling a lady's hair that was sitting on the seat in front of us. At the conclusion of the flight, she told my parents in a thick German accent "You have the worst behaving brat I have ever seen." In addition to learning basic

214

child rearing, my parent's had to enforce discipline and be patient because I was hard to handle from the get go.

My father returned to Israel as a new man; a father and an American. Being an American not only gave him a dissimilar accent, but made him stand out from the other Israelis in other noticeable ways. Not that being an American was bad thing, relations between the two countries had never been better. American Jews were influential members of the Diaspora that helped shape US foreign policy toward Israel. President Nixon and Secretary of State Kissinger established Israel as a surrogate power for US interests in the Middle East so increasing arms and financial assistance became a justifiable security policy. In addition, the Israeli Ambassador to the US and future Prime Minister Yitzaq Rabin had an incredibly good rapport with the US Administration, particularly Kissinger. Even though my father was a registered Democrat, he repeatedly supported Nixon primarily because of his policies towards Israel.

At times, my father held complex and seemingly conflicting political stances on various issues. Since my dad was somewhat conservative in nature anyway, it was just a natural progression for him to adopt some of the other ideals of the Republican platform. When you support someone in foreign policy, you like them more as a person and it makes it easier to accept their domestic agenda despite their personal shortcomings. Nixon was a perfect example. My father never embraced many of the ideals of the Great Society of LBJ. He never collected unemployment and didn't tolerate the growth of the welfare state. He saw people that took advantage of the government subsidized social net as lazy freeloaders. In an era where a popular hippie slogan "Don't trust any one over thirty," my father was already in his late thirties. He did not see eye to eye with these increasing vocal and influential liberal young adults on either a social or political level. Also, fighting for the civil rights of people of color was not a battle that he cared to wage despite the religious persecution that he experienced in Europe. He saw America as a land of freedom and opportunity that was not in need of any revolutionary social change.

However, Jews were still a minority group that suffered from discrimination in the US both legally and illegally. The Democratic Party was known as the greatest supporter of the Civil Rights Movement which speaks up for all oppressed minority groups including the Jews. Consequently most Jewish Americans—including my parents—were registered Democrats which is still true today. Certainly, there were more issues than civil rights, but the Democrats courted the Jewish community while the Republicans had not yet embraced the ideals of the modern civil rights nor did they make a concerted effort to reach out to the American Jewish community. The Republican Administration of Eisenhower was cold and unsupportive of Israel while JFK and LBJ were increasingly warm and supportive of the fledgling Jewish state. Nixon continued the US foreign policy trend of insuring a stronger alliance with Israel and this was a major factor in my father's advocacy of certain Republican administrations.

The older I get, the more my political philosophies mirror my father's. Over recent years, I've transitioned from being a liberal Democrat to more of a conservative Democrat. I believe that it is a natural waning of my youthful idealism and simplistic world view that we are all one and why can't we all just get along. The more world

216

events prove to me that my father views were correct, the more I begin to think like he did. I once perceived him as rather jaded, but now I see him as wise and realistic. His lack of tolerance for those he perceived to be lazy or unpatriotic was a byproduct of him working hard to support his family for his entire adult life and his duty to country. He certainly did not hate people that disagreed with him, but didn't understand why people did not have the same drive and ambition as he did.

My father saw some of his old Israeli colleagues as stuck in a routine with limited potential and thought that they lacked the fortitude to leave their familiar surroundings for better opportunities. He embarked on a journey back to Israel as merely a visiting friend, and not a returning resident. His initial plan was to expediently resolve his clearly defined business matters and return to his life in California.

The main purpose of going to Israel was to dissolve his business partnership and take care of any other matters that were left in limbo when the couple moved to California. Simontov was not cooperating with my father and the dissolution of the partnership became contentious. He resented my father for coming back to claim his rightful portion of the partnership, because he thought that when Seeco went to America that he "inherited" the rest of the business. My father was the brains behind the business and felt entitled to receive a fair buy out so Simontov could continue on his own. Seeco obtained the clients and signed the contracts while Simontov mostly did the manual labor in the shop. There was obviously a big misunderstanding and it took seven long months of civil court proceedings to resolve the matter.

217

The trial took so long that my parents were forced to rent an apartment in Bat Yam close to where my grandmother Rachel resided. My parents were in limbo and I was a screaming baby that required constant attention. The rest of the family in Israel showered me with love and attention. They were happy that my parents were finally able to have a baby and thought I was adorable. My parents, however, had to contend with the reality of taking care of my every need. Disposable diapers were not available in Israel at the time nor did they have cloth diaper delivery services like in America. My mother had no choice but to clean my diapers by dumping the soiled cloth into a large pot of boiling water on the kitchen stove. Yuck. My sensitive ass didn't agree with these crudely sanitized diapers which resulted in a preponderance of diaper rash. No wonder I was screaming and crying all the time.

The stress of a prolonged stay in Israel and having a red assed baby boy was alleviated a bit when my grandmother Gert visited Israel for the first and only time in her life. It was a treat for my mom to be with her mother in a place that she had lived for several years. It also gave my American grandmother a better understanding of where my Israeli father was coming from.

My father was now a US citizen and proceeded to flaunt that fact with a little bit of American flair. He had his car shipped over from the States. He was most likely the only person in Israel with a Ford Mustang. He cruised his hot rod down Disengoff Street—the main strip of Tel Aviv—which attracted an overwhelming amount of attention. He eventually sold his prize car for top dollar to an officer of the United Nations because UN Officials were exempt from paying certain customs taxes that were prohibitive for Israeli citizens.

218

Eventually the partnership was legally dissolved, Simontov paid my father an amount equal to one half of the company's assessed value and he continued the business under a new name. The ugly break up destroyed more than just the relationship between the two partners. My aunt Sarah was friends for several years with Lucy—the wife of Simontov—and they were neighbors in Holon, but the bad blood that resulted from the breakup caused their friendship to fizzle. After the dispute was finally resolved, my parents immediately moved back to the US. My mom was extremely excited about returning to her American way of life again—especially the diaper service. Everyday she received fresh clean white cloth diapers with the pleasant aroma of talcum powder, what a change from the putrid stench of boiling baby poop. It was one more simple reason to love America.

My family continued to live in the East San Fernando Valley where they briefly rented another apartment on Oxnard Street in North Hollywood. From 1971 to 1972, we enjoyed our first swimming pool at the new complex while my father continued to work at P & J Engineering. The Mustang that was sold in Israel was replaced by a brand new auburn Chevy Nova which was an affordable sedan that was more suited for a family, yet still sporty enough to be considered a muscle car which kept my dad satisfied. By the following year, my father had finally saved enough money to begin seriously looking to purchase a sizable house in the West San Fernando Valley.

My parents were ready to set down roots in Southern California and start building an American family. Once my father made the decision develop a career in the US, he realized that he would most likely live here for the rest of his life. He didn't like Israelis who took

219

advantage of the US economy and moved back to Israel once they had earned enough money to return relatively wealthy. He felt that they should love the country that they live in and make it their home. No one should treat their residence like a long distance employment opportunity.

Even though he was still considered a foreign immigrant in the US, he strived to be what he perceived to be a good American. Generally, he did feel better or worse than the average American or Jew. Many other Israeli Jews have a superiority complex towards American Jews. Some see them as wannabes who weren't tough enough to handle the rigors of living in Israel. I think those Israeli immigrants have a rather hypocritical attitude because they left that so called rigorous life to take advantage of the splendors of America. My father didn't think that every Jew must "do his time" in Israel to earn the respect of the war-hardened Israeli veterans.

However, I think my father—as well as many Israeli immigrants—outwork their American Jewish counterparts. My father held a bit of the Israeli machismo and felt that some of the Jews in America took their lifestyle for granted. He was a tough man with strong callused hands and had a similar physical appearance to other hard working immigrants. He didn't really identify with the multitudes of Jewish doctors, attorneys, accountants, and other professionals in Los Angeles. Even though he thought some of the Americans were tad bit soft compared with the Israelis, he wanted a cushy life for his family in future. He worked hard so his family could reap the benefits and enjoy a better life than he had in Bulgaria and Israel.

Determined yet still a bit uncomfortable in his new home, he continued to make progress in his business life while he slowly adapted his social life. The life affirming accomplishment of fathering his own child gave him the confidence and faith that an extraordinary effort and steady patience will yield fruitful dividends. When my parents fell in love at first sight, they never imagined that it would be so difficult to conceive a child. Perhaps, the long waiting period made them truly appreciate the miracle of life. They were finally blessed with a gift from God and beneficiaries of the scientific breakthroughs of modern medicine. The possibilities for my father in upbeat Southern California seemed limitless. No longer would war, government policy, or family obligations constrain the full potential of his ability and desire. Rather than history dictating to him, he could now guide his own destiny in the land of the free.

PART III

America

CHAPTER 12

Welcome to Your Destination

B y the early 1970s, my father had become a US Citizen, acquired a good paying job, was ready to purchase a sizable house, and was happily married with one child. After only a few short years of living in the richest country in the world, he was well on his way to achieving the so called American dream. Balancing business and pleasure would prove to be a life long struggle for my dad, but in the 1970s he was young, strong, and determined to live life to its fullest according to his own personal vision of success.

My dad was the type of person who could never fully relax and totally escape from his working world. Somewhere in the back of his mind, he was always thinking about business. Most of the vacations that our family went on usually had some business related component to them. When he worked for someone else, he was continually plotting his next move within the company or strategizing about how to start his own business again. When he had his own business, he needed to be in control of the day to day operations even when he was not physically present. He rarely trusted his employees and made every reasonable effort to scrutinize and second guess them.

He expected his employees and his family members to be as dedicated as he was, but was often disappointment in what he saw as their lack of commitment. His daily work helped identify who he was and how he judged others. He insisted that every single day you must be productive, which translated to making money everyday. If a work day went by without closing a deal or completing a job and getting paid, the day was viewed as a failure. His self-imposed pressure might have caused unneeded tension, but it did yield dividends that benefited our family in many ways.

In 1972, my family purchased a three bedroom, two bathroom house on Crespi Street in the Los Angeles suburb of Woodland Hills. The home was over 2000 square feet and the previous owners were a Japanese couple that sculpted beautiful Japanese gardens complimented by concrete Asian lanterns in the front and back yards. The fashionable décor of the era consisted of beige shag carpeting through out the house. The kitchen featured avocado green kitchen appliances with red/brown patterned vinyl flooring. The adjacent dining room had an Asian-motif wallpaper left over from the previous residents that clashed with our a brown and orange area rug topped by a fake wood grain dinette set, imitation brown leather upholstered chairs, and heavy beige fabric drapes like the kind that you might find in a cheap motel room.

In the family room sat a chocolate-colored vinyl couch in family room that was peeling apart. Most of the furniture was heavy wood and darkly colored. There were lots of valance lamps with the brass chains that had interwoven electrical cords dangling from the ceiling. The main fixture in the family room was a Spanish-style lantern with wrought iron decorations, a walnut colored body, and a thick emerald glass cover. I was always worried that gargantuan fixture would crush me to death in the event of a big earthquake.

224

My room resembled a typical child's room with sports posters on the walls, toys and baseball cards on the floor, a twin bed with nautical-themed headboard and matching dresser. The extra bed room turned into the junk room where my parents dumped their old bills, assorted papers, and unused "chachkas."

We enjoyed all the technological amenities of the early 1970s including a fifteen inch Sony color TV with turn dial (no remote control and no cable), a rotary dial phone in the kitchen and my parent's bedroom, our stereo system was a phono/am/fm hi-fi floor console unit. A few years after we moved in, my parents splurged for an eight-track tape player.

Our new neighborhood was nestled in the west end of the San Fernando Valley on a hill that was just two blocks from the 101 Freeway and Ventura Boulevard. Even though we were close to retail locations, people rarely walked to the stores or restaurants. In the Valley, it was primarily teenagers and poor people who rode the bus. There were a few Asian and Black neighbors but most of the homeowners were White. Latino families lived in the nearby apartments. Everyone on Crespi Street had a two car attached garage facing the street so that they could park their car and get into their house without having to speak to their neighbors. Our track development had no porches, street trees, and only one side of the street had a side walk. In the early 1970s, there were still strawberry patches where the office towers of Warner Center are today. There was also lots of empty brush areas adjacent to our home where the neighborhood kids could play.

Woodland Hills combined the convenience of being within the city of Los Angeles with the semi-rural/suburban refuge of the end of the Valley. It was unlike any place my urbanized father had ever lived. For my consideration, good schools were within close proximity and there were plenty of other children in the neighborhood. The soothing suburb in the West Valley was a place where families "settled down." It gave my father a sense of permanency about living the rest of his life in a typical American family.

A new neighborhood usually means new friends and acquaintances, but my family was still making the transition to the Southern California lifestyle. My parents' friends mainly consisted of couples with at least one relatively recent immigrant. Oli and Uri were an Israeli couple that originated from Bulgaria who were some of the first friends that my parents made when they moved to America. Oli was a dress designer and Uri was an engineer, both were successful, educated, a relatively affluent. They lived in a nice home in West Los Angeles and had lots of Israeli immigrant friends. It seemed like their house was the headquarters of Israeli immigrant social activities for the entire Westside of Los Angeles. They were considered to be the social welcoming committee for all new Israelis mostly because they had lots of large open parties.

Through one of these parties, my parents befriended Mira and Alex who lived in the Valley. Mira was an Israeli immigrant to America originating from Hungary. Alex was a German-American Jew that was a psychiatrist and an attorney. The two of them seemed to be constantly fighting, but stayed together because of their three kids. All three were around my age and we played together for a few years.

226

Unfortunately, Mira and Alex got divorced which hurt our relationship with them as well. My mom, however, maintained her friendship with Mira for many years afterward, but the two families never got together again. Divorce tends to break up friendships, as well as marriages.

Another transitional family of friends was the Hananels from the predominantly Jewish Fairfax District of Los Angeles. Sylvia Hananel, was a full-figured Jewish American and Izzy Hananel was an Israeli immigrant. Along with their son Michael and daughter Jennifer, they kept kosher and lived a Conservative life. Unfortunately, they lived in central Los Angeles which was over twenty miles from our house. The two families spent many weekends together and I enjoyed playing with their son Michael who was about a year older than me. He was an hyperactive boy who loved to cause trouble just like me. Food fights, crank phone calls, wrestling, and door bell ditch were just a few of the hijinks that drove our parents' crazy.

The only good friends that my parents had made in Woodland Hills were Dorothy and Yoav Kamer. Dorothy was a fair skinned blonde-headed American Jewish trophy-wife and Yoav was a dark skinned black haired Iraqi Jewish immigrant. The couple lived in a cavernous house with their dysfunctional boy Ezra. He acted like a foreigner—particularly an Arab—even though he was an American. He suffered from bad hygiene and had some learning problems. He was not like my other friends and I really couldn't relate to him very well. He didn't want to talk about school or play sports. He didn't have any video games or the same toys as other children, and generally seemed unhappy. His mother Dorothy was not intellectually compatible with my mom, but both were in need of friends. Every time

227

they went out for lunch it was an adventure because Dorothy was a notoriously terrible driver in her big white Cadillac. In retrospect, I suppose the basis of the two family's relationship was my father's compatibility with his fellow Sephardic immigrant Yoav.

Back home on Crespi Street, my folks didn't make much of an effort in the 1970s to gain friends in their private suburban neighborhood. There was a common bond with some of the Jewish neighbors but most fellow homeowners were just acquaintances. My family never had large parties or BBQs or participated in community events. In the workplace, my father didn't socialize with co workers either. Getting a drink at "Happy Hour" after work was never done because he rarely drank alcohol and when he did, it was only infinitesimal amounts. Despite the lack of a large pool of quality friends, my parents were generally content in their new family life in Woodland Hills. However, my father had the itch to be an entrepreneur like he was before in Israel and like his father was before him in Bulgaria.

For several years my mechanically inclined father was working at P & J Engineering, steadily climbing up the ladder and slowly saving money for future investments. He was finally in position to look for other business opportunities and ways to invest his savings other than interest-bearing accounts at the bank. He briefly dabbled in the stock market, which resulted in some modest losses. From that point on, he was always apprehensive about investing in stocks, even during the strongest bull markets. His natural inclination was to open his own business, and he seriously considered opening a Harley Davidson Motorcycle dealership, but the company was ailing at the

228

time, so he opted for a more reliable route. In 1974, he saved enough money to purchase a Laundromat on Ventura Boulevard in Studio City.

As the name of the city suggests, Studio City was the location of many film and television production facilities in the East San Fernando Valley. Ventura Boulevard was main drag of the Valley and featured the best cuisine and nightlife for the area. The Laundromat was located in a middle class neighborhood shopping center, next to a Market Basket grocery store, dry cleaners, and a nightclub. Most of the local customers were single and white. Today, the area has become so affluent that a coin laundry business is no longer feasible at the same pricey location. At first, he acquired the business simply as an investment hoping to earn some supplemental income. However, owning the Laundromat had unintended consequences that would eventually cause a shift in careers.

In addition to the revenue collected from the washers and dryers, the Studio City Laundromat would occasionally earn substantial rental income when the entertainment industry would lease his facility for film shoots. The highlight of these showbiz activities occurred when an episode of the Rockford Files was shot at my father's stereotypical Laundromat. In between shoots my father would chat with James Garner—the star of the show (a.k.a. Jim Rockford)— who was purportedly a very nice man who walked with a slight limp. My father found him rather unassuming and he lacked the gigantic ego of the TV star that he was. There was a big car chase scene in the shopping center parking lot, as well as scenes shot inside the Laundromat. NBC Television rented his entire coin laundry business for a week and paid my father handsomely. The glamour of being part

229

of a TV production was one side of the business, but the day to day operations were quite another.

Unscrupulous customers and vandals were constantly trying to wreak havoc on the business. My short tempered father occasionally initiated altercations with dishonest patrons. Sometimes, he would catch unscrupulous people washing their clothes in the utility sink which was designated for washing your hands only. "Free dry with wash" was a frequent promotion advertised. The same people who would wash in the sink for free would then dry for free, costing my father utility expenses and earning him absolutely no money. To say the least, he did not care for these customers. Nor did he care for the people that used counterfeit or foreign coins in the machines. One evening he caught a perpetrator of these illicit activities red handed and attempted to "subdue" him until the police arrived. The police arrived and the situation was eventually cooled down. Since there was no video taped surveillance and it was one person's word against another—arrests were infrequent.

I was impressed with my father's strength when I saw him throw a steel shopping cart at the man. It was scary yet exciting to see my dad in a fight. It showed me that even grown-ups had to hit someone if a certain line was crossed. My parents would always tell me not to get into fights and here was my dad throwing punches, just completely going ballistic. The incident also showed me that all humans were flawed and that people can not always practice what they preach. Do as I say, not as I do.

Sometimes my father's passionate behavior worked to his advantage. It gave him a competitive edge that enabled him to

230

intimidate others and persevere through tough times. When he got into the fight at the Studio City Laundromat with the unscrupulous patron, his intimidating behavior and forceful actions expeditiously compensated for his disadvantage in physical size and age.

On other occasions, my father's temper was frightening to me. He could explode over seemingly small incidents and it was terrifying to be on the receiving end of his angry tirades. When I was a child, my parents would yell at each other so loudly and passionately, that I would start to cry in fear of a separation or divorce. My weeping eyes would make them feel guilty and they would eventually calm down. It was usually my mother that did the apologizing because my father rarely thought that he did anything wrong. His confidence combined with his hot-headedness made him a difficult person to cross. One of the few people in society that my father was forced to acquiesce to were the police.

My father did not have a good relationship with the Los Angeles Police Department when he was a new immigrant. The notoriously racist police force was in full swing during 1970s. The ethnic wounds from the Watts Riots of 1965 had not yet fully healed while the growth of Black and Latino gangs was on the rise. Ethnic profiling and overtly bigoted directives were common tactics employed by the police force. They mistook my father for a Mexican-American quite often. He was pulled over for many minor traffic infractions and subjected to misguided racial slurs such as greaseball, beaner, and spick. I remember greaseball being the most widely used derogatory term because it wasn't necessarily specific to Latinos and could refer to a host of dark skinned people.

One time my dad was pulled over on Ventura Boulevard only a few blocks from his coin laundry business for speeding and was instructed via police cruiser loud speaker to "Step out of the vehicle and assume the position!" The cops spoke to him as if he were a hardened criminal. He thought to himself "What position?" Were these KEV Officers in fascist Bulgaria or Peace Officers in a free country?

Although these incidents were minor and isolated, it proved that he had not been fully integrated into the American middle class culture. He needed to learn more about the local customs if he truly wanted to "fit in." True to his confident personality, he never showed any signs of insecurity about being different. As a consequence of what he had been through in his life, he was very thick skinned in regards to the prejudice of strangers.

To a certain degree, he relished being different from the average American male and felt that not conforming with cultural norms was his own form of rebellion. He continued his Israeli bluntness and abrupt pacing of speech, speaking Hebrew loudly with his fellow Israelis. Like any foreigner, he could selectively use his ignorance of culture or language to his advantage, even though he might have been faking it as a strategy. He rarely conformed to the typically polite behavior that most Americans use everyday like "Please," "Thank You," "You're welcome," and "I love you." His rebellion against societal niceties reflected his own prejudice against the typical ugly American who he viewed as carefree, gullible, spoiled, and non-worldly. The average American businessman that he encountered was too straightforward and bureaucratic, not at all like the crafty and sometimes shifty ways business was conducted in Israel with all the haggling and dramatics. For the most part, my father still conducted himself as an Israeli and only made subtle changes to become more America which were rarely recognized by his family.

Even Seeco's in-laws sometimes xenophobically referred to him as the "fuzzy foreigner." True, my father had a thick accent and did things a little differently than a typical American. As a little kid, I was sometimes embarrassed by my father's lack of assimilation, but in time I realized that what made him different gave him his character. In suburbia amongst other children, ethnicity was more suppressed and Americanized rather than celebrated as a distinctive characteristic. During the 1970s, the Civil Rights Movement had made strides for acceptance of different peoples, but the country as a whole was not nearly as politically correct as it is today. Having an accent was something that was ridiculed rather than envied as an exotic feature. People used to unflatteringly compare my father's accent with the Latka character played by Andy Kaufman on the TV show *Taxi*.

While other kids had the all-American dad coaching the little league team and driving all the kids to Disneyland in the station wagon, and I had the dad with the thick accent who was a bit abrasive and was too busy with work to hang out with groups of kids. I wanted my dad to be like Mike Brady on the TV Show, *The Brady Bunch*.

My friend's parents would take the thirty minute drive from Woodland Hills to the beach and were allowed to invite friends. My parent's rarely went to the beach, but we would sometimes take family outings to our Laundromat on the weekend. My father would fix machines and collect coins while my mother and I watched guard. When he wasn't working, we would not spend our time doing all-

American activities like baseball, BBQ, and beer. Most of my father's friends in those days were other immigrants and he spent most of his social time going out to long dinners in the European-Israeli style. Mostly, though, it was just the three of us during non-business hours.

One time, we were in a fancy department store and there was some disagreement about the bill. I don't even remember exactly what is what about. I do remember that my father started yelling and caused a big commotion. It seemed like every shopper and sales clerk in the arena-like store stopped what they were doing just to stare at the crazy foreigner making a scene. Some whispered to each other and some made overt comments to my parents which only enflamed the situation further. I was so embarrassed; I just wanted to hide somewhere, anywhere. But there was no escape until my dad was finished making his point. In Israeli society, it might have been acceptable to argue in that manner, but in a pricy American department store stocked with prissy salespeople, it was a shocking display. Eventually the manager—who my father had been demanding to speak with—showed up and some resolution was made. My father was still fuming, as we slithered out of that place.

The department store incident was not an isolated event and similar events caused much embarrassment for me during my childhood. The lack of "fitting in" by my dad helped define our early relationship. I did not want to be like my dad. I wanted to be a typical American kid that "fit in" everywhere. I would rebel against being involved in most parent related activities. I didn't really embrace Israeli culture—except for playing soccer—until much later in life.

In retrospect, I miss his uniqueness and find myself using some of his foreign phrases which helps keep his memory alive for me. Some of the phrases he used in everyday chatter drew from Ladino, Hebrew, Bulgarian, and even Yiddish slang. "Schmeygegi & Schemderick" were favorite terms to describe a foolish and/or nerdy person. "Polisha Dripke"—referring to Jews of Polish origin even those of neighboring origins such as the Soviets—was the equivalent of the "Polack" insult. "Labrayut!" was exclaimed as a blessing whenever someone sneezed. "Big Golemo" described a large gorilla-like man. "Balegan" was a synonym for a messy or chaotic situation. For some, such foreign phrases were distinguishing or worldly. But for many, my father was simply a target for ridicule.

Even with such unfortunate incidents my father's thick skin, which was developed from a long history of discrimination, did not distract him from making the most of his economic opportunities in the purportedly pluralistic US. He began to explore other career options in the commercial laundry field. He purchased another Laundromat on Roscoe Boulevard in Canoga Park which was closer to his home. Canoga Park was located in the northwest Valley, close to Woodland Hills but was not as affluent. It was farther from Ventura Boulevard and 101 Freeway which meant land was cheap. During the 1970s, the area was dotted with lots of empty lots, car dealerships, and drive-in movie theaters.

As a rule of thumb, a coin laundry business generated more revenue in neighborhoods with large families, renters, and people who don't own their own washers and dryers. Canoga Park had a large population of Latino families that could not afford to own a house or

235

live in an apartment building with a laundry room. Also, large families require multiple loads which cannot easily be accommodated by a laundry room with only a single washer and dryer that one might find in most homes and small apartment buildings. Therefore, from an investment standpoint, it seemed to be a logical choice.

The Canoga Park laundry took in more revenue but also had much higher expenses. There was more vandalism; customers didn't treat the facilities as well. The inside was dirty and graffiti ridden. The color scheme was classic 1970s: daisy flower wallpaper, brown wood grain paneling, and harvest yellow and avocado green washers. Mothers would change the diapers of their screaming babies on the orange folding tables. Discarded candy wrappers and melted slurpees from the adjacent 7-11 mini-mart littered the industrial linoleum flooring. The stench of urine from a little boy often emanated from a corner of the Laundromat because the child's parents were unwilling to pay for the coin operated rest room.

Equipment needed to be serviced, walls needed to be painted, and the entire place needed to be cleaned much more often than in Studio City. The machines were routinely overloaded which also increased maintenance costs. Stolen shopping carts were strewn across the parking lot. There were definitely no studio rental opportunities because of local crime problems. In General, Canoga Park was not as pleasant a place to spend time as Studio City.

Much to my mother's dismay, my father purchased a third self service coin laundry on Sherman Way in Canoga Park soon after acquiring the Roscoe location. At this point he was committed to making a living with washers and dryers. He resigned from P & J

236

Engineering and took a job as a salesperson at PWS Commercial Laundry Equipment Distributor and Business Brokerage. He sold Speed Queen Brand washers and dryers for PWS by day, and fixed and collected money from his own Laundromats at night. The career shift was completed.

Now that he had a day job and side business, he could no longer drive my mother everywhere she needed to go. For the first time in many years, my mother would need to provide her own means of transportation. He handed down his Chevy Nova with automatic transmission to my mom, and bought a new Ford Pinto. His Pinto was a small yellow sports car with a manual transmission. My mom couldn't, and still can't, drive a stick shift so the Pinto was exclusively my dad's car while they shared the Nova. The Pintos had a notorious defect of exploding when struck from the rear. My father was rear ended twice while he had the car but luckily it never caused a massive detonation. He actually enjoyed the surprisingly peppy but much maligned Pinto. I remember him putting my hand on the stick shift and directing me to change gears as we raced up and down the rolling hill straight-aways on Avenue Saint Louis that lead up to our house.

In his personal life, my father really tried to make the precious time that he had with his family count despite his work obligations. My first memories of my father started in about 1973 in Woodland Hills. He had a beard in those days for the one and only time in his life which was fashionable at the time. As the decade progressed, he replaced his beard with hefty side burns, but still seemed slightly different than the rest of the American dads. He never wanted to be "Father of the Year," and never really cared what other people said about him. He just acted himself, and did what he thought was in the best interest of his family. He was reluctant to take advice from others and felt his mission was to be a provider for his wife and child.

My mother and I never lacked material possessions or love, but perhaps we desired a little more Americanism from him. He still wasn't polite or refined. He continued to have poor grammar and a noticable accent. His proverbs and sense of humor didn't always translate well. My father also did quite comprehend the many nuisances of American culture. He didn't really understand baseball or football, but was always very passionate about soccer. Throughout the 1970s, he was still a European-Israeli at heart and hadn't fully made the transition to the American way of life yet.

He did not embrace American sports as a fan or a participant. Adult softball or soccer leagues were not something my dad was interested in nor had time for. Even though health clubs, health food, and hot tubs were on the rise in active LA, neither of my parents ever fully embraced that aspect of California culture. In Israel, the young newlywed couple was naturally active within the frantic energy of Tel Aviv. The calm suburban atmosphere of Woodland Hills and the energy-consuming obligation of raising a rambunctious young boy did not provide sufficient daily aerobic activity.

Furthermore, the Israeli routine of walking a lot, riding a bike to the beach, and eating a vegetable-rich Mediterranean diet was replaced by driving a car everywhere, eating fast food burgers, fried chicken (my dad especially loved Pioneer and Ambers Broasted), Mexican food (he loved Menudo because it was similar to Bulgarian tripe soup), Chinese take out, and generally less home-cooked meals with fresh ingredients. Even as he grew into his mid forties, he still worked as hard as when he did in his twenties. With age, his metabolism gradually slowed and that combined with a high cholesterol diet caused a significant weight gain that lead to health problems. High blood pressure, unknown arterial blockage, and high blood sugar set in, even though my dad was only perhaps fifteen to twenty pounds above his ideal weight. He still looked and felt fit; not suspecting any change in lifestyle was required.

As a family, we were always busy doing activities and side trips that were mostly enjoyable. Like any other family, there were always silly fights about one thing or another. My father would mostly get angry at me over issues of disrespect or being an obnoxious spoiled brat. I was usually angry at him when he embarrassed me or didn't buy me something that I wanted. I never thought that the stress related to our arguments was more than the average father and son experienced. Mostly, our family got along well and we enjoyed our time together.

On the weekends, my parents and I would explore Southern California and try to soak up as much culture as we could. We often went on weekend trips to the typical local getaways such as Las Vegas, San Diego, Tijuana, and Palm Springs. To enrich our collective knowledge and to enhance our leisure activities, we also took frequent day trips to Ports of Call in San Pedro and Fisherman's Village in Marina Del Rey. Once a year, we attended seasonal events such as the Catholic blessing of the animals at Olivera Street, the Greek Cultural Festival in Northridge, and the Jewish Festival at Rancho Park.

Some of the events were odder than others, such as the Hare Krishna Festival in Venice. These events were merely entertainment

239

for my parents and they didn't politically embrace their causes. It was just a spectacle to them. Maybe for my immigrant father, it was nice to be the "normal one" who looked at the other freaks for a change.

One of most memorable and flamboyant events we went to was the Gay Pride Parade and Festival in West Hollywood. There were no gays in our family that I am aware of, so my extremely heterosexual father never had to deal with the issue directly. He certainly was no gay basher and didn't discriminate against them in any noticeable way, but would refer to them as "Faygalas". To him, the festival was like watching live theater. Some of my father's greatest joys were being entertained and traveling.

In 1974, my family enjoyed a longer exploration of the state of California when my grandmother Rachel made her first trip to the US. She stayed in Woodland Hills with us for a few days and cooked delectable cuisine that reminded my father of his childhood. The entire family took a tour of the Golden State in the Nova which was the larger of our two cars. We drove up the scenic Pacific Coast on Highway 1 to San Francisco. In the city, I vaguely remember going to all the tourist traps at Fisherman's Wharf and staying in a hotel room with funky velvet wallpaper. I was just along for the ride. The significance of trip was more about my father and grandmother enjoying the completeness of their lives together. After so many years of struggling through political turmoil, untimely death, and pressing obligations, my father and his mother were able to enjoy some degree of stability and prosperity with a refreshing vacation in scenic California.

A visit from the Old World safta (grandma in Hebrew), gave our family a healthy dose of the traditional ways that were most often absent from our daily lives. Although I went to Beth Kodesh Temple Pre-school in Woodland Hills, my parents were not really active members of the congregation and attending services was a rare occasion. Even though my father spoke Hebrew and had first-hand experience at a crucial time in Jewish history, he—like many Israelis—was relatively secular and not nearly as observant as a typical American Jew.

The 1970s—commonly referred to as the "me generation"—represented a break down of the traditional family structure for both Christians and Jews alike in the US. Unlike many Americans, my parents' vices were not drugs or alcohol but workaholism and overeating. A lazy home lifestyle of take-out dinners, hours of TV watching, and mom reading romance novels while dad read the newspaper, was not the traditional world of my father's early youth. Perhaps the national trends towards self-indulgence and anti-authority played a role in my family's lack of institutionalized religion and other non traditional family values, but I believe the seeds were sown in Israel. After escaping the persecution of the fascists and the communists, he never wanted to be pigeon-holed again. His level of religious and political affiliation or observance was going to be on his terms.

My father was an avid follower of world news—rarely listening to music—the radio was usually tuned into to KFWB News 98, 980 a.m. Yet he certainly was not someone who jumped on the bandwagon of national trends. During the 1973 Yom Kippur War in

Israel, my father received updates from his family via telephone just as he had done during 1967 conflict. Even though the Yom Kippur War was a harder military struggle for Israel, my father was an American citizen and didn't feel compelled to actively assist the IDF. The Civil Rights Movement, the War in Vietnam, and the Watergate Scandal were all gigantic political issues in the US during my father's initial years of citizenship, but he was mostly indifferent.

In a similar way that my father accepted Nixon's flawed policies in Vietnam because of his good relations with Israel, he was less critical of the Watergate Scandal than the average American. He was upset that Nixon had to resign because he thought that Israel had lost a good friend and an important ally. My mom—on the other hand—did not like Nixon's policies or his persona. She described him as a creepy man with bizarre mannerism.

For the most part, my father wasn't all that concerned with US political scandals no matter who they involved. He was more concerned with developing his career and establishing a happy home life for his family. He focused his own personal life and issues that affected his local interests. He deliberately avoided becoming embroiled in national issues. Compared to what he had lived through, he was not going to allow someone else's struggles to affect his goals. He simply wanted to raise a family and earn a decent living, and he definitely did not want to get embroiled in any more political battles. His main political concern as an American was the US foreign policy towards Israel and keeping taxes low. He cherished the free market economy in the US, and resented the high taxes of socialist states.

Life for the most part was going great: peace at home, a good job, a nice house, and a happy family. Because of the conception problems that my parents had—as well as me being a handful—they decided that one child was enough. My mother did insist on the addition to the family of a brownish terrier mutt named Charlie in 1976 and by all accounts we appeared to be living a Rockwellian storybook life. However, my father was too ambitious to rest and simply enjoy what he had accomplished.

In 1977, he was approached by a fellow Israeli named Avner Wolanow who was the national sales manager for Wascomat of America located in New York. Wascomat was a Swedish subsidiary of Electrolux that manufactured front load washing machines and other laundry equipment. Avner was looking to expand their distribution network into Southern California and identified my father as a top salesman at PWS with the potential to become a volume generating distributor. After several months of employment at PWS, he had earned his California Real Estate Salesperson's license in order to sell coin laundry and dry cleaning businesses. He also had gained a reputation for being technically knowledgeable about equipment from owning his own laundries. The fact that Avner was a fellow Israeli probably helped my father get in the front door. It was Avner's call to make and I noticed that Israeli's seem to stay together in business due to a matter of trust and competence even compared to American Jews.

My father had a productive initial meeting with the CEO of Wascomat of America Bernard Milch who was a German concentration camp survivor. The WWII survivor bond furthered their personal compatibility, but issues needed to make sense on a business level as well. Avner, Bernie, and Mordecai agreed to terms in July of 1977. The business would be centrally located on Robertson Boulevard in a small brick building in Culver City and Wascomat of America would initially retain part ownership of the new company called Automated Laundry Systems. My independently-minded father was excited and eager to enter the entrepreneurial fray once again.

Locating the business in Culver City was a wise and pragmatic decision. Harry Culver—the founder of the city—once said that "All roads lead to Culver City." It was true that it was centrally located near the 10 Freeway in LA metropolis but not as congested or expensive as most of West LA. My father would work in an affordable middle class neighborhood with friendly residents, located just east of downtown Culver City. There were plenty of good restaurants, the police were very responsive, and it was a safe community with little crime or graffiti. A redevelopment plan for the incorporated city had just begun and the area steadily improved with every passing year. It was a pleasant place to work despite the long commute and would prove to be a terrific real estate investment.

Now my father really had a full plate with running his Laundromats and starting a new business at the same time. He managed to juggle all of this and take his family back to Israel to attend a special family celebration. In the summer of 1977, we flew to Israel in honor of my cousin Eyal's Bar Mitzvah. The whole extended Varsano family attended the coming-of-age event in a traditional synagogue where men and women were separated. While we were guests in Tel Aviv, we stayed in my grandmother's one bedroom apartment in Bat Yam. My grandmother was always cooking us meals though, and it felt as if we were locals.

I received my first real taste of the "Old World" through the ancient language spoken by the people, the traditional foods eaten, the common bonds of a large family, and the closeness of the neighborhood. I met all the children of the extended family which was a much larger group of relatives than my small family at home. I played soccer in the streets of Bat Yam with the local Israeli boys and I was able to even speak a little Hebrew. A soccer ball was always being kicked around the streets and we played basketball in the parking lot of the apartment building with a square concoction of piping serving as the hoop. At that time in Bat Yam, the most popular t-shirt worn by Israeli kids and tourists alike was the Coca Cola shirt written with the familiar brand name script written in Hebrew. I also remember climbing a tree beneath my grandmother's neighbor's building and an old "Babushka" lady dumped a pot of water on my head so I would get down. At the markolette (mini market), I developed a liking for Elite brand chocolates and a packaged Israeli chocolate pudding with cream topping.

It was not all fun and games, though. My parent's tried to teach me a little history by taking me to Jerusalem. I visited the Wailing Wall for the first time in my life and remember thinking how odd it was that my mom could not go on the men's side of the wall. You did get a sense that it was a very holy place because of the seriousness of the men "davaning" in front of wall and the abundance of Hassidic Jews in their strange black garb.

We even had the opportunity during that time period to go to the Al Asqua Mosque. As Jews, we received lots of hard looks and there seemed to be a very tense atmosphere that I didn't comprehend. I did understand that the Arab Quarter of Jerusalem was a totally different ambiance than the Jewish Quarter. Inside the Mosque, it was very quiet, and I found it very strange with all the rugs on floor and kneeling worshippers compared to the suited parishioners in pews at Christian churches and Jewish synagogues that I had been to in my short life. It would be years later that I learned about the specific bad blood between Jews and Arabs. That particular area was an extremely sensitive area to both sides regarding the conflict and the visit to the disputed piece of territory known as the Temple Mount for Jews and Dome of the Rock for Moslems was perhaps a once in lifetime opportunity.

After we left that area and passed the Israeli guards, I had an opportunity to pose for a picture with an IDF soldier that let me hold his M-16 machine gun. I remember the gun being very heavy and the strap weighing down on my small seven year old frame. My father asked the soldier in Hebrew if I could hold the gun as a favor because he used to tell me stories about having an Uzi machine gun when he was in the reserves and I mistakenly thought he still had one in 1977. I was just a macho boy that was fascinated by guns and my dad wanted to make me happy since he refused to buy me my own BB gun.

When we returned from Jerusalem, it was time for Eyal's Bar Mitzvah which was the main purpose of our visit. The service was held in a large, old, and traditional synagogue that segregated the sexes with the women upstairs looking over the balconies at the pulpit while

246

the men were downstairs closer to the rabbi. Throwing candy in honor of the Bar Mitzvah boy was a customary practice that I really liked as a sweet toothed little boy. I scattered the floor grabbing what I could, acting as if a non-existent piñata had just been popped. There were many kids at the Bar Mitzvah reception but most of them were older and didn't speak English very well, so I spent a lot of time with my mom while my dad reminisced with some old friends and relatives. Although we were in Israel for only a couple of weeks, we lived as Israelis not typical tourists, which turned out to be quite a flashback for my father.

A few months after returning from Israel, my father needed to fly to Innwood, New York, to meet with Bernie Milch at Wascomat of America headquarters in order to finalize their business plans. My mother had to stay home to watch me and tend to Laundromats. Due to bad weather, the trip to New York lasted longer than expected. My mother encountered Murphy's Law while my father was away. The ill-equipped young homemaker had to deal with plumbing problems in the Laundromats, car problems on the road, and issues with the bank all in the course of a one week business trip. She did her best and helped my father in a time of need. She would soon be capable of coping with similar problems and much more when she joined Automated Laundry Systems as a receptionist/ bookkeeper/vice-president, the following year.

With his loyal wife by his side, the future in America held endless possibilities for a man who could have died in a concentration camp in Europe or been a victim of terrorism in the Middle East. He embraced the ideals of a stable, secure, and peaceful life. Not that he was risk-adverse, he was a just a measured risk taker. His was never reckless about anything in life whether it was the rather conservative approach to how he made investments, undertook changes, or established personal relationships. He always said that sky diving, bungee jumping, rock climbing, and similar activities were stupid. Why risk your life unnecessarily? Life—at least for him—was filled with so many involuntary dangers and life threatening events, that you shouldn't expose yourself to them voluntarily. Years later, my friend Adam Garfield was paralyzed in a rock climbing accident which not only curtailed my own rock climbing, but gave me a newfound respect for my father's conservative wisdom. The excitement of fear or the high of an adrenaline rush did not appeal to my father, just as drugs or alcohol did not strike his fancy. He did not need to be buzzed or intoxicated in any away, he was just fine with sobriety and really got excitement about making a good deal or going on an interesting but safe vacation.

By all accounts, his new life in Woodland Hills was happy and complete. The young family had made some friends, their income was gradually rising, and I was a typical American kid. Although our family was not the Brady Bunch, we managed to ride through the peaks and valleys relatively unscathed. For the first time in my father's life, he was able to settle into a safe and lucrative routine that had eluded him for so many years.

CHAPTER 13

Docking in Culver City

After living in the US for over ten years, my father was generally integrated into American culture and enjoyed his new found financial stature. He understood more American sayings and expressions. No longer were rough translations of foreign proverbs made to illustrate his points. It also seemed to me at least that his accent wasn't as pronounced as in earlier years or perhaps I had just grown accustomed to hearing it.

His new American friends said that he had no problem fitting in with them, although sometimes he was a bit embarrassed about his accent which they would periodically kid him about it. Even though his new friends had few parallels in their own life experiences with my father, the universal truths of seeking a quality life for their families were a shared characteristic. Both my parents were determined to provide the best possible life for their only child by encouraging my participation in extracurricular activities, attending the best educational institutions, and including me in a multitude of travels around the world.

In the fall of 1977, my parents decided that playing organized sports would be a beneficial outlet for my endless supply of energy. They enrolled me in the American Youth Soccer Organization (AYSO) and my father volunteered to be an assistant coach. . Since he was a huge soccer fan in both Bulgaria and Israel, he was a natural choice for a coach of this "un-American" game. Even though he was not the typical American dad, he was very knowledgeable and respected by the other fathers regarding soccer. Our team—the Tigersharks—needed a financial sponsor for our uniforms, so my father's new business—Automated Laundry Systems—became the convenient benefactor. All of the parents of my teammates appreciated his financial sponsorship of the team.

The games were sloppy but intense, and my father followed the play with much gusto. During one particular game, he lost his temper when the referee awarded the opposing team a penalty kick. All I remember was that he was assessed a yellow card and every parent of my teammates was compelled by the referee to move back behind a designated security line. Although my dad was correct about the bad call, his raging temper overwhelmed the incident. I was quite embarrassed but fortunately that was an isolated incident in regards to youth sports. The team still had a head coach and my father rarely was involved in the weekday practices because of his work demands on the other side of the city. Even though he was passionate about the game, he never turned into an over involved and controlling "Little League Dad" because he realized that it was just a kid's game.

On the flip side, my dad was my compassionate hero that could seemingly perform magic to solve a perceived crisis. At the conclusion of the soccer season, I received my very first trophy and I was as proud as a peacock. Unfortunately, the same day I received the award, I carelessly broke the soccer player statue atop the trophy. I proceeded to cry like a baby until my dad took care of the problem almost instantly. He found a trophy shop which replaced the broken plastic

250

statue with a solid metal statue. Although in retrospect, it seemed like a relatively logical solution to stop a little boy from crying, it was just one example of my father's expeditious ability to cure whatever ailed me. Over the following years, I went on to play in several private leagues for basketball and baseball, as well, but my father never became a sponsor or an assistant coach again. The new business took up too much of his time and energy.

After being in business for less than a year, Automated Laundry Systems had already sold enough Wascomat Washing Machines to earn two bonus trips through a corporate sales promotion. Seeco and his wife/bookkeeper enjoyed a Caribbean cruise on the Carib Ship which stopped at several islands, including the impoverished territory of Puerto Rico where my dad purchase a silly white beach hat and cheap rum that he never drank. Compared to the Shalom Ship, they found the Carib to be small and unimpressive. Volcanic eruptions nearby caused the waters to be choppy and many passengers—including my mother—became seasick. In the thirty years that had passed from my father's exodus by ship from Bulgaria, his standard of living had been raised so much that a modern cruise ship did not impress or excite him. All future vacations would be measured against the previous ones, so the bar had to be raised in order to wow him.

At the end of summer of 1978, I was about to enter the fourth grade at Calabash Street Elementary School in Woodland Hills. The public neighborhood school was part of the Los Angeles Unified School District that was in the process of instituting an experimental racial integration program. Caucasian, non-Hispanic students would be

251

involuntarily bused across town to predominately non-Caucasian schools to balance the racial mix. The duration of the controversial program was only a few years and was halted after much protest accompanied by many children fleeing to private schools. My parents' first strategy to combat this unpopular policy was to claim that I was of Spanish origin and by definition could be considered Hispanic. Theoretically, this was true, since my father's family lived in Spain until 1492 and Varsano is a Spanish surname. Unfortunately the school officials considered me white, and were going to bus me across the city.

My father was outraged that they wanted to waste two hours per day in order to send me to an inferior elementary school that likely had more violence and less educational excellence. He worked hard his entire life in order to afford a house in a good neighborhood like Woodland Hills, and now they wanted to take away the convenience and the safety of attending a local public school to send me to a bad neighborhood like Pacoima. He didn't understand a system that forced racial integration and tried to solve the greater society's prejudices through the public school system at the expense of performance standards and local community support. Both my parents were dedicated to protecting me from being wronged by recklessly idealistic bureaucrats. My father felt that I was becoming of victim of the educational system just as he had been in Bulgaria. He was determined to give me the educational and social opportunities that he never had.

My parents' solution was to send me to private school, preferably one with a daycare program. The previous year, I attended privately-owned Greenbrier after-school daycare center in the West

Hills area of Canoga Park because both of my parents worked. The previous two summers I had attended Meadow Oaks Day Camp in Calabasas which also had a school. Meadow Oaks was a relatively costly private school but it did have an extended day care program. My father felt that he could afford the extra expense and enrolled me in Meadow Oaks School in the fall.

Once again, my father was willing to sacrifice some of his hard earned money in order to provide a better life for his family. As expenses increased, he would be pressured to earn a higher income, so he was constantly playing a balancing act between work and family. What was more important—spending time or money on your loved ones? When the three of us were on vacation, he could do both. Even though he still worried about his business, he was generally much more relaxed on vacation than he was at home. I had an opportunity to spend long extended periods of time with him, undisturbed by his protracted work hours or my school schedule. It helped me gain an understanding of who he really was when he was unencumbered from the pressure of being the boss. Perhaps, I even caught a small glimpse of my dad in his youth before he was burdened with so many crushing responsibilities.

As the 1970s drew to a close, my grandmother Rachel paid another visit to California. Since her last visit my father had acquired a new corporation, more Laundromats, his wife join the business and he sent his son to private school. Due to the demands of my father's young company, the entirety of the trip was spent in Southern California. A day trip to Disneyland, a viewing of the Rose Parade floats, and an hour-long drive to the Scandinavian village of Solvang,

253

California, was the extent of our travels. While on Crespi Street, my grandmother was cooking up a storm and was going through about a bottle of oil per week. After a month-long stay, the entire family had about enough togetherness and willingly slipped back into our normal daily routine.

My parents returned to their laundry businesses and I returned to private school following winter break. On the weekends, the three of us continued going to local cultural events around Southern California. Since I was an only child, my parents tried to involve me in any day trips that they took. Even though my grandmother Gert would often baby sit me on Saturday nights so my parents could go out with their friends, they tried to be with me as much as possible since I had no brothers or sisters around to keep me occupied.

My parents were typically overprotective Jewish parents— especially my mom. They didn't allow me to play tackle football, ride a skateboard, or purchase a BB gun. Sometimes this attitude was difficult to understand and other times it was downright embarrassing for a rambunctious American kid. On News Years Day 1979, my father's overprotective feelings shined through in a quick glimpse of his strength and heroism.

It was New Years Day and some department stores were open with huge after-Christmas sales. My parents were shopping downstairs at JC Penney's in the Fallbrook Mall while I was upstairs watching the Rosebowl in the TV section. Suddenly, the ground started to violently shake, the lights went out, and there were the sounds of merchandise and fixtures crashing to the floor. The store was packed with holiday shoppers and a small panic ensued. Before electricity was restored or the staff knew what was going on, my father had leaped up the broken escalator and managed to find me amongst the stunned melee of people. Being a small child, I was a bit frightened at the time, and was pleasantly surprised to see my father's bold display of love and concern for his only child. Although we were all a little frazzled, the three of us exited the store unscathed.

Later that year, the three Varsanos embarked on their first major summer road trip together. Like most typical Americans, my big daddy drove an enormous Detroit-built sedan that got about ten miles to a gallon. Nobody cared about gas mileage yet. Although the Iranian hostage crisis and petroleum rationing were still in effect, gas prices were still relatively low. Gigantic cars, recreational vehicles, and family-sized station wagons crisscrossed the nation because trips along the interstate highway system were popular and inexpensive.

We packed up our chocolate brown 1977 Ford Thunderbird full-size sedan with all the essentials—including 8-track tapes for the stereo. Those big plastic box 8-track tapes like the Fiddler on the roof soundtrack and Brazilian music sang in Portuguese by Antonio Carlos Jobim littered the beige interior carpeting of the car. My mom liked music when she was driving, usually R & B and disco. My dad—on the hand—listened to news and talk radio, or whatever my mom wanted to listen to. The three of us drove north until we arrived in the Bay Area. Staying in San Francisco was too costly, so we opted for a room in Corte Madera in Marin County just north of the city. Everyone loved San Francisco and we had a great time being tourists at Fisherman's Wharf, Ghirardelli Square, and the Golden Gate Bridge. I loved the character and diversity of San Francisco as a child and as an adult. The hippies of Haight Ashbury, the street entertainers in the tourist traps, the sourdough bread bowl clam chowder, the exhibits at the Palace of Fine Arts, driving down windy Lombard Street, and simply walking the hilly streets of the city were a good time for the whole family. I even enjoyed eating at the Peppermill restaurant in Corte Madera and playing in the motel arcade which had pinball and early video games like Space Invaders, Tempest and Astroids.

After a couple days in the Bay Area, we ventured into the great Northwest. Navigating our boat-like sedan through the "twisty-turney" mountain roads, we headed towards Eureka. After a few near misses with log-carrying trucks driving the opposite direction, we arrived at the northern tip of California. Eureka was not much of a tourist town but a hearty breakfast at the Somoa Cookhouse with its community row tables and lumberjack clientele was a memorable experience that embodied a different era in California history. The entire family—especially my father—learned about the variety of lifestyles within different regions of the West Coast. The suburbanites of the San Fernando Valley, the farmers of the San Joaquin Valley, the unique city dwellers of San Francisco, and the lumberjacks of the Pacific Northwest were just a small slice of life within California.

A long day's drive through almost the entire state of Oregon put us in Portland for the night. After a quick jaunt through the city, we continued north through Washington State. Mount Saint Helens had just erupted recently and white ash was everywhere. The eerie sight of miles of fields—that was once green and flourishing with vegetation—was now blanketed with a faint gray ash that made it look like a moonscape. Fortunately, there was no danger of an imminent

256

eruption, so we just scooped up some ash as a souvenir and continued to Seattle. Passing quickly through Seattle, we spent the night in Vancouver, British Columbia.

Vancouver was a tourist Mecca with its ample parks and cultural diversity. We caught a quick peek of the island of Victoria, and snapped some photos of flowers and totem poles. Almost all of our photos had at least one family member in them because my father always insisted that "I only take photographs with people in them, if I wanted scenery I would just buy a postcard." It was simply his theory regarding photography; he didn't like shooting static scenery because he felt a professional photographer could take a much better picture. He believed that personal photos of people were more interesting and made the scenery unique and spontaneous. My father was controlling in certain ways, but if I really wanted a "scenery only" shot, then he would have allowed me to take one. Since no reservations were made ahead of time, the vacation was completely spontaneous. Armed with AAA books and maps, we pushed further north, all the way to the Columbia Ice Fields. Riding snowmobile tour buses on ice in the middle of summer was indeed a uniquely Canadian experience.

Even though the Canadians of Western Canada spoke English, they talked a little different up there in the Great White North, eh. The pace of society seemed a bit slower and the people were simpler compared to the hustle-bustle life of Los Angeles. The Canadian people were honest and friendly compared with the paranoid privacy of suburban Southern California. I remember my parents and I having long conversations about a variety of topics for an extended period of time with complete strangers. I remember thinking to myself, "Gee, this never happens at home." Maybe it was due to my parents being more relaxed and gregarious because they were on vacation, but I think the good natured spirit of the Canadian people played a big part.

The weather was very cold, even in the middle of the summer. In many ways Western Canada was similar to northern Washington State, but we would eat at totally different restaurant chains than in America. Smitty's, a chain of family restaurants with promotional toys for kids was the Canadian version of Bob's Big Boy. Since we were on the road just about every day, we lived on diner food, so we became very familiar with Smitty's continental cuisine.

Crossing over provinces, we drove east to Alberta, Canada. Visits to Lake Louise, Banff, and Jasper National Parks showed the breath taking beauty of the Western Canadian Rockies. The pristine mountains, lakes, and rivers of this majestic land were inspirational for us all. My father truly appreciated the natural beauty of the Canadian Rocky Mountains and the cheap prices due to the favorable exchange rate to the Canadian Dollar were an added bonus.

The farthest that we ventured away from LA was Calgary, Alberta where the annual celebration of Calgary Stampede was happening. The whole town was like one big Canadian Cowboy convention. Rodeo and state fair-type events were everywhere which made a suitable climax to our Western exploration. My father was feeling what the old west was like and how elements of that cowboy past still existed in Western America. Generally, he enjoyed the chilly summer sunshine in the Western Provinces and the frontier lifestyle much better than his previous trip to Canada in 1964 where he experienced an overcast and frigid autumn in the urban environment of Toronto in Eastern Canada.

As we headed back towards Southern California, my father felt a great sense of accomplishment by driving such a great distance, without any help from my mom I might add. He ventured to a new place on the globe that he had never been to before and exposed his family to something different and fun. After a thousand mile drive home, my father returned to the daily grind of everyday life packed with pleasant memories but itching to return to work.

With the inauguration of Ronald Reagan and the simultaneously release of the hostages from Iran, a new era of both prosperity and awareness had begun. Although my father was still a registered Democrat, he continued to support certain Republican candidates. My mom would chastise him for not voting for his party just as she did in the Nixon days, but my father was stubborn and felt he would vote his conscious regardless of political party affiliation. My dad—along with the vast majority of registered voters including the so called "Reagan Democrats"—cast his ballot in favor of the former California governor. The Iranian Hostage Crisis had the entire country concerned—as well as my parents. National and international politics was generally not a big concern to my father—except where Israel was concerned. The Hostage Crisis was no different. My father was more concerned with the sluggish economy, and he believed Reagan would do a better job at stimulating economic growth than Carter.

In a few years, the implementation of trickle down economics and a large amount of government spending on defense by the

Republican administration would transform the economy of Southern California. However, in the early 1980's the region was in a recession and the new reality of higher gas prices and the urgent need for more efficient automobiles was a pressing concern. My father's hard work and diversified investments gave our family a hedge against drastic swings in the national and regional economic picture. He earned small business income from Automated Laundry Systems and the Laundromats. He was building equity through his commercial real estate on Robertson Boulevard in Culver City while paying down his mortgage payments with more than the monthly minimum so the principal amount owed would be reduced quicker. The value of our house on Crespi Street in Woodland Hills was also rising along with the rest of the residential real estate market of LA. He invested in two large plots of vacant land in Palm Springs which slowly appreciated in value as the surrounding resort areas became more developed. He had planned to build a small shopping center on this land as soon as all the vacant land around him was developed, but he would have to be patient with the turtle-like desert town growth rate.

In addition to real estate, he held a small portfolio of stocks and bonds. Although his investments in marketable securities were minimal, due to his lack of trust of the fluctuating markets. Most of his cash savings was held in interest bearing bank accounts such as Certificates of Deposit. In the 1970s and 1980s, interest rates were often in the double digits, so simply leaving your money in the bank earned a decent return.

Most of his accounts were at World Savings which had a branch about a mile from our house in the El Camino Shopping Center.

260

My father liked to keep a close watch on all of his assets, so he would make several trips per week to the local branch in the days before ATM machines and online backing. I would often accompany him because there was a bike shop next door and it gave me an opportunity to be one on one with my dad. On numerous occasions, I witnessed his "take charge" attitude that made him so successful in business. If the line in the bank had more than a couple of people waiting, he go directly to the manager and summons her to open another teller window. Instead of the manager saying "Please be patient and wait for the next available teller," like any employee of the modern mega financial institutions would, the helpful manager would usually say "Yes Mister Varsano, I can help you right here." My father had commanded enough respect and financial stature that the manager would personally take care of his transactions at her desk. As a boy— even as an adult—that impressed me and was another sign that my father was a welcomed member of the community.

Now that my parents had more disposal income and their private school son was pressuring them to "keep up with the Jones," they started to make an effort to polish their image a bit. The first step was purchasing an automobile with a touch of prestige. In the wake of the oil crisis of the late 1970s and the poor quality of automobiles being manufactured in Detroit, my father finally broke his policy of only purchasing American-made motor vehicles. In 1981, after selling a Swedish-made washing machine for several years, he purchased a new Volvo GLE Coupe. With its gold European-styled exterior, black leather interior, and sunroof, it was my father's first luxury car. He really loved this car and would eventually log over 300,000 miles with it.

Commuting around Southern California was now done with a tad more style, while vacations become more luxurious and elaborate. In the summer of 1982, the International Laundry and Dry Cleaning Equipment Convention was being held in Birmingham, England. It represented the first in a series of Laundry Conventions that would mix business with pleasure and involved our three person family trekking to various international locales. Clean '82—as it was known—was an excuse for my father to take his family to Great Britain and Israel. He had never been to Great Britain before and had mixed feelings towards the British based on their treatment of the Israelis in 1948. However, when he arrived in England, he found the people to be unsurpassed in their politeness.

We had a storybook journey through the English countryside. We stayed in a Bed and Breakfast on a pastoral farm where the children played with the farm animals and the adults enjoyed hearty home-cooked meals. We visited Shakespeare's birthplace in Stratford upon Avon where we indulged in a spot of afternoon tea. My father carefully maneuvered his steering-wheel-on-the-right rental car through the drive-on-the-left country roads until we reached Warwick Castle. After experiencing a taste of medieval history, we drove onto the rather un-scenic city of Birmingham.

Clean '82—like every other Clean Show—essentially consisted of a few days of my father schmoozing with business associates on the convention floor. My mother and I attended the event as well, but were not part of the meetings. We spent our time at the convention hall

262

picking up freebies from the various booths such as foam balls, pens, and yard sticks emblazoned with corporate logos. After we were finished making our rounds, we walked throughout the convention center eating lousy snack bar food and trying to sneak into other exhibits that seemed more interesting.

After the drudgery of the laundry show subsided, the vacation headed west towards the country of Wales. We arrived at Cardiff, Wales, and enjoyed a day of sight seeing that included yet another castle. The Welsh people were very friendly, but a bit difficult to understand, especially for my non-native English speaking father. After a quick Welsh experience, we darted down to London destined for Heathrow Airport.

The family boarded a plane to Tel Aviv to visit my father's family in Israel for the first time in five years. A week-long stay in Tel Aviv proved to be more of a family gathering than a vacation. We stayed in my Grandmother Rachel's vacant apartment in Bat Yam. She had just recently moved in with a Bulgarian man named Bookoh. My father was glad that his mother had someone to share her elder years with, but didn't have much of a relationship with him. We did go on some token tourist activities, but visiting Israel for my father was more like going back to his old neighborhood rather than being at an exotic Middle Eastern vacation locale. Israel seemed like our home away from home from the the late 1970s to the mid 1980s because of the frequency of our visits there.

Summer vacations to a variety of places had become a regular occurrence, but my mother urged my increasing affluent father to take at least two extended vacations per year. Since business was always

263

slow around Christmas and New Year's my father begrudgingly agreed, and our family made the first of several winter vacations to the Sierra Nevada Mountains of Northern California. Although we had all been to Yosemite during summertime, none of us had experienced the majesty of the great National Park during the frozen season. The peaceful serenity of snow covered granite and the lack of crowds made for a much needed, relaxing escape for my hard working father. We also took the opportunity to go to Badger Pass Ski Resort and take lessons. Subsequent years would bring more winter excursions to Yosemite or Lake Tahoe, but I would be the only one going skiing. Vacations for them were a time for shopping, eating, sightseeing, and relaxing. Exercise and physical challenges were not on their itinerary. Both of my parents—particularly my father—were more concerned with growing their business than learning new recreational activities.

By 1983, my father had been successfully expanding the scope and profitability of Automated Laundry Systems for six years. The small 2,000 square foot office and warehouse that he had originally rented, then purchased, was becoming cramped. He had saved up enough capital to purchase a larger property; it was just a question of location. Although the commute from Woodland Hills to Culver City was becoming more congested with the population growth of the Los Angeles area, he liked the benefits of being in centrally located and municipally incorporated Culver City. He developed a plan to build one 2,000 square foot warehouse on his existing parking lot and another identical warehouse on the opposite side's adjoining lot. The only problem was that the adjoining lot was not for sale and there was a rapidly deteriorating home on it.

264

Fortunately, the Culver City Municipal Government was in the process of implementing a civic redevelopment plan. First, the adjoining house was a residential property in the middle of an area that was zoned for industrial use. Second, the house was decrepit, structurally unsound, and not of historic significance. The city government used its power of eminent domain to forcibly purchase the property and deliberately burned down the house for fire department training purposes. The city eventually sold my father the vacant lot, and the construction of the newly expanded Automated Laundry Systems began shortly thereafter.

The new buildings were quite expensive, but my father was willing to spend vast amounts of money on items that he deemed a good investment or a bargain. Generally, his management style was conservative while his spending habits were practical and controlled. Frivolity and excess were not part of his business plan. That attitude carried over into his personal life as well. Even when he would indulge my wishes and grant me what he perceived to be lavish gifts such as the Intellivision video game system, he would temper my arrogant jubilance with a sobering comment that "I am doing this against my better judgment." Compared to his childhood, I was completely spoiled. So he didn't appreciate comments from me like "I deserve it" or "all of my friends have one." He wanted to teach me that "money doesn't grow on trees," by not spoiling me as bad as my Meadow Oaks counterparts.

In my parent's opinion, I took my lifestyle for granted and had a "toilet mouth." My father especially thought that I was too disrespectful towards him because of the Old World upbringing that he had. In the post 1960s and 1970s era, some lenient ex-hippie parents and a general anti-authority sentiment created children that were much more defiant than the previous generation. Following the lead of the older kids in my neighborhood, I got into quite a bit of trouble. Getting caught shoplifting and blowing up a neighbor's mailbox with my friend Mike Prizzi were a small part of my repertoire. I was constantly being disruptive in class and getting into fights on the playground. At Meadow Oaks when you did something really bad, you were forced to "sign the gray book," which meant your parents were called and you were on an informal probation. Needless to say, I signed the gray book a number of times.

My father was the parent that was responsible for most of the disciplinary action, but he rarely grounded me or punished me very harshly. He would usually take away privileges like the use of my stereo, TV, videogames, or put my bike on a ceiling hook in the garage where I couldn't get to it. Most of the time, I would understand what I did wrong and not make the same mistake again. I was a smart kid and received good grades. The fact that I was an outstanding student saved me from harsher penalties. My father realized that I was a generally a fine son, just a little too disrespectful for his liking. I had inherited his intelligence and some of the defiance that he had in his youth like the time he didn't wear his Jewish star across the bridge.

Of course, the defiant attitude that I inherited was the source of much argument throughout our lives. Parents, who are aware of their own faults, like to say "Do as I say, not as I do." For most part, my father set a great example for me and was truly the only role model that I ever had. We never lived beyond our means whether it was for

266

the sake of me or my parents. My dad would spend far less than he could actually afford while continuing to save as his business steadily progressed.

Inspired by another generous sales incentive program, Automated Laundry Systems had sold a record amount of Wascomat products and earned several free trips to Sweden. An equipment salesman named Roy and a parts manager named Joe had been employed by Automated for several years. Due to Seeco's generosity, Roy and his wife, as well as Joe and his wife, accompanied my parents to Sweden. My mother and father toured the Electrolux factory (Wascomat's parent company) in Ljungby, Sweden. Between the Volvo and the Wascomats, my father was becoming enamored with Swedish craftsmanship. An example of this fascination was the visit to the Orefors crystal and glassworks plant, where he purchased thousands of dollars worth of sculptures and vases. Such extravagance and materialistic enthusiasm would have been very much out of character only a few years earlier especially when he lived in Israel. However, there was sound reasoning behind every penny that my father spent. He was usually frugal with items that were priced high while he was relatively extravagant in regards to purchases priced below the market price. Orefors crystal was much more expensive in the US, which justified in his mind such an indulgence on an unnecessary decoration.

Attractive souvenirs helped transform our home decor from the funky 1970s track house to a glitzy 1980s updated residence. My father employed a German-born carpenter named Franz to custom-build us a floor to ceiling wall unit in the family room and a desk with

267

bookshelves in my bedroom. A semi-gloss rosewood wall unit with display lights and an unused bar was also added to the living room. With two large wall units, there was plenty of room to display the "chachkas" from our family vacations. It also helped my parents impress their friends with a flashy appearance of wealthy objects wherever you looked in the areas of the house where they entertained guests.

They usually had to do lots of cleaning up before guests came over because both of my parents were quite the pack rats. The extra bedroom was packed with old bills and random papers that they were too lazy to file or throw away. If I attempted to clean up, they would stop me for fear that I would throw away something important. I tried to reason with them that a four year old utility bill was not worth saving, but they ignored my pleas. I also struggled to get them to hire a cleaning lady like the rest of my private school friends had. With the support of my mom, my dad actually caved in on the issue of the cleaning lady, but only once every two weeks. He might have been a bit frugal, but if something benefited the entire family, he was willing to pay for it.

Another item that was important to the family and would end up costing my father a pretty penny was me having a Bar Mitzvah. He figured out how to save a little money on Hebrew School tuition by having me attend for three years instead of the recommended five years. My persuasive father explained to the administrators at Temple Aliyah in Woodland Hills that I already knew some Hebrew because he was Israeli and could learn quickly because I was an honor student. Even if I did attend Hebrew School for the recommended five years, I still would have learned very little because of the poor quality of teachers and the lack of enthusiasm by the students. The teachers were merely Israeli women who also could speak a little English but had not been formally trained teachers. There was certainly no standardized testing nor incentives to study. Hebrew School was voluntary and the assigned homework had to compete with regular school homework which was mandatory and much more important for my future.

I usually showed up to class late and was extremely disrespectful to the teachers. They didn't know English slang words, so you could curse in their face and they wouldn't know what you were saying. One day after Hebrew School while I was waiting to get picked up by my mother, some weakling boy carelessly knocked my books into a puddle of water. I could have easily just have beat him up with my own hands, but I was carrying an illegal switchblade knife on me that my friend Brad Prince had recently given me as a souvenir from his vacation in Italy. Brad and I were macho boys who collected knives and played every sport at Meadow Oaks. Instead of punching the kid that soiled my books, I simply pushed the button on the black marbled knife and showed him the small three inch blade. He looked shocked and ran off.

I thought the incident was over, until my parents received a call from the principal of the Hebrew School the following day. I received a tongue lashing and had my switchblade taken away by my parents, but that was about the extent of my punishment. Temple Aliyah—just like Meadow Oaks School—was not going to expel anyone because the parents were paying expensive tuition fees. My father told me that in a similar situation I should use my fists and should not have pulled out a knife—especially one that was illegal. I subsequently gained a bit of notoriety and schoolyard respect at my Hebrew School as the kid who pulled out the switchblade.

The curriculum of the Hebrew School only stressed the teaching of very basic Hebrew vocabulary and a few simple stories of the Judaism, followed by intensive preparation for your Bar Mitzvah. There no was attempt to teach the students to functionally converse in Hebrew. There was also very little history of Israel or Zionism, and certainly no philosophical debate in regards to the Torah or the Talmud. If you really wanted to learn Hebrew, you studied at a language school, took college classes, became Orthodox, or lived in Israel. By the age of thirteen, when most Jewish kids have their Bar or Bat Mitzvah's and drop out of Hebrew school shortly thereafter, I do not recall having any classmates that could actually carry on a conversation in Hebrew despite studying for five or more years. "Hebrew" School was to prepare you for your Bar Mitzvah and earn the temple money. My father recognized that Hebrew School in America was mostly about having a Bar Mitzvah and felt three years was ample time to prepare for the coming-of-age ceremony.

In the midst of my preparations, the family was ready for yet another summer vacation. Only a few months after my parent's Wascomat trip to Sweden, the International Laundry and Dry Cleaning Convention was being held in Chicago. Instead of flying out for a quick business trip, my father continued the annual tradition of combining business with pleasure. Our family loaded up the Thunderbird family-sized sedan and embarked on an adventure reminiscent of *National Lampoon's Vacation*. This was the longest road trip that I ever took with my parents and it tested the limits of our close-knit family. Unlike my parent's cross-country trip of 1969, they were not young newlywed trying to conceive a child, but middle-age parents with a hyperactive thirteen year old boy. On the plus side, my father was much more Americanized by the 1980s than in the 1960s. He didn't stand out like a sore thumb, even in the intolerant rural areas.

The trip began with some low stakes gambling in Vegas, and then abruptly shifted via a short drive to the natural splendor of Zion and Bryce National Parks in Utah. My mostly non-athletic parents and I went horseback riding with the cowboy guides in Zion and hiked through the red rock canyons in Bryce. Despite living in the US for about fifteen years, it was my father's first time in the Rocky Mountain or the Midwest regions of the country. The gnarled orange rock formations of Southern Utah and the gold encrusted Mormon Temple in Salt Lake City were unlike anything that he had ever seen before.

After a few days of leisure and exploration, the pressure was on to get to Clean '83. My now Americanized father bought a cowboy hat in Cheyenne, Wyoming. It was such a stereotypically American thing to do; it showed how much he had assimilated. He never really wore the hat—except at maybe a costume party—so it was not really embarrassing for my mom and I, it was just simply amusing to see this Bulgaria with a big beige felt hat.

We then drove a beeline through flat open plains of Nebraska and Iowa without even having the time to occasionally stop at the quirky tourist attraction. Within a few days of leaving Bryce, the boat-

271

like Thunderbird sailed into the Windy City. Clean '83 was much like Clean '82, a "schmooze fest" for my father and hours of boredom for my mother and me. The one highlight I recall from Chi Town was eating their world famous deep dish pizza.

As a teenage boy, I just wanted to play with my friends. It didn't matter where I was with my parents; I was only a child and wanted to play with kids my own age. Going on vacations with my parents during those adolescent years was where I missed having brothers and sisters the most. Sure the conventions were boring but I was old enough to understand that it was an essential part of my father's business. I just wished I had a sibling to help kill the time. I was mature enough, though, to enjoy seeing new places and later in life would truly appreciate the culturally enriching opportunities that my parents gave me.

After the business part of the trip was concluded, my dad promised us that the drive back would be more scenic and leisurely. The first stop was the Wisconsin Dells, which was a wonderland for a thirteen year-old boy but a nightmare for two grown adults. With its endless array of pinball and video arcades, miniature golf courses, carnival rides, waterslides, and loads of hokey entertainment, my parents had to pull me away kicking and screaming. When they finally managed to get me back into the car, we made a mad dash for the Black Hills of South Dakota.

South Dakota represented a return to the Western frontier portion of our American adventure. We had the time to stop at the roadside tourist attractions that we bypassed on the way to Chicago. South Dakota had the world famous Corn Palace in Mitchell and Wall

Drug out on the plains where we witnessed the grandest electrical storm that any of us had ever seen—white bolts of mythologically inspired electric branches painted across the black canvas of the big sky. A lightening strike had knocked out power at the eclectic drug store, so the miles of billboards that advertised the store's tourist wares were unfortunately hidden in the darkness of the South Dakota night.

Because of the ubiquity of the Mount Rushmore imagery, we were somewhat skeptical about seeing it due to the fact that it might be a pseudo-patriotic tourist trap in the middle of the woods. However, upon visiting Mount Rushmore and Crazyhorse, we were all impressed by the scope and detail of these monumental undertakings. The fact that my father made it a point to see Mount Rushmore further illustrated his patriotism, as well as his desire to learn more about American history and traditions. After my mother purchased some of the famous Black Hills gold that she had been nagging my father about, we cut through Northern Wyoming to Yellowstone and Grand Teton National Parks.

Yellowstone—with its spooky sulfur springs and shooting geysers—seemed like a mystical and magical park. The reality of Mother Nature was vividly displaced for us when we saw a French tourist viciously gored when photographing a bison too closely. The ambulance carried him off, and the three of us proceeded with a bit more caution. The National Parks were generally teeming with foreign tourists that loudly babbled in their own languages. My father gazed at these awkward visitors as outsiders while his fellow American tourists—unlike past years—began to treat him as one of their own. A naïve sunburned man from Wisconsin in a RV once

273

asked my dad for detailed directions to the Old Faithful Geyser, as if he looked like a knowledgeable park ranger. Following a memorable meal at the Jackson Lake Lodge—with its ceiling high glass window view of the Grand Teton Mountains—we made our way back to Utah.

As we pushed further south, the weather in mid summer became oppressively hot. The poorly engineered T-Bird had a radiator that was too small to cool its eight cylinder engine. After logging a few thousand miles on this cross-country journey, our family sedan was starting to bog down. We stopped in Zion again to cool down the engine but when we headed back on the road, the same problem occurred. The air conditioner had been turned off long ago and the heat inside the car had to now be turned on full blast in order to counteract the overheating in the engine. Our little family jaunt across the nation was turning into an exercise in both physical and mental discipline.

Tensions and temperatures were running high as we pulled into Grand Canyon National Park in Arizona. It was the end of three long weeks together, and we were all hot and cranky. My mom was fed up with the car troubles and demanded that my dad "take this piece of shit to a mechanic." He was insistent on fixing the car himself, and I tried to play peacemaker. The pet peeves between us had accumulated to the point where the smallest disagreement could trigger a litany of old resentments boiling over into a huge fight.

The Grand Canyon was awe-inspiring, but after seeing so much of America's natural splendor, we expected it to look like a postcard. We spent a few days in the park and then passed through Flagstaff and Phoenix. On the final leg of our twelve hour drive home, the

274

overheating was a constant worry but a flat tire became a new twist in our American highway saga. In the middle of the Arizona desert, we had a blowout and my father attempted to replace it with the spare. Unfortunately, the same Motor City engineers who designed the small radiator designed an unstable jack. With the wheel off, the jack began to slip as my father held the car up and frantically directed me to pile the extra wheel and rocks under the axle so that the propped up car wouldn't collapse. Somehow, my mechanically-minded father managed to replace the tire and drive into the late night to get us back to the friendly confines of LA.

A few months after returning from another monumental road trip, an important family milestone would be reached: my religious induction to manhood. Unlike the rest of Hebrew School, the intensive preparations for my Bar Mitzvah were very detailed and somewhat difficult to master at times. I had to write my own speech in English about the importance of the ceremony and say a number of prayers in Hebrew. I elected not to read out of the Torah, but still would have to carry the heavy scrolls around the seating area of the synagogue. The Haftorah portion was the most difficult part because it was lengthy and it had to be chanted according to ancient Hebrew musical notations. A man by the name of Mr. Reader was my chanting instructor and he demanded perfection. He supplied me with tapes of the proper intonations and pronunciations which I played and replayed at home while studying. My father would overhear the deep and holy voice of the temple elder emanating from my room and it would remind him of the chanting that he heard as a boy with his father in the synagogue in Sofia.

275

Despite my impressive memorization of the prayers and chants, my father didn't seem surprised or disappointed that I wasn't fluent in Hebrew by the time of my Bar Mitzvah. At least this way, my parents could still speak Hebrew to each other if they didn't want me to understand their secret dialogue. My father was not an intellectual linguist. By that I mean that he learned the six languages that he spoke all out of necessity through forced immersion. Besides speaking to my Israeli grandmother and possibly a few other relatives in Israel that didn't speak English, fluency in Hebrew was certainly not a pressing issue for me. Living in Southern California, learning Spanish was much more important. I was studying Spanish at Meadow Oaks and later continued to study Spanish in high school. Just as my father expected, three years of Hebrew School had adequately prepared me for what I needed to do.

On November 19, 1983, I celebrated my Bar Mitzvah ceremony at Temple Aliyah in Woodland Hills. Even though my father wasn't very religious, he seemed to enjoy the services. It made him nostalgic for the old Jewish rituals of his youth in pre-WWII Bulgaria. The whole father/son dynamic of attending synagogue together reminded him of Sofia except this time the roles were reversed and he played the wise old father. During the service and the rehearsals, he secretly laughed at the American Rabbi and Cantor because they would mispronounce Hebrew words and speak with a thick American accent. It was his little way of getting revenge on everyone who would correct his English. Similarly during Passover Seder when I read the four questions in Hebrew, he would constantly interrupt me to correct my pronunciation.

The Bar Mitzvah day was great. At this stage of his life, my father wasn't a very religious Jew but did enjoy both the religious and secular aspects of the Bar Mitzvah ceremony and reception. He was glad that I had the opportunity to enjoy such festivities, especially because he was never given the opportunity. A grand Bar Mitzvah celebration wasn't the custom in Bulgaria and WWII had just ended when my father was thirteen years old. Bulgaria was devastated by the war and the communist government was taking over, it was certainly no time for a lavish celebration. .

Initially, my father was shocked at the cost and elaborate party planning that went into the special day. The extravagant Bar Mitzvah party was mostly an American phenomenon where it became comparable to weddings, Catholic Confirmations, and Debutantes Balls. He would often lament, "Shulman will pay," which I always believed to mean that I was acting like some stranger was paying for the excess even though it was my dad's hard earned money.

All of the guests and family members joyously danced the Hora at the Westlake Inn adjacent to the golf course, followed by me having the ceremonial first dance with my girlfriend Laura Ramsden. My friends supposedly broke over forty glasses, my Meadow Oaks buddy Chris Gibson was caught chugging a bottle of champagne, and the party climaxed with a huge cake fight. My father was a little shocked at how bratty my friends were but generally had a very good time. None of our relatives from Israel were able to attend, but my grandmother did send a generous gift of several hundred Deutsch Marks. The German currency was part of the war reparations money that victims of the Nazi regime had received. I never thought that I would be the indirect beneficiary of such funds, but when I questioned why I received Deutsch Marks from Israel I was taught another lesson about Jewish history.

After my Bar Mitzvah was finished my father thought that temple membership dues were a waste of money. In Israel and Bulgaria, synagogues didn't charge yearly dues or sell tickets to High Holy Day services. If you were a Jew who wanted to go to services, they would let you attend and whatever amount that you donated was up to you. There were Tzedaka boxes on a table for small cash donations or you sent a check for what you could afford. If you didn't want to give anything that was your prerogative.

For my parents, belonging to an organized congregation was done more for social reasons rather than religious ones. Through Temple Aliyah's Havarah (Hebrew for group of friends) network, my parents befriended several new couples, but paying yearly dues was no longer necessary just to keep their new friends. The entire social aspect of belonging to the congregation was actually more important to my mother than my father. He joined the Havarahs mostly to appease her. This new social circle helped to augment their pre-existing group of immigrant friends that already seemed a little foreign to them.

The following year, the entire family would have an opportunity to travel to the source of the German reparation funds that I had received for my Bar Mitzvah. In the spring of 1984, the Clean Show was being held in Frankfurt, West Germany. My father pulled me out of school a few weeks early and our family was off to Europe. At the age of fourteen, I was able to appreciate a trip to Europe more than I had any other previous family vacations. I was certainly more mature and began to realize that not too many of my peers had multiple opportunities to travel abroad during childhood. I also recognized the fact that international laundry industry conventions were the excuse for going on these privileged European excursions. Still, attending the conventions and the related business activities was incredibly boring for my mother and me. We had grown accustomed to the drudgery of the convention hall but looked forward to the conclusion of the three days of exhibiting because that's when the "good part" of the vacation would commence.

No one in my family had ever been to Germany before and my father definitely held some residual animosity towards the people of Deutschland. However, when we arrived in the former home of the Nazi regime we felt relatively comfortable and the people—although somewhat glum—were more welcoming than many other Europeans. Even though my parents were generally very keen about teaching me Jewish history, we did not visit a former concentration camp. My mother wanted to show me the physical remains of the evil acts of the Nazi regime, but I didn't really want to see such a depressing place and I didn't think my dad did either. First hand accounts were enough for me and real life experience was enough for my dad. The non-business part of our vacations was supposed to be a fun time, and not a mournful experience.

After we were released from the bonds of Clean '84, we jumped into our sporty Opel rental car and made our way around the European continent. My father claimed that he spoke a little Germany as his seventh language of fluency, but after getting lost and asking directions, it was clear that no one in our family spoke German. That fact made driving through Germany and Austria a bit challenging, but not impossible. We enjoyed a taste of sacher torte in Vienna and filled our bellies with wiener schnitzel in Kufstein in the Tyrol. Since we had no reservations and our route was spontaneous, we chose Italy as our next destination.

The easiest way to drive from Austria to Italy was to go through the communist nation of Yugoslavia. Yugoslavia had just hosted the Winter Olympics and was not as feared by Americans as the Soviet Bloc nations. We cut through the northwest corner of this distressed nation, stopping only once in the city of Ljubljana. We went to a "department store" where the shelves were sparsely stocked and the lines were unreasonably long. We made a few purchases of ultra-cheap products like small and modest Olympic pins from the 1984 Winter Games in Sarajevo adorn with no corporate sponsors, as well as carved wooden and brightly painted knick-knacks. The Yugoslavian soft currency was worthless outside their country, so hard currency from West Europe or US Dollars had a terrific exchange rate. Consequently, everything was very inexpensive for us. Unfortunately, most items were poor quality, so even though you could afford anything, there was little that was worth purchasing.

Disappointment by the selection of communist crafts, we drove towards the Italian border city of Trieste. Unfortunately, the Yugoslavian government did not encourage its citizens to leave the country so there were no signs directing motor vehicles to any foreign cities. We were forced to stop at a residence where my father managed to get directions speaking a bastardized Slavic tongue combining elements of Bulgarian and Russian. Our quick glimpse of a communist nation made my father wonder what his life would have been like if he had remained in Bulgaria.

He counted his blessings as we crossed the well hidden border and we ultimately arrived in Trieste, Italy, where the surrealistic events of the day persisted. Trieste—the former international city—was holding the annual Alpinire Festival. The Alpinires appeared to be lumberjacks or mountaineers that dressed in lederhosen-type outfits with green felt hats decorated with various pins. Several were driving three wheeled cars and most were completely drunk and over jubilant. It truly felt like we were in some Disney-inspired cartoon. Suffice to say, there were no available hotel rooms in the whole area.

After an already long day of driving, my father was forced to push onto the next town. Rather than panic, my father handled the situation well despite being road weary. My mother could not drive a stick shift and rarely, if ever, shared the driving duties on family vacations. We arrived late at night in Udine, Italy where there were some remnants of the Alpinire swarm but we did manage to acquire a hotel room. The chef at the hotel held the kitchen open late for us and cooked us one of the most delicious meals that we had ever had. It was the first time any of us had eaten the now ubiquitous pesto sauce.

After an extra long night of sleep we drove to Venice. We spent only one day in Venice where we saw a few of the historic attractions like San Marcos Square but did not have time to visit the Jewish quarter. We took a ferry boat to the island of Murano where the famous blown glass was made. My normally frugal father was wheeling and dealing with the Italian sales people and ended up purchasing thousands of dollars worth of glass sculptures. Just like when he purchased excessive amounts of Orefors crystal from Sweden, his extravagant acquisitions from Murano were motivated by the perception that it was a bargain rather than to simply impress his friends back home. Even if the prices were a good deal, he did get a bit carried away from his usual conservative nature. I suppose that being in a far away place sometimes brings out of side of some one that you've never seen before. We were on the island so long that the rest of the tour groups had left and we were forced to take a boat taxi back to our hotel.

After leaving the canals of the north, we went south to Bologna then Florence. For the most part, everyone in our family enjoyed the delicious food and the warm expressive people of Italy. In Florence, we saw the giant marble statue of David and purchased leather products in the flea markets. Driving in Italy was quite a feat for my father because many roads were cobblestone, lanes were not marked, and an imposing mass of Vespa Scooters and small Fiat cars tried to thrust into whatever space was available. We thought our final Italian destination was Rome but my father informed us that we could not go to the Italian capital because he had to meet a laundry equipment manufacturer in Michelen, Belgium. We had only a few days to drive from central Italy to central Belgium, which was not very conducive to sight seeing.

My mother and I were eagerly anticipating our final destination of Rome with its rich history and myriad of tourist activities. However, my father disappointed us dearly when he informed us that we would be turning around before Rome and heading north to a small boring town in Belgium for business meetings.

We managed to see some designer fashions and fascinating urban architecture as we made a quick stop in Milan. By chance, we ended our next day of driving in Lake Lugano, Switzerland, a place of unparalleled natural beauty nestled in the Swiss Alps. Despite the high prices of the resort area, the whole family wished that we could have spent more time surrounded by the steep snow capped mountains, the clear mirror-like lake with lush green banks, and the quiet serenity that inspires poetry. We rushed through Basel and spent the next night near the train station in the historically rich city of Strasbourg, France. We darted through tiny Luxembourg and low and behold we had finally made it to Belgium.

In Michelen nothing ever came out of the meetings and my father remained loyal to the Wascomat line which he had been carrying for the past seven years. The rerouting of our trip was a total waste of time, but my mother and I—although disappointed—realized that it was part of the package when you attend a Clean Show. Whenever a vacation combined business and pleasure, the business part would usually taking precedence. The fact that my father stayed with Wascomat was predictable because his trait of loyalty persisted throughout his life. With the European portion of our vacation sadly drawing to a close we drove south to Paris, France.

My parents had not been to Paris since my mom's surgeries in the late 1960s. They both had pleasant memories of the great city, but this time the people seemed nastier and the tourist attractions seemed more gauche. The area of Monmarte was checkered with portrait painters wearing berets that seemed too stereotypically French. The Eiffel Tower admission price was high and that was just to walk up the stairs. The charge for the elevator was even higher, so my father decided that we would just take pictures from ground level. The immediate area surrounding the tower was loaded with cheap souvenirs and I convinced my dad to buy me a plastic wind-up flying bird since he wouldn't pay for us to go up the tower. We visited the gaudy Palace of Versailles and dined on overpriced French food while being subjected to terribly rude waiters. The menus at the tourist restaurants were in five languages so most people could read them but the typical French cuisine was mediocre and intolerably overpriced. The table service was poor and waiters were nasty whether you dined at a tourist trap or a local's hangout. Since my father spoke French, he was able to understand the comments that people made behind our backs and developed a somewhat antagonist attitude towards the French people. As we boarded our airplane and flew out of Paris' Orly airport, we were glad to be on our way to Israel.

The style in which we visited Israel was representative of my father's steady upward mobility. This time, Seeco arrived in Israel as an affluent American businessman, rather than an expatriate Israeli. Finally, my father had broken down and rented a luxury hotel room instead of staying with family. We spent about a week in Israel visiting relatives, handing out small gifts, and telling tales of the US. We did take one long drive to the Good Fence border between Lebanon and Israel during the Israeli occupation of the southern part of the war-torn Arab nation. We saw captured tanks conspicuously covered with fluorescent tarps to avoid IDF air reprisals, and truly saw first-hand the might of the Israeli military's power. I tried to take a photograph, but my father cautioned me to put the camera down immediately or the

284

soldiers would confiscate it because it might jeopardize the security of their operation.

My father found it curious that some of the Israeli soldiers had gray hair. These chiseled veterans looked too old to be guarding a border lookout post. Usually, older soldiers or reservists received easier assignments as they age. It just showed how the occupation of Southern Lebanon was extending the resources of the small Israeli fighting force. He wondered if he was still living in Israel, would he have been still been required to serve his milium duty even as the age of fifty-one.

Despite his speculation about reservist obligations, my father was generally in favor of most of the actions of the IDF. He reasoned that the initial military incursion into Lebanon was a justified and a necessary action to suppress cross border attacks by Hizbollah militias, but the lengthy period of occupation and the brutality of regional conflict eroded some confidence in the operation. At the age of fourteen, I pretty much went along with what my father said about Israeli foreign policy, but I was not in favor of Israel being or even perceived to be an imperial power that arbitrarily captured foreign land. The debate raged for years whether the IDF operations in Southern Lebanon represented a military buffer zone or a long term occupation. After a decade of occupation and the deaths of many Israeli soldiers, public support in Israel and many in the US turned against the military occupation.

My father felt almost anything was justified as long as peace with all Arabs had not been achieved. He did not favor giving back any land to hostile Arabs in exchange for peace. He felt it was

285

blackmail. After years of occupation, the IDF unilaterally pulled out in quick order and the Arabs viewed it as a victory. It gave them the reassurance that years of terrorism will wear down the resolve of the Israelis. The IDF placed itself in a "lose-lose" situation in Lebanon despite their military dominance. Just like the US in Vietnam, they won the battles but lost the war. I'll never forget seeing the endless line of captured tanks being towed back to Israel, but a superior army can't stop isolated terrorist attacks. Although a bit scary, it did add a little excitement to what had become a ho-hum visit to the Holy Land.

Excitement of a different sort occurred only a few weeks after returning from overseas. In the summer of 1984, the games of the twenty-third Olympiad were hosted in Los Angeles. Many long time residents feared massive traffic jams and terrorist bombings, so they went on vacation during the two week period. My father—on the other hand—embraced the Olympic spirit and shared his enthusiasm with his family and employees. We endured one hundred degree temperatures and massive crowds to attend the free road race cycling event in Mission Viejo where the US won the gold medal. My parents had preordered the expensive and hard-to-find tickets to basketball games at the Fabulous Forum as well as the track and field events at the Los Angeles Memorial Coliseum. As the whole family caught Olympic fever, we purchased memorabilia such as pins and t-shirts, while my father even decorated his business with large Olympic street banners. It was yet another example of his burgeoning American patriotism. Anyone who was in Los Angeles during the 1984 Olympics will remember a time when the city and its people shined their brightest. I even remember a cop catching my dad speeding on freeway and just giving him a warning. Kudos to the Olympic spirit!

Later that year, the city of Los Angeles affected our lives once again but in a much different way than the joy and success of the Olympics. In the fall of 1984, the Los Angeles Unified School District—in another ill-planned move—decided to expand most high schools from tenth grade through twelfth grade to ninth through twelfth. I was still attending Meadow Oaks School which was private and had a junior high school that went from seventh grade through ninth grade. Of course—like any kid—I wanted to grow up fast and go to high school.

This decision left my parents with a dilemma. The commute from Woodland Hills to Culver City was becoming overwhelming. If they were going to move, they thought it would be best when I was transferring schools. We looked at homes in Beverly Hills and Rancho Park which were only a few minutes from Culver City. Even though my father could afford to purchase a home in these pricey communities, the houses were smaller and older than our Woodland Hills home. Furthermore, after living in Woodland Hills for twelve years, they had friends and relationships that they did not want to distance themselves from—which was further evidence that my father was an accepted member of the community. We opted to stay put and I enrolled in El Camino Real High School which was public. The commuting problem would have to be solved another way.

Although the commute was awful, my dad had become quite familiar with the Culver City area after seven years which lead to valuable knowledge regarding the local real estate market. One

287

particular financial transaction in 1985 exemplified my father's business acumen. A struggling Laundromat on Washington Boulevard near Automated Laundry Systems was listed by my father for sale. The coin laundry business entity was sold and my father earned a generous agent's commission. Shortly after escrow (needed for the sale of a business in the State of California) closed, the inexperienced new owner could not keep the business profitable and my father took ownership for a nominal expense. The landlord wished to negotiate a new lease with my father, but really just wanted to unload the problemed property. My father purchased a 2,500 square foot commercial space plus a fenced parking lot in an all cash sale for the below market price of $35,000. He proceeded to renovate the washers and dryers, then sold the business entity for more than he purchased the entire building which he now owned free and clear. He continued to collect rent as landlord until the lease expired. At this point the area had improved and the properties' highest and best use was not as a Laundromat. The property went through many incarnations including the offices of an architect and La Brea Bakery. For the past several years, the property earned more in net rental income per year than the original acquisition cost.

Around the same time as the Washington Laundry deal, my father had entered a limited partnership with five other people for ownership of another Laundromat. The partners agreed to exchange the Laundromat for a condominium in the burgeoning resort of Palm Desert. For a few years our family enjoyed weekend getaways in the Palm Springs area about once every six weeks according to the negotiated schedule. It was the first time that our family had a

288

swimming pool since I was a baby and the only time I ever played tennis with my father. My dad was a decent tennis player for a beginner, but generally he was overweight and out of shape. He was not really interesting in exercising for more than about half an hour. The highlight of the condominium complex amenities for him was laying in the Jacuzzi.

Unfortunately, the other partners did not utilize the condo as much as we did and wanted to sell it for a profit. Much to my chagrin, the condo was sold a few weeks shy of my sixteenth birthday. My father quickly realized that having lots of money and vacation homes was not the key to happiness. A favorite saying of his was "the only problem money solves is the problem of not having money." He vowed to purchase another vacation home, but never did. Perhaps if he viewed a vacation home as a good investment, then he would have purchased another one. I think he saw it merely as a luxury and a risky investment in a peaking real estate market. Additionally, I don't think that he wanted another property that he would need to take care of because he had his hands full with his other business interests.

Although he never invested in a second home, he did increase our overall level of luxury by not using business as an excuse for a vacation and finally decided to simply take a break. In 1985, our family took its annual summer vacation to the Hawaiian Islands. The lack of any distractions from business related activities was a sign of growth by my fathers and the five-star accommodations were a reflection of his increase in disposable income. More importantly though, both my parents and I had the feeling that the era of our family traveling together as two adults with a child was coming to a close. I

289

had already gone on some vacations separate from my parents with friends on skiing trips. I was also approaching my sixteenth birthday and was determined to get my driver license the same day. My parents realized that being able to drive my own car would mean that I would be more interested in going on vacations with my friends rather than my parents. Our family still might travel together, but future vacations would consist of three adults and most likely be far less frequent.

During my time in Hawaii, I became preoccupied with meeting girls and my parents could sense that their little boy was growing into a young man. We spent several days at the Royal Hawaiian Hotel on Waikiki Beach, Oahu and a few days in a condo in Maui. The whole family had a relaxing and non-business oriented vacation, although my dad would frequently call back to the office for status updates. We simply "lei'ed" on the beach, drank a few tropical drinks, and drove on the infamous road to Hanna.

My parents' relationship had literally taken them around the world and back again. Like any marriage it had its ups and downs. I remember several devastating arguments that I was sure would lead to separation or divorce. As a small three person family that did a lot of traveling together, every argument my parents had between them inevitably involved me. I often acted as the mediator by taking an active role in resolving conflicts. Although I tried to be neutral, I would often make them feel guilty about how their fighting adversely affected their innocent child and how a separation would devastate me. I remember pleading with them that they were "made for each other," and that they had been through so much together between their years in Israel, the hospitals in France, and life in America. A silly argument

290

could not break up decades of love and marriage. I would like to think that my pleas helped to keep them together but I gather that I only illuminated what they were secretly thinking and they knew deep down that the words I spoke were true.

It was just the high emotion of the moment which clouded their judgment and made them say regrettable and hateful things to each other. My father had a bad temper and my mother had a foul mouth, so arguments got pretty damn ugly. Sometimes I would cry and beg them to stop. Sometimes they would stop the yelling only to give each other the "silent treatment," which sometimes resulted in several days of quiet tension. Eventually, level heads would prevail and the conflict would resolve itself.

It was at this point—when my mother knew I was vulnerable—that she would plant seeds in my head about her own personal philosophy on arguments with your spouse. She told me that her parents told her that if you marry a Gentile and get into an emotional fight like the one that she had just had with my dad, the Gentile will call you a "dirty Jew." Her implication was that all Gentiles are covert Jew haters and just need an emotional trigger to release their venom. Of course, I never really believed her but she was certainly insistent and her words stuck in my head.

In retrospect, I can't even remember what most of the biggest arguments were even about or how they ended. I supposed that's why they resolved themselves and never escalated to marriage counseling or worse. In fact, despite much name calling, yelling, throwing of small household objects, they still loved each other and were not only compatible but best friends. No irreconcilable differences existed, no infidelity occurred, and no physically or mental abuse was imposed. They simply had disagreements that seemed to me to be catastrophic and life altering events, but then again I was just a child observing adults at their worst. A large percentage of my friend's parents were divorced and I thought that my parents could be next. Divorces were in vogue during the 1980s in Southern California, but that was just one more example of a trend that my unique parents did not follow.

In fact, trends and fashions were not my father's thing. He certainly never Americanized his name, nor did he spend a lot of money on the latest clothes. He had a simple haircut that remained consistent for several decades. With his new found wealth, he most certainly could have afforded a more prestigious car or a pricier home but chose to build around what he already had.

Part of that building process included developing a social life with a new group of friends. Even though we were no longer members of Temple Aliyah following my Bar Mitzvah, my parents continued to participate in Havarah activities and retained a few lasting friendships, but they yearned for more. It wasn't until the late 1980s when they joined the newly opened West Valley Chapter of B'Nai Brith, that they really became part of a solid group of friends.

Through the B'Nai Brith's Knesset they associated with Jewish couples living in the West Valley with whom they shared common interests. Members of the West Valley chapter were generally well-to-do and threw a lot of large parties. My parents always seemed to have a good time at these parties and other social functions. My father and his friends Mickey Wolf, Leonard Chesler, David Zollman, Bob Sirkin, and Harvey Levine had a lot of laughs together. The group of men

292

would often engage in heated debates about a variety of topics, and they described my father as rather opinionated which doesn't surprise me. Perhaps, David Zollman understood my father's point of view the most because he too was an Israeli. On the lighter side, they said that my father loved when there was a musical presentation at any of their events and appeared to really like to dance with my mother. When his friend found out that he used to play the accordion, they urged him to get one and play it at parties, but he never played again following his father's untimely death.

I never saw my dad dance with my mom when I was around and couldn't imagine him playing the accordion at a party, but he had a social side to him that only came out among peers. I suppose that my parents needed to act a little different with their friends to help balance out their demanding work and family life. In addition to local friends, my globetrotting parents had developed long distance relationships with other Wascomat distributors and employees. My parents finally had a good circle of friends and the financial ability to enjoy themselves.

Perhaps, the comfort of friends was what my father needed to prepare him for the impending tragedy that was to soon grip him. In the bitter winter of 1986, my father received an early morning phone call that left him in complete shock. His mother Rachel had died of congestive heart failure at the age of seventy-eight. She had been the symbol of female strength in his life and he could not believe that she was gone. He wondered if he was in Israel, could he have obtained better medical attention for her? My father was a natural problem solver who had grown accustomed to talking charge of virtually any situation. He felt helpless being so far away from his mother as she struggled for her life. For several years following her death, he carried a nagging guilt about whether he could have made a difference if he had been in the Israeli hospital during the critical hours. After coming to terms with the loss, he realized that he simply could not control everything—try as me might. He subscribed to the philosophy; "there is my plan, there is your plan, and there is God's plan." From a medical standpoint, it probably wouldn't have made a difference because genetic heart disease, years of a rich fatty diet, and old age had taken their toll. He took an emergency flight to Israel to grieve with his relatives and the large mass of friends that attended the funeral. My grandmother was a very popular and beloved woman throughout the greater Tel Aviv area.

The loss of his mother from heart disease also made my father question his own mortality. He realized that weighing almost two hundred pounds was too heavy for even a stocky man at five feet eight inches of height. He agreed to a simple exercise regiment that I diagramed and posted on the refrigerator door. It was quite unusual that my father took advice from me, but maybe he finally realized that I was correct or perhaps my continual nagging took its toll on him. I was an athlete in several sports and my latest focus was on cycling which taught me a great deal about conditioning. I was actually able to impart some the knowledge that I had learned to my father and maybe for the first time he respected my opinion enough to realize that there was something in this world that I knew more about than him.

For a short period of time, I did feel like an amateur personal trainer to my overweight dad, but he needed to get in shape on his own initiative. Simple aerobic exercises coupled with push ups and sit ups lasted for several weeks but his heart wasn't into it. I could not force him. It also would have been useful if he had some friends that were his age that could have been his "work out buddies," but he never sought anyone out and remained in poor physical condition.

Unfortunately, his workaholic tendencies did not transfer to his physical exercising and his business continued to consume the vast majority of his energy. Also, I was a teenager whose social life took precedence over exercising with my non-enthusiastic father. It would take several more years of increased dosages in his high blood pressure medications and a traumatic incident to actually change his eating and exercising habits.

Rather than recognizing that the death of his mother meant that he had a genetic predisposition for heart disease and that he should do everything in his power to help counteract this, he continued the status quo. To help cope with the loss of his mother, Seeco tried to become even closer with his sister. He would make more frequent calls to her in Holon, Israel. He also commented that the older Sarah grew, the more she took on the appearance of his mother Rachel at a similar age.

To numb the pain of the loss of his mother he mostly sought refuge in work, but he also indulged in some uncharacteristic material consumption in the form of a new tropically themed backyard. In 1987, the economy of Southern California had been prospering for several years and nearing a peak. My father's most extravagant display of his new found wealth was the purchase of a gigantic seven person faux-rock Jacuzzi with waterfall that was lifted by crane into the backyard of our Crespi Street house. It relaxed him at first and was symbolic of the material indulgence of the times. One of the most important things that he missed about Palm Desert was the Jacuzzi, so he decided to have one at home. I think he just went a little overboard. The gargantuan water feature was almost as large as a pool, but he thought that it would require less maintenance. It was also a paradox that he was so frugal on most items but blew thousands of dollars on a rock spa. I think that the loss of his mother made him realize that he couldn't take his money to the grave with him, so he might as well enjoy some of it. Also, the doctors told him to reduce his stress and the relaxing warm water and massaging jets did a good job at that.

After much argument from me about years of landscaping neglect, my unpredictably frugal father actually hired a gardener. I was not a shy kid and I had always voiced my opinions, but it wasn't until I reached my early manhood that my father would listen to any shred of advice that I might try to give him. I was always speaking up because according to my father "I had a big mouth." Maybe he was getting older and my years of nagging had finally worn him down or maybe he actually respected my opinions. Perhaps the death of his mother showed him the importance of respecting the wishes of his family members. Listening to my mother and me more often might actually give him a different perspective on things and improve the harmony amongst our family. I believe that a combination of all of those factors enabled me to get my point across and finally get a gardener.

My father believed that anything a gardener could do, he could do better. That boastful "can do" attitude helped him in many situations throughout life, but the demands of working full-time didn't afford him the necessary amount of energy or time for gardening. As

296

one becomes older it seems as if their will and desire do not necessarily decrease, but their capacity to fulfill their desires diminishes. Age was starting catch up with my overachieving dad and for brief moments he could take a step back and live vicariously through the son that was living the life that he never could have.

For my seventeenth birthday, he bought me a brand new jet black Ford Mustang with a red pin stripe, after I drove the hand-me-down 1977 Thunderbird for a year and proved I could take care of a car. My father had affection for Mustangs because it was the same car that he had driven twenty-five years earlier. As I cruised around in that sporty little hatchback, my father couldn't help but see a little of himself in me. When I started dating girls or going to my Senior Prom, my father might have even been a bit envious. After all, he never had the opportunity for a Prom or any of the traditional celebrations of the American high school experience. As a high school graduation present, I traveled to Europe with my friend Chris Gibson which was a luxury my father never enjoyed. His first significant trip on his own was at the age of thirty-one and he paid for it himself.

I was lucky enough to do the things that he never got to do, but he didn't want my spoiled life to make me soft. He still wanted me to have Israeli toughness and "sechel" which was a Yiddish term meaning smarts or intelligence. I think that every father inevitably lives through their son to a certain extent, and does not want their child to make the same mistakes that they made. Unfortunately, I was a stubborn teenage boy that was reluctant to listen to the advice of my father because I felt that his upbringing was so entirely different from mine. He had his unique life and I wanted to have mine. I didn't really appreciate his wisdom and understanding of the universal truths of growing up until I was older. Despite the typical head butting of an adult/children relationship transforming into an adult/adult relationship, I think he enjoyed seeing me progress through life without the stress that he had during the same youthful years.

He would rarely pressure or manipulate me for a specific result, trying to teach by example. He was mostly concerned with broad results. He never said that I needed to get straight A's in school or urged me to lead the league in scoring, but he expected me to live up to his high standard in everything that I did. There were no hard and fast rules, just an implicit understanding. Sometimes that was frustrating because I was never sure what exactly he expected, but that was just the way he was. He never liked to itemize his goals and expectations in business or in fathering because he was afraid that it would be used against him or I would rest on my laurels once I had achieved something. In one way I was competing to live up to him and in another way he lived through me.

In June of 1988, I graduated from El Camino Real High School and would be enrolling in the University of California at Santa Barbara in the fall. My father was proud of my accomplishment and that I was the first Varsano to attend a university. 1988 was a year of transition for not only me but for my father as well. He had finally found a solution to his time-consuming commute to work. Rather than move his residence, he would move his business. The Robertson Boulevard area was becoming more of a high rent commercial district and less of an industrial location suited for a laundry equipment company.

Customer parking availability on the street was difficult because so many businesses had moved into the area.

The decision was made to rent the three buildings on Robertson Boulevard and relocate the business closer to Woodland Hills. After being outbid in the super hot real estate market of the late 1980s, my father was able to purchase a large 10,000 square foot warehouse and office building with an additional 10,000 square feet of parking on Fulton Avenue in North Hollywood which was located in an industrial area just a few miles from our old apartment from 1971. The building was being used as a factory for the manufacture of intercom equipment which employed about eighty people. My father would be moving in only five full-time employees but lots of heavy commercial laundry equipment and a drive to expand into his new ambitious space. In the extra space of the rear parking lot, he planned to eventually build a loading dock for large trucks and a small factory that he had wanted to construct since his initial trip to the US in 1964.

The future looked bright and the road ahead held no visible obstacles. Business had never been better, I was off to a respectable university, and there were lots of new friends to enjoy the good times with my parents. They weathered the storm and seemed to be growing into middle age quite well. Although some health problems affected Seeco, it was just another responsibility that my parents would adequately manage together. The 1980s were a time of unbridled prosperity and worldwide adventure for our family. Although the workaholic nature of my father overwhelmed many occasions, the fond memories of family vacations seen through the cleansing mirror of reflection symbolized the decade from my perspective.

299

CHAPTER 14

Choppy Waters in North Hollywood

A s the year 1988 concluded, my father had an optimistic outlook and a prospering business. Unfortunately, the economic boom had hit its peak and Southern California would soon endure a crippling recession. At the conclusion of the 1980s, the economy in Southern California fundamentally changed. The Cold War was over and the demand for defense contractors had diminished. That structural change in the local economy coupled with the cyclical downturn created a stinging recession across the board. In the laundry business, an over saturation of coin laundries, increased water/sewer charges, and price wars caused the industry to be much less profitable than it once was. To combat the rapidly shrinking profit margin and negative outlook, my father decided to search for related revenue sources within his industry and area of expertise.

In the summer of 1990, I was in between my sophomore and junior years of college and in need of a summer job. My father had recently hired a new salesperson named Paul Bottone that formerly worked at another laundry company that specialized in apartment building laundry room contracts. He was younger than most sales people in the industry and my father thought that I would work well with him. My father uncharacteristically gave him perks such as a company car and actually allowed him some autonomy in regards to establishing the apartment routes. Over the past years my mechanically minded dad/boss also had trained several competent service technicians. An Italian immigrant named John Paul—who arrived in California with meager skills and a poor command of the English language—turned into one of the best servicemen that the company ever had. My dad used to say "If I had another three John Pauls, I would stop selling machines and just become a service business." Unfortunately, many members of the service staff would leave Automated for a higher paying job when their personalized training was over. Other technicians such as Steve the alcoholic, or Craig the overzealous Raider's Football fan, were skilled on one level but ultimately unreliable.

The decision by me to take a job in the family business was more voluntary than compulsory. My father encouraged me to take a job elsewhere the previous summer, but by the summer of 1990 I felt I was experienced enough from other part-time jobs and my business economics studies to contribute to the business in a material way. During this summer of immersion into Automated Laundry Systems, I was taught gems such as "Don't give customers anything for free because then they come to expect it," and "There's a fine line between honesty and stupidity." In reference to the latter, my father was by no means a liar or a dishonest person, but he was trying to explain the nuisances and shades of gray that a salesman must use to be effective. Often what is not said was as important as what was said. Although working in a family business was a stressful and relatively underpaying proposition, I learned a lot about the laundry industry and the daily struggles of running a small business. Despite the inevitable friction between a cocky college student and a stubborn father, I believe he was happy to have me on board.

Although the national economy was beginning to falter and my dad's business was looking to diversify, overall sales of Wascomat machines—the staple product over the past twelve years—were still relatively strong. The previous year's sales were brisk enough for Automated Laundry Systems to earn several Wascomat-sponsored tickets to Spain. My father's first and only visit to his historic homeland was a typical tourist vacation. Although he was able to speak to the Spaniards in their native tongue, he was forced to spend the majority of his time in Spain with business colleagues. Bus tours to the Costa del Sol, Granada, and Seville were supplemented by flamenco shows and group dinners.

I found it interesting that my family was exiled from Spain in 1492, and no one returned until almost 500 years later. Being that my family had carried a Spanish name for hundreds of years, I would have been naturally curious to explore my roots on the Iberian Peninsula if I had the financial where-with-all to do it. Unfortunately, my father was forced to focus on business networking activities instead of roaming freely around the country. Even though my father was intelligent and well traveled, he was much more of a businessman than a scholar. He had the opportunity to spend additional time in Spain if he chose to pay an extra fee, but he felt compelled to get back to his sputtering business as soon as possible.

The next year sales dropped but were still sufficient enough for him to earn an "Outstanding Salesman of the Year" award, and for my parents to take a second complimentary cruise through the Caribbean.

This time Wascomat sprung for a fancier cruise ship called the SS Norway. My parents enjoyed this trip much more than the previous one because the accommodations were more luxurious, there were less business-related activities, and they knew even more of their fellow Wascomat salespeople. They spent day and night with their vacation buddies, Avner and Carol Wolanow. They also befriended a Puerto Rican-American distributor from the New York area named Angel. Since a yearly Wascomat trip had become a tradition, they had established friendships with fellow distributors, as well as Wascomat employees. Their long term relationship resulted in a higher comfort level and constituted part of the payoff for their years of loyalty. After the cruise, they traveled around Florida—stopping at Epcot Center and Orlando. With the national economy headed towards a recession, the Caribbean cruise marked the end of promotional trips from Wascomat which served to sour the relationship with their distributors.

In fact, this was the beginning of the end of Automated's exclusive and profitable relationship with Wascomat. Wascomat's policy of loyalty and cooperation was forced to change due to the nature of the national economy and competition from other laundry equipment manufacturers. As the 1980s fell and the 1990s rose, the times were indeed changing on both a national and international level.

After the fall of the Berlin Wall in 1989, all of the former Soviet satellite nations began to follow suit. My father felt that the dismantling of the Iron Curtain was inevitable once the Glasnost of the Soviet Union became apparent, but he certainly wasn't overjoyed about it because he didn't really know anyone personally stuck in the communist bloc nations. Furthermore, any Jew who lived in Europe during WWII was understandably apprehensive about a united and more powerful Germany. Realistically though, he was not too worried about a repeat of the Holocaust or the rise of a fascist government, but was not jumping for joy over the emancipation of the oppressed East Germans.

He was happy that the Cold War was over and that the world—theoretically—should be a safer and freer place to live for everyone. I was a freshman in college when the collapse of the Soviet Union began, and subscribed to a philosophy of neo-hippie idealism. "Right here, right now there is no other place I'd rather be, watching the world wake up from history." A song lyric from that era summed up my optimistic view of the world following the fall of the Berlin Wall. I hoped that the world—as a global community—had turned the corner and the oppression of the past would never be repeated again. I felt the elusive goal of world peace could actually be achieved, while my dad took a much more realistic approach. It was a classic case of the conservative wisdom of age versus the liberal idealism of youth.

While my father and I debated the theoretical merits of globalism, the end of the Cold War did have a direct effect on our family. Monumental world events again influenced my father's decision making but this time it was simply regarding a vacation. By the summer of 1990, Bulgaria had opened its borders, and my father decided that it was finally time to return to his place of birth. The Varsano journey through Eastern Europe began in Munich, West Germany.

We rented a Mercedes Benz 190 L and drove south to Vienna, Austria. Although my father would have never purchased a German

304

car on moral grounds, he could justify merely renting it for a couple of weeks. He had never driven a Mercedes before and was a bit curious about the famous German automotive engineering. Just as he enjoyed his quick Mustang in the 1960s, he wanted something with a little pep for driving on the speed limit-free Autobahn. Also, I think he wanted to return to his homeland in a bit of style, not in a pretension way but enough to show that he had achieved substantial resources.

After a couple of days of enjoying modern Western Europe, we gingerly crossed through the former Iron Curtain. However, the strongly anti-Semitic nations of the former Soviet Bloc—namely East Germany, Poland, and Romania—were not on our tourist agenda. We spent a few days in Budapest, Hungary, where we stayed at a luxury hotel that was trying to keep up to Western standards. The tourist programs were a bit amateurish because for decades they only needed to cater to a meager amount of visitors. There was a lack all-inclusive tour packages to capitalize on the well-to-do tourists spending habits. Few restaurants had multi-lingual menus or local cuisine that catered to foreigners.

Like much of the market economy reforms, a new tourist industry had to basically be built from scratch. The programs and tours that did exist were cheap imitations of Western-style sightseer activities. In Budapest, our tour bus broke down and the driver got lost during a short four hour drive around the city's monuments. Most of the tour guides lacked the language skills to converse with a wide range of foreign-speaking tourists. For the most part, if you didn't speak German, French, or English then you were not going to understand any audio portion of the tour.

305

There was a general lack of amenities and money-making opportunities at the few tourist destinations that did exist. There were no T-Shirts that read "My parents went to Budapest, Hungary, and all they got me was this crummy T-Shirt." I don't know if the lack of cheesy souvenirs was a good or bad thing, but I had grown accustomed to seeing those typical items at every other tourist location that I had been to around the world. Some of the items for sale were unique such as local handicrafts, but rarely did they design products to be a memento of a particular monument or city that we could bring home and said "I was there."

After an exhausting day of wandering around the city and my mother being disappointed by the lack of jewelry to buy, we plopped down in the lobby of the four star hotel where we were staying for a short rest. We soon realized that the lobby was loaded with prostitutes and gangster pimps milling about trying to blend in with the patrons and look classy in their sequined mini-dresses and broad shouldered suits. They just looked cheap and overdressed while they stood out like a sore thumb.

Despite the city's shortcomings, you had a sense that it had a proud past and would rebound relatively quickly with the help of democracy, capitalism, and foreign investment. The neo-Gothic and neo-Renaissance architecture in Budapest was magnificent even though most of the older buildings were covered in a layer of thick black soot from years of unregulated pollution. The vast majority of cars still ran on leaded gasoline and God only knows what the factory smokestacks were spewing out. Contrasting the poisonous byproduct of man-made machines was the harmony that skilled architects, engineers, and craftsman created with their beautiful bridges across the Danube River. The semicircle of statutes in Heroes' Square and the dominating grandeur of Parliament building were standing examples of the country's proud past.

You could sense that the Hungarian people's rich past had been stymied for decades and now that they had the freedom to determine their own destiny, there was an anxious uncertainty about how to proceed. My first glimpse at the overreaching influence that the Soviet Union used to suppress the natural aspirations of a neighboring country was disturbing. I had a reluctant compassion for them because on the one hand they were poor and had been oppressed for a generation but I was also taught to be distrusting of communists. The Soviet Union had collapsed, but there were still many communists that were plotting for a resurgence while many of the former communist countries were only making slow and cautious reforms.

Continuing south, we entered the Serbian portion of Yugoslavia. We stayed in a spectacular Hyatt Regency in Belgrade with all the finer amenities of home. There was a large TV in each of the two king-sized bedrooms, as well as in the living room. The two bathrooms had a Jacuzzi tub with a separate shower, a telephone by the toilet, and each closet was supplied with white terry-cloth bath robes and matching slippers. Every morning, a complimentary *USA Today* newspaper and a deluxe fruit basket was delivered to our door. To round out the luxurious experience, the lobby was crawling with beautiful female models because of some fashion show that was happening nearby.

Yugoslavia—although communist—never became a full fledge Soviet satellite and you could see and feel this in the people. It was certainly more plentiful in Serbia than the other regions of Yugoslavia and neighboring communist nations. There was a great selection of available dishes at the local restaurants and there didn't appear to be any significant shortages of any products because there were no huge lines of people in front of retail locations. There were even some signs of foreign investment from the West with familiar corporate logos conspicuously displayed on prominent buildings. The Serbs appeared to be a proud people that had not retained the melancholy demeanor of their neighbors who had been beaten down by being on the losing end of the Cold War. Belgrade was the capital of Yugoslavia and the people enjoyed the spoils of being in the seat of power. In 1990, the people of Belgrade were still prospering under the old systems and had very nationalistic tendencies. Many took pride in keeping Yugoslavia united under Serbian rule at all costs—despite the brutal regime of Slobodan Milosevic.

After a day in Belgrade, we entered my father's homeland. At the border crossing, we handed the guards our US Passports and waited. All of the border guards came over to inspect our passports and then broke out into a round of hearty laughter. When they returned with the passports, they asked my father in Bulgarian, "How were you able to emigrate out of Bulgaria." They had noticed that he was born in Sofia and had apparently never seen a native Bulgarian of US citizenship return to this impoverished Balkan state. My father explained his story to them, everyone had another laugh, and they waved us into their beleaguered country.

My father was fifty-seven years old and had left the country when he was only fifteen. He was actually worried that the government would hassle him about not serving his required military service. As outlandish as it seems, he could never quite trust the Bulgaria authorities based his past experiences. He had lots of cash hidden in various pockets in case he needed to bribe his way out of a situation. Luckily, it was not needed. We also carried several gallons of extra gasoline in containers in the trunk of the car because of the fear of gas shortages and petty criminals siphoning the gas from our tank.

We had reservations at the Novotel which was supposedly a four star hotel. When we arrived, the lobby was filled with gypsies and other impoverished Eastern Europeans that were chain smoking cigars and cigarettes. On the elevator ride up to our room, a shifty-looking man was brazenly smoking a cigarette in total disregard for the clearly marked sign that prohibited it. My mother—who was very sensitive to smoke—told the man that he was not supposed to be smoking inside of an elevator. He belligerently responded in broken English, "What are you, doctor?" and proceeded to shamelessly puff away, but luckily exited the enclosed lift on the next floor.

When we entered our room, the air conditioning did not work properly and the windows did not open. The television only received one signal which showed a test pattern line while you heard communist news in Bulgarian. I was curious to hear what kind of news that they received but Bulgarian was the only language spoken on the local station and they didn't have English language newspapers available in the country yet. The only things that were in English were

309

the limited number of tourist brochures that were also written in French, German, Russian, Spanish, and several other unrecognizable Slavic dialects.

After several days in formerly communist countries and the utter disappointment of arriving at our ultimate destination, my mother was totally fed up. She was accustomed to certain amenities as a traveler that she wasn't getting on this unusual trip. She sometimes had a tendency to get bratty and the atmosphere at the Novotel was the final straw. As soon as we were alone in the room, she immediately threw a tantrum and threatened to leave the country. My father and I—although more tolerate of the rough conditions than she was—were not too pleased about the accommodations either. Apparently, the Bulgarians have a different interpretation of a four star rating.

Our only other option was to stay in one of the country's two five star hotels. We chose the Japanese-owned New Otani and rented a two bedroom suite for several days. The room had to be paid for with hard currency—preferably US Dollars or Deutsch Marks—while meals in the hotel were paid for with Bulgarian currency. The results of this arrangement were that the room cost about $250 per night while a full five course meal cost about $1.50. Hard currency was in high demand because you could exchange it outside the country which made acquiring foreign-made products much easier. The currency of most of the communist countries was worthless outside of that particular country which meant American tourist dollars were like gold. Opportunistic black market currency converters would accost us in the hotel lobby offering a better exchange rate than the hotel or other legitimate services. Consequently, Bulgarian citizens that were not employees of the hotel were not allowed in the lobby because of fear of theft or illicit money exchangers. Spending our valuable hard currency on the luxurious room was well worth it. The hotel was first class and it served as the focal point to any social activities that we were able to engage in while in Sofia.

There were no organized tours of Sofia, so my father gave us a personal tour in our rental car. Unlike his trip to Spain a few months earlier, he did try to retrace his past in Bulgaria in order to show my mother and me. He was a bit nostalgic, but he was generally not a very sentimental man. Unfortunately, the Bulgarian government had changed every street name to honor communist generals and political leaders which was reminiscent of the street name changes that honored the fascists of the 1940s. Sofia in 1990 was a city of neglect. Over forty years of communism made its citizens lazy and apathetic. There was no incentive to work hard; you received the same pay no matter how hard you worked under the communist model. The people didn't trust anything that the government promised them after living through fascist then communist regimes. A few protesters were even nostalgic about their former monarchy and were optimistic that bringing back King Boris' son Prince Simeon II would return Bulgaria back to its former glory.

In fact, the monarchist's efforts proved somewhat fruitful because Simeon did return to Bulgaria after spending decades in exile. On June 17, 2001, King Simeon II of Bulgaria won the Bulgarian parliamentary election with promises to improve the lifestyle of Bulgaria's 8 million people, and prepare to bring the country into the EU and NATO. Since the vast majority of the country did not want a

311

monarchy, Simeon Saxe-Cobourg became Prime Minister and leader of the National Movement Party. Simeon was the first of the former European monarchs to lead a political party to victory with a platform that promised to turn the economy into a working market economy, abandon political partisanship, and to eliminate corruption. In a passionate statement he said "For decades, I have suffered, as you, our unhappy fate. But I have never lost my belief in a free and strong Bulgaria. I was happy at the end of 1989, when the dictatorships collapsed, and in all Eastern Europe opportunities for dignified and successful life returned. It was painful for me later to see how the dreams in Bulgaria have been replaced by poverty and desperation."

Political rhetoric aside, Simeon has made some progress on transforming Bulgaria. Bulgaria recently was admitted to NATO and a close alliance with the US has helped spur foreign investment. Even before Simeon's government took power, the Bulgarian economy was slowly improving. Since the mid 1990s, per capita income and Gross Domestic Product have been steadily rising despite being low by European standards. The unemployment rate has slowly been declining while tourism—surprisingly enough—has been increasing due mostly to the popular beach resorts along the Black Sea.

When we visited Bulgaria, my father wanted to take us to the coastal resort town of Varna on the Black Sea which was a vacation spot for my father's family as a child, but the driving distance from Sofia was longer than a tank of gas would take us. Despite having about five extra gallons of gas in spare tanks in the trunk, we decided to stay in the greater Sofia area to avoid the possibility of running out of gas and waiting for days to refuel. Bulgarian gas stations at the time

312

were suffering from severe shortages. People would park their cars in line in front of the station and sometimes wait for days to refuel. We drove by one gas station and saw long lines of frustrated Bulgarians sleeping in their cars, fixing their jacked up cars, some cars were empty but in line, and the most peculiar thing about this unreasonable long line to buy gas was that the gas station was not even open.

The public transportation system was an even worse transportation option. The trolleys and trains seemed to consist of the same 1940s era equipment of my father's childhood which was maintained in only the most basic working order. There were no traditional souvenir shops, only stores that sold essentials. When we wanted to purchase a hat or bowl, the shopkeeper was impatient and unwilling to be helpful. The more we purchased, the more resentful they became because they didn't receive any more pay or better job security, and they just had to work harder with no incentive.

We took a day trip to the ski resort of Mount Vitosha which was just a few miles from the center of Sofia. Even though it was summertime, the weather up on the top of the mountain was very cold. I realized how cold the climate in Bulgaria could be during the non-summer months and how different the climate was from the warmth of Israel and Southern California. I also could see a bird's eye view of the Bulgarian landscape and the greater Sofia region.

It was truly a beautiful country with lots of green sloping hills and small farming plots. The majority of the country was still an agrarian society that looked like a series of quant farms strewn across a rich land. Contrasting the scenic countryside was the reality of city up close with its run down public transportation system; pollution stained

313

buildings, half constructed or debilitated projects, corrupt government bureaucracies, and a disenchanted populace.

Like almost everything else in Eastern Europe, the resort of Mount Vitosha was not comparable to the standards of any Western ski resort that I had visited. I ordered a hot chocolate to warm myself up a little but even that was a disappointment. The hot chocolate—like the rest of the country—was lacking of the necessary amount of ingredients. It looked like a pale version of a Swiss Miss hot chocolate but tasted like a watered down brew that suffered from a shortage of sugar and cocoa. It seemed like the poor citizens of Bulgaria were living under the same strict rationing standards as in WWII.

After I poured out the rest of my hot chocolate, I saw my father leaning against his rented Mercedes-Benz sitting high atop Mount Vitosha. I wondered whether he fantasized about returning to the heights of his hometown or if he had a chance to envision an idealistic Bulgaria. Here he was coming back to his former home as a triumphant American citizen, enjoying the spoils of the victors in a German-built car and staying at a Japanese-owned hotel. From his perch on the Bulgarian peak, he looked down upon the country that had once oppressed him. You could almost see a glimmer in his eye dreaming about "What if?" What if WWII and fascism had never reared their ugly head in Bulgaria? Would he still be living in Sofia? What if Germany had been more successful in pressuring Bulgaria to deport their Jews during WWII? Would he have been alive to see this day? As he quietly contemplated these awesome scenarios, he counted his blessings, gathered his family, and zoomed off in his little blue sports car to indulge in a lavish five course meal at the luxury hotel where we were staying. Life as an America had been pretty damn good to him considering the alternatives. He did miss some nostalgic memories of his youth, but certainly did not yearn to live in his homeland once again after finally returning for the first time in forty-two years.

My father did manage to locate his old apartment and his synagogue. His apartment building looked the same as it did fifty years earlier. The synagogue was in disrepair after looting during WWII and forty years of neglect. There were scarcely any Jews left in Sofia. Those who remained were communists or intermarried. We did meet the synagogue caretaker, who explained the reasons for the decay and my father made a contribution.

Overall, my father was rather disappointed with what had become of his once beloved country. For years, he held a romanticized memory of his homeland that he had reconstructed from his early childhood which was starkly replaced by the reality of an impoverished communist country that was actually much worse than he remembered. Although he was aware of the pitfalls of the country's old economic system because he lived under three years of communism, he hoped that a transition to a market economy and a modernization to the standards of the Western World would be smoother and faster than it actually was. Years of living in the US had made him accustomed to fast results, smart marketing, and a certain level of luxury.

He was frustrated with the lack of smart reforms and the utter confusion over the street names being changed. The idealistic stupidity of the communist system had destroyed the plentiful land of his youth.

315

Under communism, the only way to get ahead was to break the law, so the craftiest elements in their society were also criminals which resulted in a plagued corrupt culture that would take many years to reform.

His disappointment was reinforced when he—by chance—ran into his uncle Shlomo and cousin in the lobby of the New Otani Hotel. His father's brother had spent a month in Bulgaria staying in an old friend's apartment. The eighty year-old man had waited over forty years to see his old friends and the country where he had spent half of his life. He complained about shortages of food, gas, cigarettes, and other important items. He wanted to cut his vacation short and was completely shocked at the poor living conditions. This was not the homecoming my father had expected, but it made him glad to be an Israeli-American.

After we drove out of the traffic jammed border, we re-entered Yugoslavia, which was going through a tense transition. We spent a night in Skopje in the Macedonian region of Yugoslavia. It seemed like a fruitful paradise compared to Bulgaria. Skopje was a very picturesque town with a visible Ottoman Empire influence. We drove through the parts of Macedonia that were annexed by Bulgaria during WWII which corresponded to the reverse route of the exiled Jews who were deported through Sofia on route to the death camps at Treblinka. Not surprisingly, my father was able to converse fluently with the Macedonian people, but certainly didn't talk about politics.

We made our way up the west coast of Yugoslavia along the Adriatic Sea until we reached Split. We enjoyed steep beach cliffs along the Adriatic Sea with quant small villages and towns that had

316

ancient architecture and great beach resorts. Split was a scenic coastal resort town in the Croatian region of Yugoslavia. We stayed at a first class hotel that had a shortage of fresh water. When you turned on the faucets only salt water flowed out of the pipes. There were massive shortages of food and only one or two dishes could be ordered. As we drove through the countryside going north through Bosnia, people were driving erratically and there were mass gatherings in the fields. People were waving Yugoslavian flags with the center emblem cut out while chanting loudly in unison. We were quite ignorant of the impending civil war that would result only a few weeks later. Over the next few years, these historically independent regions would break off from the Serbian-dominated Yugoslavian authority and become sovereign nations.

We finally left Yugoslavia after spending a final night in Reyaka in the Slovenia region. My father had distant memories of northwest Yugoslavia because in 1948, his family embarked on their Aliyah to Israel from a port near Reyaka. He didn't remember too much about the place because the last time he was there, he was not doing much sightseeing. All of the Jews were just trying to keep a low profile and expediently make their way to Israel. Many years later, the west coast of Yugoslavia appeared to be a peaceful vacation-goers paradise, but the underlying hatred would soon boil over into an ugly civil war. Our ignorance of the political turmoil helped us glide through the country with a minimal amount of fear and we were lucky to leave before any of the fighting started. After a quick lunch run through Italy and a few more nights in Austria and Germany, it was back to the friendly confines of the US.

317

Unfortunately, home was not as warm and friendly as it once was. Southern California was the last region of the country to feel the crushing national recession. The financial pain of the nation—and indeed the world—was now felt from the shores of the million dollar beach homes to the hills of the Hollywood mansions. Many of the lower middle class and the working poor lost their homes entirely and were desperate for some good news. As almost every American felt the sting of the economic downturn, the majority temporarily forgot their worries to band together in order to support our troops in Operation Desert Storm.

My dad really did not express any strong opinions about the war. As a former Israeli, he was supportive of the IDF bombing of the Iraqi Nuclear Reactor in 1981 because he knew Saddam Hussein was an enemy of the Jewish people and Israel. The world would be a much safer place without nuclear weapons in the hands of such a tyrant. However, the nation of Kuwait was no friend of Israel or the Jewish people either. He was not gung-ho about American young men—that were the same age as me—dying in order to reestablish an Arab monarchy.

There was the possibility that the draft would be reinstituted and that worried him as well. There was a general fear of the unknown and the potential for an escalation into another Vietnam. The US military had not been engaged in a large scale operation since the days of Vietnam, and the concept of an all volunteer Armed Forces had not yet proved feasible for a victory in a sizable war.

At the time, I was a liberal Democrat college student that followed the Grateful Dead around the country and did not support the

318

concept of war much at all. I wasn't about to risk my life for the economic security of cheap oil and the political autonomy of an oppressive country like Kuwait. My father didn't think much of the peace protestors because the war was too short to build up any sense of an anti-war movement like during the Vietnam crisis.

My family—like most Americans—watched the video game-like images on CNN that made the fighting seem sanitized and painless. While we were happy to see a US-led coalition oust Iraqi troops from oil-rich Kuwait, we were horrified when Saddam Hussein launched Scud missiles at Israel. My father was quite surprised when Israel did not strike back due to the US pressure to maintain the sanctity of the tenuous coalition. The depersonalized TV war began to hit home when a Scud missile was reported to have landed in the Tel Aviv suburb of Holon. My father watched the TV images in horror realizing that this war to liberate a non-democratic Arab state was now resulting in missiles landing in his sister's neighborhood. He immediately tried to contact Sarah, and after some anxious moments of busy signals, he learned that the missile landed several blocks away.

Once Israel was attacked by Iraqi Scud missiles, my father and I strongly supported the US-led Operation Desert Storm and hoped that they would go further than the stated mission objective of liberating Kuwait, and continue onto Baghdad to overthrow Saddam's evil regime. As it turned out, the victory was a route, and many Americans—including my father and myself—theoretically rallied around the victorious troops as we watched the CNN TV show war. Despite our pre-war apprehensions, I guess that everyone likes a

319

winner especially when its quick, decisive, televised, and apparently antiseptic compared to the brutal images of Vietnam and WWII.

A few months later, pictures of a different kind of suffering would be beamed into our living rooms as a war-like atmosphere engulfed the mean streets of Los Angeles. Even though the Gulf War was viewed as a rousing military success that helped America regain some prestige lost during the Vietnam War, the country's economy did not rebound. With Los Angeles mired in economic doldrums and years of a purportedly racist police department furthering civic tensions, the conditions were ripe for an ugly nationally televised riot. A Black motorist named Rodney King was severely beaten by several White policemen and the whole incident was caught on videotape. The entire nation was outraged, but the longstanding Chief of Police Daryl Gates was a blunt and defiant which only exacerbated the problem. The same police department that used bigoted comments against my recently immigrated father during the 1970s had never undergone any effective reforms to address the systematic issues of racism.

When the policemen who administered the beating were not found guilty, many angry citizens started shooting and looting. Los Angeles seemed to be at its worst during those few heated days in April of 1992. My father's building on Washington Boulevard was in a predominately Black neighborhood and according to the current tenant; the local gang contemplated burning down the building but luckily chose another one nearby. In the midst of the madness, my stubborn father had previously scheduled to have a booth at a laundry convention in Cerritos and he was determined to drive across the city despite the urban uprising around him. Practically nobody attended the event and my work-at-all-costs father wasted his time, but at least he returned home safely. I didn't know about my father's workaholic heroics until after the fact. I was still living in lily white Santa Barbara where the riots consisted of some isolated incidents of intoxicated college students vandalizing property. After a few days, the urban uprising petered out as a tearful Rodney King attempted to quell the remaining violence by uttering the simplistic but timely words, "can't we all just get along?"

Los Angeles was a city that was both integrated but divided. The riots illuminated the underlying tensions between the Blacks, Asians, Latinos, and Whites. Koreans shopkeepers didn't trust Black patrons, Armenians fought with Mexicans, Latinos and Blacks quarreled over gang territory, Blacks and Whites had a long history of segregation, and a myriad of other ethnic and racial divisions came to the surface when it seemed like the law of land was absent. My father was never a liberal that insisted on a color blind society. He held his own prejudices.

His friends would say that he sometimes appeared to have been intolerant of the behavior in people that he deemed to be not smart. To a certain extent, he avoided forming long term friendships with couples that with weren't White or Jewish. He referred to Blacks with the Yiddish term "Shvartza" and called most Latinos, "Mexicans." These were not politically correct terms nor did he generally hold those ethnic groups in high esteem. His mostly liberal Jewish American friends did not agree with his narrow mindedness in that regard. In his defense, I would not categorize him as a racist. He hired both Blacks and Latinos at his various businesses, and treated them in the same manner that he treated any other employees.

I think my father tried to base his feelings regarding someone on how hard they worked and how effective they ultimately were. Social niceties and being culturally sensitive were not his forte. He was concerned with the bottom line and when business was bad, he was angry. His workaholic attitude seemed to strengthen with age while his feeling of desperation grew with every bit of bad news.

Even though Automated Laundry System's revenues were drastically declining, my prudent father had significant savings and owned the Robertson and Washington Boulevard properties free and clear while having his buildings fully rented at leases signed during the high rent of the late 1980s. Therefore, he could still afford luxurious vacations in the midst of a recession.

In 1992, my parents went on yet another cruise. This time they ventured to the remote locale of Alaska along the Noordam ship of the Holland America Cruise Line. They visited Skagway, Sitka, and Juno, and were impressed by the awesome beauty of jagged glaciers and snow capped mountains. While many Southern Californians were having their homes foreclosed, my parents were spending a week at the four star Sheraton Bouganvilla in PuertaVallarta, Mexico, gallivanted around the jungle in a rented jeep with their friends David and Leona Zollman. They also spent several weekends together at the California resort towns of Cambria and Solvang where David was impressed by my father's patience when my mother would spend countless hours combing through jewelry stores in search of the right piece to add to her treasure chest at home.

While the majority of country suffered, my father's net worth had never been higher, mainly due to the appreciation of his real estate holdings. However, he did not judge his success based on what he had accumulated in the past, but by what he was doing currently. Sales of washing machines were down and his company was struggling to make a profit, so he was more distressed than he had ever been.

In spring of 1992, I was set to graduate from UC Santa Barbara with a Bachelor's Degree in Business Economics with an accounting concentration and thought that I might be the savior of the laundry business. The previous summer, my father had paid for me to attend Cambridge University Summer Session in England and I spent the rest of the summer traveling around Europe. He gave me the opportunity to sow my wild oats and take a grand tour of Europe with my friends Alan Rosenblatt and David Wartell, as well as some other classmates. At that time in my life, I wasn't interested in researching my genealogy even though I visited Spain. I spent most of my time on the beaches of the Costa del Sol and the bars of Madrid. My goal was to simply have a good time and enjoy the carelessness of my last summer as a college student.

Upon returning home, I felt a debt of gratitude towards my father's generosity. During the following school year, I considered myself personally obligated to work part-time for my father's company and tried to make sales in the Santa Barbara area. His business was suffering and his new, larger quarters were being under utilized. I felt that with my college education and youthful exuberance, I could reinvigorate Automated Laundry Systems.

On Saturday June 12, my father watched his only child graduate from a respected university, and on Monday June 14, he hired me as a full-time sales person. Inwardly, it was a proud moment for my father to see his son earn the degree that he never had the opportunity to achieve. I think that deep down he was reluctantly proud but quietly jealous. Outwardly, he seemed unimpressed and even belligerent. He made comments such as "Now you have a piece of paper to put on the wall (referring to my university diploma)." The translation being that college degrees do not buy his respect, only results do. When I felt that I was entitled to more pay or respect, he countered with "you can wipe your ass with that piece of paper (again referring to my diploma)," which was a less than tactful way of conveying that a degree alone lacks the ability to make money—especially for a entrepreneur.

Secretly, though, he gave his friend Mickey an entirely different interpretation of the significance of my education. My father confided that regardless of whether I wanted to be in the family business, he could take pride in providing me with a good education that would eventually take me to wherever I wanted to go. He also sought advice regarding how he could bring me into the business and how I could be most effective. Both concluded that I was probably smart enough to make my own way if necessary and that I would find some manner of integrating my education into the business. I was a bit disappointed that my father couldn't convey those feelings to me personally even after achieving an educational milestone.

The many celebratory events that I had scheduled during the weekend of graduation with friends and family made it virtually

324

impossible to spend much one on one time with my dad, so he never directly expressed his emotions to me. He wasn't the type of person who would sit me down and have typical father/son talks anyhow. I don't recall hearing any story about the birds and the bees, nor any hand on my shoulder saying "today you are a man." He figured that I was independent enough to learn certain things on my own and smart enough not to repeat his mistakes. On a certain level, my life was completely foreign to my father and he simply couldn't relate. He never went to college or played organized sports. He never worked on a computer, played video games, or even used an ATM machine. Going to rock concerts and listening to loud music was not a part of his teenage years. Binge drinking or smoking pot were indulgences that he never experienced. He never had the opportunity to date a non-Jewish girl. All of those experiences that he missed were a huge part of my college and high school years. Because my friends and I were so much different than my father and his friends as young adults, he felt that we had it a little too easy with our extended educational process. He thought that being smart in school wasn't nearly as important as proving yourself in the working world.

With a grand challenge in front of me, 1992 was a year filled with hope and promise. Despite my father's recent conservative leanings, he did vote for Bill Clinton because he blamed George Bush for the bad economy and his Secretary of State James Baker was an Arabist who threatened to withhold loan guarantees from Israel in order to get concessions. In addition to his policies with Israel and economic affairs, I also didn't like Bush's environmental record, and thought it was time for a change. I would have preferred someone more liberal like Jerry Brown—who I voted for in the primary—but Clinton was the better choice over Bush. The memorable theme music of Fleetwood Mac's "Don't stop thinking about tomorrow" played at the Clinton Inauguration Ball and a new era began.

The nation sensed a changing of the guard and I felt the business plan for Automated Laundry Systems needed the same. My father and I continued to methodically build up the business with a new emphasis on obtaining profitable contracts with apartment buildings. Another aspect of the laundry business with a potential for sizable profits was the brokerage of coin laundries and dry cleaners. My father held a California Department of Real Estate Salesperson license since the mid 1970s but was never able to pass the more difficult test for a broker's license. I was always interested in Real Estate and was taking the required classes for the broker's test starting in Santa Barbara and finishing in LA. In August of 1993, I passed the California Department of Real Estate Broker's license exam on my first attempt. My father was extremely proud and somewhat surprised. We immediately began the challenging process of developing a business brokerage to buy and sell coin laundries and dry cleaners. An obligatory step in this process was our attendance in the "who's who" of the laundry business—of course, the Clean Show.

In the spring of 1993, Clean '93 was once again being held in Chicago, ten years after the all-American road trip to the Midwest. Unlike the Chicago convention of a decade ago, the three of us flew out to this one. A few half day trips around the Second City and dinners with Avner and his family were the only non-business activities of the week. The former Wascomat manager who set my father up as a distributor was now an independent distributor of non-Wascomat products himself in Texas. The Wolanaws were little younger than my parents, but the two couples were good friends after spending so many business-related vacations together over the past fifteen years. The only time they really saw each other was at dinners and shows when they were on business trips around the world. Everything at Clean '93 seemed to be boringly similar to every previous laundry convention. We had made our rounds around the exhibitor hall, went to our Wascomat breakfast meetings, socialized with the Wolanows, and were prepared to conclude another Clean Show.

On the last day of the convention, my father collapsed without warning as he was leaving the exhibitor booth area. My mother and I were horrified as the convention center's medical staff attended to him. We were both extremely nervous because something like this had never happened before. I was shocked and afraid because I had never really seen my father in a weak or vulnerable position ever. After a few anxious moments, he appeared to be okay but the medical personnel urged him to go to a hospital for further tests. My father stubbornly refused, perhaps fearing his own mortality while reasserting his own personal strength. He had suffered from high blood pressure for several years and was taking medication for other minor health conditions such as mildly high blood sugar and above average cholesterol. Through sheer will and determination he gave the outward appearance of feeling healthy, but this did not last for long.

A few days after returning home from Chicago, he suffered another traumatic episode and this time went to the hospital. His

327

doctors diagnosed a fairly significant heart attack. Did it start in Chicago and reoccur? How much damage was done? How much could have been prevented by going to a hospital in Chicago? These are questions we will never know the answer to and will haunt my mother and me forever. On the other hand, my father had an extremely strong will and we could not force him to do something that he refused to do. I had a sinking feeling in the pit of my stomach as I wondered if my father was going to die. He didn't appear to be struggling for his life, but who knows what kind of damage was done to his internal organs. How long did he have left? He ended up being hospitalized for several days and was cautioned by his doctors to change his diet, start a consistent physical exercise regime, and work much less or simply retire.

Starkly confronted by his own mortality for the first time, he and my mother embarked on a quest to learn as much as they could about heart disease and how it could be prevented or reversed. My father changed his diet dramatically. All meat, saturated fats, fried foods, and anything high in cholesterol was eliminated. Plain fish and vegetables were the staples of his new diet. Daily walks and some golf were combined with a battery of drugs prescribed by his cardiac specialist.

When facing a life or death decision, many people find solace in their faith, but my parents did not turn towards Judaism during this moment of crisis. In fact, since my Bar Mitzvah they didn't even belong to a congregation or attend High Holy Day services. We still fasted on Yom Kippur, held a Passover Seder, and exchanged gifts during Hanukkah, but that was the extent of our secular and

Americanized Jewish faith. Whether it was a steady decline in his belief in organized religion or a general apathy towards old values, my father was clearly writing his own rules and picking out what he felt was relevant and important.

The one medical warning my father did not heed was the request to work less or retire. He tried at first to not work as much, but ended up calling the office more and becoming even more distressed when he was not able to solve a problem in person. His friends urged him to retire so that he could get serious about golf but they felt that he could not really separate himself from his work. It became apparent that his genetic history of heart disease and his self imposed identity of being a lifetime workaholic were major contributing factors to his health problems. Years of working too hard and not eating right had finally caught up with him. The most difficult challenge for him was curtailing his work schedule because his success in business stood as his barometer for personal accomplishment.

Years of self reliance had morphed into a controlling management style that made him virtually incapable of delegating authority and relieving the stressful burden from his shoulders. His unwillingness to allow me to relieve his duties caused many arguments between us which resulted in more stress that was detrimental to his health. I was frustrated by his inability to accept my help and I couldn't be too pushy about it because it would only make things worse. He rarely allowed me to learn from my business mistakes because he never permitted me to take the chance on my own. He would almost always interfere or disallow my initiatives. He had the wisdom of a man who had learned many different skills and accomplished many difficult tasks but was not a patient teacher and rarely gave a detailed explanation of how to do something or why not to do it. His answer was often a simple "No!"

However, in retrospect he was usually correct in his assumptions. But as a young and ambitious son/employee, I needed well justified reasons why my way was wrong and I wanted him to cite specific examples to support his theories. This type of probing didn't usually illicit the response that I was hoping for. It would just antagonize him and he would say I was disrespectful. A heated argument would often ensue and the learning process would be stunted and tainted by spiteful emotions. He also wasn't very impatient in his manner of teaching me a new skill. He expected me to observe the other employees or him performing a particular task and absorb the method. He would often say that he was too busy to sit down with me and go through step by step. Just watch and learn.

He would complain to his friends that he was impatient with my learning curve, so they urged him to go slow but to keep giving me more responsibility. My father's festering edginess grew into a questioning of my lack of commitment. He was worried that I wasn't really interested in his business. He felt that I should be honored to be the recipient of his special legacy that he had built from scratch. After all, he never had such an opportunity. I must admit that there were times where I had mixed feelings. I wanted to work with my father, learn about being an entrepreneur, and make money but I did not want to be selling washing machines for the next twenty years or more. The business had been in decline for several years and his friends assumed that he was really keeping the thing going for my eventual takeover. I realize that he had some faith in my intelligence and capability, but he was frustrated that I wasn't as "aggressive" as he was.

I proposed to give the other employees more responsibilities and put more trust in their abilities, but my father didn't allow any of his power to be diluted nor his tight grip to be relinquished. He never really showed any employees—including myself—any overt signs of respect or gratitude. In his eyes, we were doing what we were supposed to be doing and didn't need any positive reinforcement for earning our paycheck. If we screwed up, then he would be sure to impose the negative reinforcement, but compliments and "thank yous" were not in his vocabulary. It seemed like any person who fell short of his life's achievements was not worthy of any public displays of respect. Not that he was completely rude to everyone; he just wasn't the most flattering gentleman in the world.

The pitfalls of our family business were numerous and it was definitely not the best environment for my father's heart condition. Work related arguments inevitably spilled over into our personal life. Consequently, we spent less time together on weekends and the time we did spend together was strained and overshadowed by lingering job related disputes. Spending less time together on the weekends was also a result of me being older and having a busier social life. The era of going on day trips or weekend getaways with my parents was definitely over. Both my parents and I still loved to travel, but we now did so separately with the exception of going on business trips. I suppose that the distance and the friction between my father and I was partially a result of the fact that I still saw him as a strong and defiant man.

331

The change in diet and exercise had a positive effect on his health and he began to work harder as he regained his energy and enthusiasm following his heart attack. He would need every ounce of energy that he could muster because the general economy and the laundry business showed little signs of improving. To make matters worse, Southern California was suffering a series of natural and manmade disasters of almost biblical proportion. Riots, floods, mudslides, and fires contributed to the exodus of residents from the shaky economy of the region to the greener pastures of neighboring states with a higher growth rate. And to add to the confusion and urban flight, the greatest disaster was yet to come.

In the darkness of the early morning hours on January 17, 1994, the city of Los Angeles was literally shaken to its core. My parent's home in Woodland Hills was only a few short miles from the Northridge epicenter of the 6.7 magnitude earthquake. The tremendous impact hurled my parents from their king-size bed to the floor, then quickly to a sturdy nearby doorframe. After the shaking and pounding ceased, my father scrambled through the darkness to retrieve his heart condition medication. Even young and healthy people panicked in the midst of the widespread catastrophe, but for a sixty-two year-old person—who had recently suffered a heart attack—the mere shock of such a cataclysmic event could have been deadly. Ailing and barefoot, he fought his way through broken glass, broken plates, spilled water, and a hodge-podge of unintentionally dislodged household items to recover his medication. His heart was okay, but on route to the kitchen cabinet he had cut his foot on broken glass and turned his ankle when he slipped on the spilled water. He was hospitalized on a very business day at Kaiser Permanente in Woodland Hills—not for heart problems—but for a broken toe.

I was sharing an apartment on Beachwood Drive in the Hollywood Hills with my roommate James Min. He was actually already awake and getting ready to go to work when the quake struck. We were both extremely lucky because our apartment only suffered minor damage. However, a report from a battery-operated AM radio said that the epicenter was in Northridge. Both of us grew up and worked in the Valley at that time, so we had major concerns about the safety of our families and the security of our jobs. I tried to contact my parents but the phone lines were dead and we didn't have cellular phones yet. I was finally able to speak to my grandmother in North Hollywood first and she had spoken to my parents and told me that they were alright. Since the power was out citywide, James and I waited until daybreak to drive into the Valley and survey the damage which was extensive. Crumbled retaining walls on the freeway, broken water mains gushing water, severed gas lines spewing flames, and no functioning street lights were just some of the obstacles in our painstakingly slow commute.

Fortunately, the damage both to property and person was the worst in Woodland Hills for my father's real estate portfolio. None of his properties had earthquake insurance, but luckily the damage was minimal and a major financial disaster was averted. Relative to many Angelinos, we were fortunate. Besides my father's broken toe, the worst part was that my parent's house lacked hot water for about a week and the general chaos within the city.

Many sections of LA resembled a Third World country that had been ravaged by war. Thousands of impoverished Angelinos were rendered homeless or simply afraid to go back into their damaged buildings, so they lived in tent cities that were erected in public parks and administered by the National Guard. Several foolish people started hoarding goods and some minor shortages occurred. Streetlights and traffic lights continued to be non-operational for several days, so every time you entered an intersection you had a much higher probability of ending up in an accident.

Many buildings that were deemed unrepairable were marked with a red tag and properties that were unsafe but could be restored were yellow tagged. Those condemned properties were strewn about the San Fernando Valley as well as the City. Many middle class families—even some of our friends—lived in hotels for several months while their homes were rehabilitated to a safe condition which was marked by a green tag. Most neighborhoods in the Valley were a virtual construction zone for the entire following year. The rebuilding process was lengthy due to many people battling with their insurance companies and the Federal Emergency Management Agency (FEMA) for a settlement payment.

Fortunately, all of my father's five commercial buildings and one residential property received a green tag but did sustain some costly damage. Other homes on Crespi Street received yellow tags and considerably more destruction due to the rolling wave effect of the earthquake. My parents received a mere compensation from their standard fire insurance policy and a token amount from FEMA compared to the windfall from earthquake insurance that helped

334

completely remodel many of the their neighbor's homes and skyrocket future insurance rates for everyone.

In the first few days following the initial quake, there was a constant barrage of substantial aftershocks. An Automated Laundry Systems employee named Sergio Silva—who was from Nicaragua— frantically ran out of our warehouse every time there was a minor aftershock. He told us that in his country of origin, tens of thousands of people perished during earthquakes and aftershocks of similar magnitude mainly because of lesser building standards. It was unusual to see how different people reacted to a natural disaster. It ranged from complete panic to total indifference and everything in between.

In retrospect, though, it wasn't that bad. LA would rise like a phoenix from the ashes. For the city, it was the beginning of the economic recovery because so much money was reinvested into the damaged properties that it provided employment and eventually increased property values.

Another regional infusion of revenue and spirit came in the unlikely form of a soccer tournament. In the summer of 1994, the World Cup was being held in the US for the first time ever in the history of the event. The Bulgarian team had defeated the defending champion Germany, and had their best showing in their history of international competition. Although they lost in the semi-final game, Bulgaria played Sweden for the consolation game for third place at the Rosebowl. I purchased Bulgarian Soccer hats that my father and I wore as we proudly cheered on his home country's team. For my father it was reminiscent of his childhood experiences with the Maccabi Sports Club. It was also the only time that he was around so

335

many fellow Bulgarians in the US. My father made some chit chat with the other Bulgarian fans but the day represented a quintessential father/son outing rather than some quasi-homecoming game. Because of WWII, he never had the opportunity to see the Bulgarian National Soccer Team play with his father. In fact, the untimely death of his father had robbed him of many father/son events that we had the privilege to share. The game itself was a blowout since the Bulgarian team supposedly got drunk the night before the consolation match. Since they were only playing for third place, the players lacked motivation and my father would have preferred see the US or Israeli team make to the semi-finals, but he was still able to root for Bulgaria as his third favorite national team. It was further proof that he did not hate his former country like so many other Holocaust survivors did.

Cheering along side my father for a sport that he was familiar with was not only a great bonding experience for us, but also worked as a transition to attending other sporting events. Since Magic Johnson was drafted by the Lakers and the "Showtime" era began, both my dad and I were avid fans. We were able to relate in a very typically American male way over NBA basketball which was a triumph of cultural integration that worked to the benefit of our father/son relationship. As my disposable income gradually increased and my father's interest in the NBA, NHL, and MLB grew, I made a habit of purchasing tickets to a few games per year. We started to experience in person what we usually only watched on TV. My dad never became the drunk guy with the game jersey and the ridiculous headgear, but we were both true fans that finally shared some common non-work related interests.

Because of cultural and generational gaps, we didn't relate the same way a traditional American father and son did. Work became a place for us to be together and speak the universal language of making money. When business was good, our work relationship was smooth, but when business was bad, arguments from work spilled over to our personal life and spoiled our social interaction. Work related disputes certainly didn't help our family life—it was a pitfall of spending too much time together.

Other adult children might have issues with their parents, but a work-related argument was not one of them. That dynamic made it much more difficult to bridge the cultural and generational gap. Work did give us the opportunity to strive towards a common goal and gave me the sense of duty that I wasn't merely laboring for a paycheck. I was helping my family and managing the Varsano assets that would eventually help sustain us in the future.

Besides sporting events, meals, and an occasional shopping trip, there was no social time spent with my parents when I was a so called grown-up. There were no parties, no concerts, no theater, no non-business vacations, no weekend getaways, no day trips, no amusement parks, and no recreational activities of any kind. I had my friends, my parents had their friends, and we both "did our own thing." My mother, my father, and I often went dining out together and sometimes went to the shopping mall, but attending sporting events was strictly a father/son outing. It was the only time as an adult that I spent with just my dad alone socially and therefore, it was a much cherished memory.

I remember attending a game at the Great Western Forum between the Los Angeles Lakers and the New York Knicks where I

337

almost got into a fight with three obnoxious New Yorkers. These provocateurs were relentlessly ridiculing the Lakers players and fans for the entire game. It built up to the point where it was beyond bragging and gloating, and it just became plain rude and insufferable. Finally, I couldn't take it anymore and told them to "shut the hell up, go back to your ghetto in the Bronx, and don't come back to LA to brag until the Knicks win an NBA Championship." (The NY Knicks last won an NBA Championship in 1973 and as of 2002-03 had not won another) I told them to look up at the Lakers Championship Banners (5 at the time, the most recent being 1988) and show them a little respect. In LA, we judge our teams based on championships, so beating the Lakers in a regular season game "don't mean shit!" I felt that I was defending the honor of the typically low key LA fans that refused to stand up to this band of New York fools.

I realized that my dad was a little to old and didn't want to put his heart at risk to engage them in a confrontation, but as a young man I needed to do something. My father had indeed changed. The same man who waited hours for the soccer referee's armored car to leave the arena in Israel so he could attack it with stones and who threw a shopping cart at an unscrupulous Laundromat patron in Studio City would have kicked their New York asses all over the Forum. But now I was the strong young man who was deliberately taking over the reins of manhood from my father. In the end, only tough words were exchanged, but it was very close to fisticuffs. At around sixty dollars per ticket, none of us really wanted to get kicked out of the arena for fighting. I also didn't want to ruin my father/son night or damage his ailing heart. Heavy emotionally charged situations—whether at work

338

or in social setting—were definitely not good for his health, but were often difficult to avoid because he didn't really curtail his lifestyle too much following his heart attack.

I believe that no matter what my father was doing, work was almost always on his mind. As the local economy began to show signs of improvement, the laundry industry did not follow suit and appeared as though it would never be as profitable as it once was. For the past several years, my father chose to maintain a high profit margin with less volume of sales and consequently, a smaller staff. Used equipment, new on-premise laundry (non coin-operated commercial equipment commonly known as OPL), replacement coin equipment, service calls, and even retail parts fetched a fatter profit than high volume sales of new coin laundry equipment. While other distributors packed with salespersons and brokers pleased the manufacturers by selling big numbers of coin machines at a lower profit per unit, Automated's lean but viable approach soured our long term relationship with Wascomat. In the business world of the 1990s, loyalty and quality of service meant very little while the number of units sold became the only significant measure of success. My dad/boss and I started seriously looking for other laundry products to sell while also researching other investment opportunities entirely.

In June of 1995, the Clean Show was being held in muggy New Orleans and the three us attended once again. By mid 1990s, the laundry industry had been suffering for several years and the restructuring of distributor networks caused us to branch out and sell the Dexter line equipment in addition to Wascomat. Besides doing business with a different group of manufacturer's representatives, the

339

convention experience was similar to the previous shows. A few tourist activities coupled with dinners with Avner and his family in the French Quarter added levity to the trip. Despite the New Orleans theme of "let the good times roll," my father was eager to get back to work and once again chose not to extend his vacation to explore Cajun country.

Later that summer, we finally discovered the other investment opportunity that would help us diversify and take advantage of the impending recovery. I was a twenty-five year old real estate broker and laundry equipment salesperson that had been renting an apartment for the past seven years. The market was down and I had the knowledge and desire to acquire a property of my own. With my father's expertise and 50% financial backing, we purchased a twelve unit apartment building that I would manage and live in rent-free on Grace Avenue in the Hollywood Hills. Even though we apparently got a good deal, the building needed work and neither of us had experience owning or managing residential rental property.

One week after escrow closed I went to Europe with my friend Mark Sundahl on a vacation that had been booked several months earlier. One of the smaller apartment unit's was inhabited by a band of about seven people who were intravenous drug users with a violent streak. By the time I returned from Europe, my father with the help of the LAPD had managed to oust these tenants without going through the normal eviction procedures. It was a testament to my father resourcefulness and it also showed a marked change in his relationship with the police department when he was a new immigrant.

340

For about one year, every Saturday afternoon my father, a day laborer from Peru named Benji, and I would work to renovate the apartment complex. I remember my father feeling healthy and vibrant as he helped to dig a trench for a sprinkler system in the smoldering midday heat. After a tumultuous first year of evicting deadbeat tenants and slowly reinvesting in the property, the Grace View Apartments were redeveloped and profitable. To improve things further, I felt the need to address issues related to the greater Hollywood community. I volunteered for a local property owners and mangers group named the Yucca Corridor Coalition (YCC). When I asked my father to attend one of our meetings his response was the same as when I told him that I volunteered for non-profit groups at UCSB, he said "I learned not to volunteer for anything in the army."

It was more of a welcoming challenge than a betrayal of support, so it did not require any reason for argument on either side. YCC and the Grace View Apartments gave me an opportunity to prove to him that I could be a success in business and make a difference in the community, completely independent of his criticism or control. Managing the apartment building in Hollywood that we had recently purchased together as a partnership was solely my responsibility. Hollywood was my baby and by that point in our business relationship, I didn't even care that he didn't want to get involved in the community.

I was becoming more of an independent business man in several ways. Within the laundry business I had carved out my niche supplemental to my father's existing business. I managed the apartment laundry routes and coin laundry brokerage while my dad made most of the sales of equipment and supervised the service staff. He wanted me to do my own thing and be self reliant from day one. Sometimes, I was frustrated by this philosophy of self education because I wanted to be taught and nurtured. After several years of observing and absorbing, I had gained the confidence and ability that my father wasn't willing or able to teach me.

As the economy improved, rents were steadily raised and my father's skepticism about the apartment investment turned into a cash cow. I managed the building and was able to solve most of the problems regarding my portion of the laundry business which helped to relieve any extra burden on him. My father had gained enough confidence in me that he could leave the country for several weeks to attend a family milestone with at least some measure of assurance that I could hold down the fort.

In 1996, Seeco's one and only niece Dorit was getting married in Israel. My parents took the opportunity to travel to Turkey as well as Israel for the wedding while I ran the business back home. Dorit married a Turkish-Israeli man named Dov whose family gave my father numerous pointers on the next destination of their eastern Mediterranean vacation. From Israel, my parents flew to the former head of the Ottoman Empire, Istanbul, Turkey.

My parents spent about ten days in Turkey and saw a great deal because they went on ambitious tour. They stayed in first class accommodations and dined on fantastic cuisine. There was plenty of fresh fish which was now the staple of my father's restrictive diet. They traveled from place to place via a luxury bus tour with scheduled stops at all the tourist attractions. Many of the passengers on the bus were Americans and most were very friendly. The easy going atmosphere allowed everyone to become friends and enjoy the tour as a cohesive group rather than individual couples. Unlike the amateurish tours of Eastern Europe a few years earlier, a local guide—who spoke English flawlessly—showed them everything worth seeing.

Istanbul had many museums, amphitheaters, historic cemeteries, and the Grand Bazaar shopping area. After spending several hours shopping the cavernous Grand Bazaar, my parents came away with a souvenir dagger for me, a variety of jewelry for my mom, wall sculptures of old Ottoman characters for the home, and as usual nothing specifically for my father. He never collected anything and rarely indulged in souvenirs that were just for him. My mom would have stayed in the Bazaar the entire day looking at jewelry, but she was a little fearful of "some scary looking Turks," who would aggressively show her their great deals in a dark corner of the marketplace.

Ismir was another city that was known as the capital of the affluent Turks with a rich history dating back to the Ottoman days. It had a significant Jewish history which my parents uncommonly explored. They also enjoyed the natural splendor of the town of Pamukkale which featured graduated layers natural deposits of calcium laden waters in wading pools. One waterfall after another cascaded down as my parents gleefully soaked there feet in the warm water while basking in the sunshine. On one tour stop, my father was dressed as a belly dancer in a restaurant and danced with the rest of the costumed patrons. It had been years, since he was able to be so carefree. It was perhaps his last hurrah. Both of my parents had a really great time on this grand tour of Turkey.

Unlike the business oriented trip to Spain and the confusing poverty of Bulgaria, my father was free to explore his historic roots and ventured to the Jewish quarter of Istanbul. The Islamic country was in far better shape than the former communist state of Bulgaria had been six years earlier. Unlike Bulgaria, the Jewish landmarks were well preserved and much easier to locate. My father found an ancient Sephardic synagogue that was like a fortress from the outside due to the threat of terrorist attack. As they walked inside they gazed upon the gorgeous sanctuary with awe inspiring crystal chandeliers overhead and were greeted by the caretaker who my father was able to speak at length in Ladino.

Although not privy to the conversation, it must have been a satisfying experience for my father, coming from a family that had lived for five hundred years in the Ottoman Empire and was still practicing some of those ancient customs. Now he was a wealthy American on vacation reminiscing and identifying with this ancient synagogue keeper. His life had come full circle. At age sixty-three with failing health, he had returned to his Ottoman roots to complete his ancestral voyages. In the past six years, he had visited Spain, Bulgaria, Israel, and finally Turkey. It represented a reunion with the four countries encompassed a thousand year history of our Sephardic family. Upon returning to the US, he would prepare to make the final move of his long journey.

Fed up with the run down neighborhood of North Hollywood, I urged my father to move Automated to the municipally incorporated and middle class neighborhood of nearby Burbank. I reasoned that the commute would be about the same distance for my parents and it would be much more profitable in the long run. By 1996, the laundry industry had systematically changed due to a saturated coin laundry market in Southern California, increased sewer and other utility costs, an influx of immigrant owners willing to endure a lower standard of living at smaller locations, multiple mergers and acquisitions with larger corporations dominated market share, and a prolonged recession in the general economy. My father and I finally succumbed to the notion that we would not be able to fully utilize the large space in North Hollywood with our current business plan. We both researched supplemental business opportunities within the laundry industry as well as investing in an entirely new business. The best option seemed to be purchasing a smaller building in the better real estate market of Burbank and renting the North Hollywood facility to our well financed adult entertainment product distributor neighbor who was chomping at the bit.

The daily work of a porno distributor was basically the same as any other shipping and receiving business. There were a lot of fork lifts moving boxes around, packing materials, and mailing labels. Once you got over the shock of what's in the boxes, it was a tedious business just like any other. From a moral perspective, my father was able to accept them as tenants, but certainly didn't want to be a partner or an investor in their business. He did, however, accept some free product samples such as a ridiculous-looking penis shaped golf putter. It actually was not a bad golf club, but who had the balls to whip it out on the greens. Novelty items aside, they were hardworking people and

345

their business was extremely profitable which my father respected. Similar to us they were a father/son operation that was constantly arguing. They were Puerto Rican Americans from New York—who we found to be a bit crude and uncultured compared to us—but they were decent tenants.

In the spring of 1997, Automated Laundry Systems moved for the third time to a 5000 square foot warehouse and office on South Victory Boulevard in Burbank. The property only required a quick overhaul to accommodate our needs and we negotiated a very reasonable purchase price. The move, however, took several weeks and proved to be laborious and stressful. Automated's 10,000 square foot yard was filled with literally tons of extra supplies and used equipment which were eventually given away as scrap metal. Most of the stuff was junk anyway, but my father was a still a pack rat and departing with this "wealth" of potentially profit making merchandise further contributed to the stress of the relocation.

By the time that we finally finished moving in, there was an air of optimism abound. The commercial entertainment district of Burbank was a much more pleasant locale to spend a working day than the graffiti-ridden industrial streets of North Hollywood. It was more reminiscent of the younger and more prosperous days of being in another entertainment industry town, Culver City.

Everything seemed to be coming up roses. The business was finally starting to be modestly profitable again and the new location gave us all a fresh approach. All of the rental properties were fully occupied with rising rents and my frugal father had tucked away hundreds of thousands of dollars in the bank. My parents had a great

346

group of friends and their son was even dating a nice Jewish girl. Even though we weren't particularly religious, marrying a Jewish woman was still very important to my parents. My mom was especially vocal about it, while my father would just tell me that I could "fool around with shiksas, but make sure to marry a Jew."

The one important factor of life that was beyond anyone's control, though, was my father's health which appeared to be stable, but everyone knew his condition was degenerative. Failing health caused him to slow down and give me more responsibility, but a controlling attitude and workaholic mentality made this a painful process. He tried to travel and enjoy his wealth in his golden years but a lifetime of pushing his limits overwhelmed the constant urging of his wife to take it easy. Unwilling to face his own mortality, he tried to continue his old ways and remain outwardly strong.

CHAPTER 15

Last Port: Burbank

A new business location, optimistic revenue projections, and a busy social life gave my father a sense of hope that he had been lacking for much of the 1990s. He exercised his rapidly aging body with determined regularity while disciplining his eating habits for each and every meal. Physically, he was able to maintain a sufficient level of health given his pre-existing condition. But mentally he struggled with an overwhelming frustration of not being able to control his life as he once did. He never came to terms with the ultimate terminality of his medical condition, and I don't think he really took solace in the success of his lifelong achievements. He kept pushing and fighting for relatively unimportant tasks with a disregard for the toll that the stress would take on his legacy. Even though he earned a majority of his current income from his real estate holdings, he still tightly controlled the reins of Automated Laundry Systems and felt obligated to continually improve his apparently underperforming small business.

As summer of 1997 approached it was time for another Clean Show, with Las Vegas being the location of choice. By Clean '97 we had dropped the Dexter line, so we hung out with the Wascomat folks who had changed quite a bit since the high flying days of the 1980s. The familiar faces of the veteran employees and fellow distributors were gone, replaced by a fresh batch of untried new recruits. My father seemed to be at peace with himself and enjoyed the business-oriented trip more as a vacation with his family rather than a rigorous working affair.

Now that I was over twenty-one, my parents and I were able to play at the casino together for the first time. Neither my parents nor I were big gamblers, but we did enjoy plunking down quarters in the slot machines and video poker. I hadn't really played any types of games with my father since I was a little boy and even then it was rare. After we lost our roll of coins on the one-armed bandits, we strolled down the Vegas strip until we reached Gameworks which was a state-of-the-art arcade geared towards young families. My father and I had a nice bonding moment over his first ever game of air hockey. It was a welcomed sight to see my dad acting a bit silly trying to hit the bouncing plastic puck. He actually beat me and I was able to see a tiny glimpse of his long lost youthful joy as he clinked in the winning goal.

When we came back to Burbank—on a summer afternoon car ride—my father and I had a prophetic conversation. I told him that I thought some customers didn't respect me because of my youthful appearance. I also told him that I would prefer to be introduced in business settings as "Jonathan" rather than "my son." My dad empathized with me and told me a related story about his experiences as a machine shop owner in Jaffa. When he was about the same age as I was at the time, he also had an unusually youthful face. When potential clients would visit the machine shop and ask to speak to the owner, a fresh faced Seeco would tell them that he was the owner. Many of these customers did not believe him and insisted on waiting until the owner arrived. My father would laugh and tell them to wait as long as they wished but he was the true owner. It was a basic lesson about the importance of self-confidence and determination over appearance that my father was trying to convey to me.

A few weeks earlier, I had met a nice Jewish girl named Lauren Fink in a bar on the Sunset Strip in West Hollywood. We were dating steadily for several weeks and it was developing into a serious relationship. I had shown my parents a photograph of Lauren and was even contemplating making a rare introduction of my girlfriend to my parents. Conflicting schedules and a slight bit of apprehension on my part had prevented this meeting from occurring.

The majority of the girls that I dated when I was in high school and college were not Jewish partly because I felt that I was too young to even contemplate marriage. I rarely brought them home because I would be subjected to the scrutiny of my parents whom I knew did not approve of me "getting serious" with non-Jewish girls. They weren't going to be rude to my girlfriends, but they certainly were not going to give them a warm reception. The very few times that my parents did meet a girlfriend, it was brief and they were cordial but not embracing. I never went as far as to invite any girlfriends—Jewish or Gentile—to holiday meals, just an occasional meet and greet.

After college, I started to date more Jewish girls, but still kept the practice of not introducing them to my folks until I felt that it was "getting serious." My mom was generally more interested in meeting the girlfriends than my dad was. He was not going to pressure me to bring anyone to our small family events. When I was ready, he would welcome the right kind of girl into his home for a Passover Seder or Thanksgiving Dinner. A few years earlier, I remember him expressing

350

approval over one girlfriend that he briefly met. She was Jewish, her dad was a doctor, and she dressed in tight clothes that complimented her well toned body. He liked her whole package and I could even sense a tad bit of envy. However, I older I grew, the more hesitant I was about bringing a girlfriend to my parents house because the pressure to get married and start a family was intensifying.

On Friday, July 18, my parents and I spent the day together at work just as we had done for the previous five years. It was just like any other day that's ever been, the sun going up and down. At the day's end, I said "good-bye" to my father and headed out to a date with Lauren. It was unusual that I said "good bye," because I would normally say see you Monday or Saturday or whatever the case may be. A few days earlier, we had a pointless argument that was finally resolved earlier that afternoon. I went into my dad's office to make sure he still wasn't angry and that we left for the weekend on good terms. He was sitting down in his executive chair going through his phone messages and seemed distracted by the worries of business as usual. He might have been a bit fatigued but he didn't seem to harbor any animosity towards me regarding the petty argument that we had just resolved.

We were both looking to the future. After about two months in Burbank, the company was finally settling into our new space and our operations were starting to run smoothly. Business was starting to pick up and we had a special occasion to celebrate in our new facility. The following week would mark the twentieth anniversary of Automated Laundry Systems' founding and we were planning a modest party. After spending a Friday night of romance at Lauren's apartment, I returned to my apartment to find a message on my answering machine that would change my life forever.

It was my mother's frantic voice fighting through tears, to say that my father had suffered what they think was a stroke and that I should immediately go to the hospital in West Hills. I began to hyperventilate for the first time in my life and rushed from Hollywood to the West Valley. I found my mother distraught and my father semi-conscious, unable to speak. He strongly gripped my hand as he slowly drifted into unconsciousness. He was put on life support systems and the doctors waited for test results which confirmed that he suffered of a massive stroke. My mother and I were extremely confused, depressed, emotionally distressed, and afraid of what was to come. After four unimaginably agonizing days, the doctors said that there was no hope and Mordecai Varsano was pronounced dead on July 22, 1997 at the age of sixty-four.

It was worst moment of my life. The life support machines just stop processing, and my father succumbed to a sterile hospital death. I was in disbelief that this would be the last time that I would see his face or touch his skin. I held his cold lifeless hand and prayed for his soul and hoped that we would meet again on another spiritual plane.

The last four days still seemed unbelievable, like the life that I knew ceased to exist.. I was scared, shocked, and depressed. I lost my father figure, boss, mentor, role model, hero, competitor, confidant, teacher, and prime motivator. My life was irrevocably changed forever. I sensed that I would no longer be able to feel joy or act youthful again. I secretly wondered whether the trauma would change my personality and I would turn into a bitter and serious person. At that point, I didn't care about my life much; I was just empty—like an enormous part of me just unexpectedly disappeared.

I wondered if my dad felt the same way when his father died and he was only a fifteen year old boy. At least I was twenty-seven with a well developed personality and a diverse life experience, so I could theoretically cope a little better with the enormity of the loss. My dad never seemed youthful or jovial to me. He almost always was very serious and hard working. I hypothesized that he developed this serious adult persona after his father died tragically. I thought that the trauma of his father's untimely death stunted his normal adolescent development and his capacity to be playful and unconditionally happy. I wondered whether this would now be my fate. I was always somewhat of a class clown and a sarcastic kidder who loved to laugh and be playful. Would I now turn into a workaholic like my dad?

My mother and I had our world turned upside down. The symbol of stability and wisdom in our lives was now gone. My mother lost a husband, best friend, and supporter. I could not replace those roles. For most of my life, I never really cared about having a brother or sister because I always had a lot of friends. In the abrupt aftermath of my father death, I wish I had a sibling just so I could cry on their shoulder and have someone else who felt the same pain that I felt.

As Sarah and Shimon arrived from Israel and tens of friends and relatives expressed condolences at the funeral, my mother and I were still in a state of disbelief. Shimon tried to encourage me with stories of Seeco's clever inventions at the machine shop, while Sarah reminisced about childhood memories of Bulgaria, but no kind words or inspirational sentiment could comfort our gaping loss. We were in no way emotionally prepared for this tragic event. We thought his health was somewhat stable and there would be more blatant warning signs of any catastrophic episodes. The end was abrupt, unpredictable, and it taught us a valuable lesson about the fragility of life and the finality of death.

I regretted all the arguments I had in the past with my dad. I felt terribly guilty about any insults that I had ever directed at him. After he was gone, the only thing I could think about was how much I missed him and how I would do almost anything to have things back to the way they were just a few days ago. One day he was working hard and arguing with me over meaningless things and the next day he was gone. To me, he seemed as strong willed as ever and physically able to handle his smorgasbord of daily tasks up until the very end. Then, without warning, his true health status revealed itself as he desperately clung to life in an intensive care unit. Others would say that he looked a little pale and seemed fatigued in his last weeks, but I believe that was just 20/20 hindsight. No one ever cautioned him or told him to go to the doctor. Would it have mattered anyway? There are certain things in life that we can not control.

It really made me reflect on what is most important in life and reassess my values system. Corny book titles like "Don't Sweat the Small Stuff, and it's All Small Stuff," started to sound very profound to me. It didn't have to be a stroke, it could have been a gun shot or a car accident, we never know when we are going to live our last day. You get so caught up in the day to day trials and tribulations that a sudden tragedy jolts your mind to contemplate the very essence of mortality and the meaning of human life. It is ultimately the most important question for a human being to answer, but nobody knows for sure what the correct answer is. For me, it was also a very scary state of mind to be in for a long period of time. Constantly dwelling on unanswerable existential questions was both fruitful and frustrating, but ultimately distracting to living a "normal" life. Life—even the simple daily chores—must go on in order to retain good mental health and to reemerge into the social fabric of the world around you.

Even though it would take a long period of time for my mother and me to pass through the initial phase of recovery, my father had taken care of our financial needs posthumously. A living trust of his multi-million dollar estate provided my mother with assets that would give her financial security for the rest of her life. My father was an advocate of maintaining a high level of savings and would often theorize, "It's not how much you make, it's how much you keep." There were provisions for my benefit as well, but I was more concerned with stabilizing business and family matters. I was now the man of the family and inherited the burdens of my father.

One of my father's greatest fears was giving up control of his self-built company to me and watching it crumble before his eyes within the first year. Fear of failure caused my father to be somewhat overbearing and not give me as much authority as he probably should have. I resented his lack of trust in me and was eager to prove him wrong. How could I prove my worthiness if I was never given an fair opportunity? He felt that he would control as much as possible until he was no longer able. I think he was expecting a much more gradual decline in his ability to work and then he would slowly turn over more responsibilities to me. Unfortunately, my ascension to power at

Automated Laundry Systems and my assumption of the responsibilities for other Varsano assets was just as abrupt as his passing. I was only given a true opportunity to pass his unspecified tests after he was no longer around to judge me. I had to demonstrate my abilities to my father posthumously, which really meant proving it to myself. There were so many times that I wished he was there so I could ask him a simple question. It would have been so much easier for me to make the transition if my father was able to relinquish his grip on power and become the wise old teacher. He was going run his company his way regardless of the long term ramifications of his actions.

In the final months of his life, he was bogged down with worries about meaningless daily concerns such as the punctuality of employees and customers paying late, while neglecting to address the much more significant issues of putting his newly acquired property in his living trust and properly training his only child for succession. Doubt and mistrust of my abilities coupled with the unknown side effects of the battery of prescribed drugs that he was ingesting daily caused periodic lapses in judgment and reason. In his final years, he would internalize much of his pain and frustration exemplified through retorts such as "I am listening" when he would not speak for long periods of time while conversations went on around him. Whether he was "stressing out" about work or just displaying passive-aggressive behavior regarding whatever we were discussing, there were a lot of thoughts going on inside his head that he did not care to share.

Like most men, he had a hard time expressing his feelings. He wouldn't speak open and honestly about his inner thoughts and fears.

My father and I both put up a macho front because you never want to show your opponent your weaknesses. In business or any other competitive relationship, if you expose your vulnerabilities, then people will take advantage. My father never let any business associates know that he suffered from health problems for this very reason. We both had similar attitudes regarding not budging on our convictions which made our dialogue about emotional issues almost nonexistent. Tender feelings such as love and fear were assumed instead of actually spoken. After he was gone, I just wished that I had told him that I loved him and respected him more often. My mother—like most women—was much better at communicating her true emotions. She wore it on her sleeve and wasn't afraid to cry or say "I love you." Since I was unsure about a lot of my father's feelings, I had to make assumptions and try to think what he would have done after he was gone.

I would have to pass the test of my father's mostly unspoken expectations for me. I attempted to use what I thought were my father's fears as a motivating factor to successfully run his business. For the first year following his passing, I managed Automated Laundry Systems in a manner that mimicked my father's style as closely as possible. My first task as boss was to terminate an employee that my father didn't like and who took advantage of the lack of supervision while I was dealing with my father's death. My mother continued to be the bookkeeper for several months before becoming the first employee of Automated to officially retire.

After the first year, I felt I had overcome my father's fear and would choose my own destiny. I didn't want to be in the laundry business indefinitely, so after three years of successfully running Automated Laundry Systems, I went out on my own terms. In June of 2000, I married Lauren Fink—the girlfriend my father never had the opportunity to meet—and in August of 2000 I sold Automated Laundry Systems.

Selling the business that was my father's driving force was a very difficult decision for me emotionally and I probably dragged it out a little longer than I should have from a purely financial standpoint. I felt like I was ending yet another chapter in my life, and finally closing the book on my father's long legacy of hard work. I also felt an obligation to the employees, some of whom my father hired and trained. However, I did not want to be in the laundry business for twenty years like my dad, it was his business and he chose that industry because it suited his interests. I wanted to choose something else.

I made a promise to myself and my father's memory that I would run the business for a full year to demonstrate to myself that I could do it, to gain valuable experience, and to prove my father wrong. I not only accomplished that feat, but continued to run it for an additional two years. From my college graduation to the day I finally sold the business, I had been working in the commercial laundry equipment business for over eight long years; five years under my father's thumb and three years on my own. Now, at age thirty I was getting married and had other business and professional interests. I needed to move on in order to satisfy my own personal ambition. Despite the emotional attachment that I had to the business that had sustained my family for over twenty years, I ventured forth to unknown future endeavors.

Even though the business was sold, my father's legacy would certainly continue. Condolences were given to my mother and me for years after the fact. Kind words regarding my father were conveyed to me by customers, competitors, friends, and employees. In the immediate aftermath, friends Mickey and Barbara Wolfe were a compassionate and stabilizing influence that helped us cope with the gravity of the situation. Along with other B'Nai Brith friends, they conveyed stories of past conversations with their friend Seeco. Successful people themselves, they were impressed by my father's knowledge of global events and business acumen. Mickey reminisced that the women would gather to gossip, while the men would theoretically solve the world's problems.

Mickey described my dad as a very "earthy" fellow, meaning that he managed to sweep away unnecessary detail to uncover the grit of reality. He could read people pretty well and expose the motives behind their behavior which came from growing up "in the streets." Although my father's background and experiences were totally different than most of his friends, they talked about a variety of world issues as well as family problems. Sometimes they would agree and other times they wouldn't, but they respected each other thoughts without getting upset. They weren't afraid to take on any issue. Whether it was regarding their family, local events, national politics, or world news, they had a private forum of men to honestly voice their opinions. My father was most respected among his friends in the Knesset B'nai Brith group—both male and female. He in turn had respect for most of the members but was bluntly outspoken about any nonsense in the group.

Whether amongst friends or employees, my father possessed natural leadership qualities while not being bossy. The priceless lessons about a vocation and life in general that he taught to his service technicians spawned several independent companies. The experience gained under his tutelage also enabled many former employees to thrive at more prestigious careers. He was proud that he helped them and gained a good reputation in the industry as a knowledgeable and honest mentor. The former machinist taught his laundry equipment technicians to fix things the correct way so that they would not have to come back a second time for the same problem.

His motto was as follows: Use only factory parts, do quality work, finish the job and get paid. Do not overcharge and do not make up problems that do not exist just to pad the bill. Other competitors in the laundry industry made a bad habit of "stealing" his protégés away from him. Because of his high sense of loyalty, he often felt betrayed by some of the employees who would leave for a higher paying or more prestigious job as soon as they had learned enough from Automated's training procedures. It gave him a rather jaded attitude towards employees, so he was always reluctant to offer high salaries or job perks. He was going to do things his way and his own willpower would continue to guarantee his success.

The lessons my father taught me made me who I am today. I only truly had one role model in life. I was instilled with an ethic of hard work that would only be judged by results and not merely words or educational degrees. My mother learned that my father was capable

360

of handling nearly all of the family needs. From making money and fixing what was broken to driving from point A to point B and helping with the cooking, my father showed what being a good husband entailed.

For the most part, my father was my role model for being a decent husband as I embarked on my own voyage into the choppy waters of marriage. It was up to me to pick out his good qualities while discarding the bad. My father would give my mother most of what she wanted especially when it came to jewelry. It wasn't that he was trying to buy her love or happiness, but simply indulging her small materialistic desires. The most important aspect that I saw in my parent's successful marriage was that they were best friends. They were able to enjoy each others company at work and socially. Since they spent a lot of time together, they tended to get in lots of petty arguments. I learned that it sometimes healthy for a couple to not spend every hour of every day together. My father stubbornly urged my mother to continue working even when she wanted to retire because he thought it was best for the business and our family. My father was persistent in his desires to fulfill his own personal vision of what was right.

However, the man was not without faults. Being a workaholic plagued him his entire life. He was ultimately a product of his environment. The survivor mentality that he had developed during the hard times of WWII and the tragic loss of his father, were an integral part of him. He could not shut off his learned instincts just because he had a lot of money later in life. He just kept pushing himself against the better judgment of his friends and family. The resulting effect was lots of stress and a bad temper. Lack of exercise and a poor diet coupled with overworking directly caused the health problems that would prematurely deprive him of his life. Nobody is perfect and as time passes you tend to remember the good rather than the bad.

Following the tragic loss, the value of his estate served as a testament to his lifelong financial accomplishments. The rents generated from the properties that my mother inherited fully sustained her in retirement. The properties that I inherited provide a solid income and grant me a certain degree of economic security. I also inherited enough to teach me about the responsibilities of being a boss and a property owner while not having enough to be complacent.

Besides money, my father also took a humble pride in his personal accomplishments. He managed to have a successful marriage for over thirty-two years and showed his wife the worldly adventure that she had been seeking back in 1964. He helped to raise his only child, who became the first Varsano to be a university graduate and would accomplish other significant achievements that would make him proud.

Although my dad shied away from formal Judaism in his later years, he never abandoned the principles that formed who he was. For the most part, he lived by the teachings of the Torah, but bended the laws to fit his vision of life. Major holidays were still recognized, but observances were non-traditional. In the last years of his life, the only formal observances of Judaism were fasting on Yom Kippur and having a Seder on Passover. After he had his heart attack and his health was failing, he did not find solace in religion or consult a Rabbi for advice. How could over sixty historic years of being a Jew

362

degenerate to such religious apathy? Our ancestors in Spain endured torture to preserve their religion and my father's immediate family went to great lengths to continue their Jewish traditions, but towards the end of his life, none of this seemed important. My father was more concerned with working on Rosh Hashana and trying to sell one more washing machine rather than contemplating the spiritual meaning of his life's work. Had he lost his vision of the big picture or was he so accustomed to working hard that he was unable to change? Rather than being at peace with himself and content with a life full of grand accomplishments, he was irritable and distracted. His mind was as cluttered as his messy office, and he continually obsessed about his business, while taking advice from no one.

In his final years, the only affiliation to Judaism that my father held was his friends and family. My parents always had their social network of Jewish-only friends and donated to Jewish charities. Although not a devout follower, my father embraced the cultural aspects of Judaism more enthusiastically than the spiritual ones. However, he was born a Jew and died a Jew knowing that he was part of a tradition that dated back to the Biblical age. Just like everything else in his life, Judaism would be defined in his terms.

His passing marked the end of an era in the timeline of our family's Jewish history. He was the last of the Old World generation that spoke Ladino and lived through such globally transforming events like the Holocaust and the birth of Israel. His generation was instilled with a work ethic and a perseverance creed that could only be gained through experiencing the hardships of history's darkest hours. He had developed a survivor's mentality through his suffering in Bulgaria and

363

Israel that was simply foreign to a carefree American in sheltered suburbia. Sometimes, it felt like the cultural and generational differences between my father and I were utterly incompatible.

He was indeed a very complex man. Rarely revealing his true feelings, he was a proud but modest person who always retained his Israeli sense of uneasiness. A favorite saying of his was "The only problem money solves is the problem of not having money." The enigma of Mordecai Varsano was that he was a workaholic who amassed a huge fortune but was not greedy or materialistic. In his latter years, he worked for the sake of his own self-worth and simply to avoid the boredom of dreaded retirement. Finding a balance in life was his Achilles heel. He was always able learn the lessons of his forefathers and to rise to the challenge when confronted with a crisis, but his biggest enemy was recognizing when to relax. Despite his internal health problems, he never appeared weak or not in command of his small business empire. He refused to do less than he could physically muster and died doing what drove him throughout his life. Although he died at age sixty-four, he was always able to live life in his own unique way and he left a legacy which was a testament to his laundry list of praiseworthy achievements.

EPILOGUE

The Second Leg of the Journey

On a crisp autumn morning in 1964, my father boarded a ship that would take him on a journey to the second half of his life. After a somewhat lackluster visit to America, he was glad to be going back to the friendly confines of his home in Israel. America was a bust for him. Years of dreaming about going to the greatest nation on earth anticlimactically turned into disappointment. The Big Apple was just a big nightmare for him. Canada and his family's attempt at Old World style matchmaking were no better.

As the Shalom ship disembarked, he made his way around the main deck scoping out any attractive young ladies that had romantic potential. My father took a ship rather than fly because it was more fun and glamorous, he received three good meals per day, and it was a new experience for him. The only other large ship that he had ever been on was the converted freighter from Yugoslavia to Israel. Much to his dismay, the ship didn't have many people on it at all and the few passengers it did have were mostly old ladies. Oh well, I guess America wasn't meant to be, he thought. He still held out hope for a good time in France, though, because he would spend about a week in Paris before going back to Israel. For the long trip across the Atlantic Ocean, he would just have to kill time with the old kibitzing yentas.

Then God finally smiled on him. An attractive young American woman came out of nowhere and started flirting with my dad. Of course, the woman was my mom and they were both standing in front of the quintessential symbol of America—the Statue of Liberty—when she began picking up on him. Before the ship even pulled out of the harbor, he had fallen in love. He didn't know it yet, but his life would be changed forever. As Lady Liberty shined down upon them, my dad probably reconsidered his pessimism about America that he had been brooding over only a few minutes earlier.

My father would teach my mother a new Hebrew word which was bersheret, meaning destiny. It's hard to describe the feeling that you have when you fall in love with someone, but when it happened they knew it. My father was nine years older than my mother and had much more experience dating. By the time he met my mom, he was very adept at courting pretty women, but true love had eluded him. In my mother, he not only found a woman to love but the key to new opportunities and a chance to raise his own family. As I reflect on his entire sixty-four year life span, the moment that my parents met was almost exactly at the midpoint of my father's earthly existence—where everything took a new direction.

Mordecai Varsano was determined to make the second half of his life better than the first. The next few years would bring much change and lots of hope, but in the end I believe he was content with the outcome. In a way, my father's journey through life resembled the pattern of evolution of the Jewish people. They both started as a cohesive group of peaceful and prosperous people, but were attacked and displaced by others who hated them. Though the tragedies were cruel and unpredictable, they persevered and ultimately emerged stronger than they were before God and man tested them. Life was a struggle, but love brought hope. My father was able to hold onto enough faith in his heart that his future would be bright one day.

The second half of his life brought both good times and bad times, so what did love truly bring him? I am sure he pondered the question of what his life would have been like if he had never met my mother. I think it's an impossible question to answer, but it is certain that his life would have been entirely different. For better or for worse, those words were part of common wedding vows, and those were apt words to describe the commitment my parents made shortly after meeting on that fateful autumn morning. I believe—and I think my father would agree with me—that meeting my mother on the deck of that ship in the New York harbor was truly the best thing that ever happened to him. Hello to a new beginning, good-bye to the Old World, and the second half of his life would indeed bring him peace. Shalom.

Index